D1281358

THE BIG HITTERS

THE BIG HITTERS

Kevin Koy

Copyright © 1986 by Intermarket Publishing Corp.

All rights reserved.

Printed in the United States of America
Published by Intermarket Publishing Corp.
401 S. La Salle, Suite 1100
Chicago, Illinois 60605

ISBN O-9374-5300-5

HG
4910
.K66
1986

To Joseph Johnson, Raymond and Rachel Obermiller, and Thomas and Charlotte Smith, for their inspiration and motivation; to Maureen Hughes Koy for her understanding and proofreading skills; and to my wife, Nina Brannigan without whom this work could not have been done.

134979

Contents

Our world is a difficult place in which to find expert advice. Those whose opinions I value will not volunteer it; those who volunteer it I find of no value.

—Bertrand Russell

*L*egitimacy in the investment world is conferred by credentials in economics, finance or other dry disciplines of natural science. In the field of economics, as in others, talk is cheap. Experts abound. Yet few economists who express strong opinions on a marketplace actually prosper from it.

There are those who do, however. And the multitudes of investors and traders who regularly put their money on the line respect them— not for their credentials, but for their successful performance, especially when it is achieved consistently.

This book features interviews with a number of these select individuals, originally publishing in Intermarket Magazine. I believe that the insights, observations and practical information from these select few—until now unavailable—can be most valuable to anyone wishing to enter the world of risk.

These are individuals with intellect, integrity and color. Each uses his own approach and decisionmaking process. Each has found his own answers by himself. Each has had the courage to sit through the learning experience as it unfolds, often slowly, painfully and expensively. I would like to thank each of these gentlemen for granting the time and effort required to provide the following and for being unafraid to share their ideas and experiences with the world.

1

Richard Dennis

Richard Dennis has an *office* tucked away on the antiquated twenty-third floor of the Chicago Board of Trade building. The outside hallway has dingy brown paneling. Etched in small lettering on his office door is "C & D Commodities, Richard J. Dennis and Company." No marble. No glass. Immediately next door is a grimy-looking men's room.

The office entrance disguises the performance of an individual who, in his own estimate, has made "somewhere between $100 million and $200 million" trading futures in the last 15 years. Such understated performance seems to attract a kind of fraternity. Down the hall is an office belonging to the O'Connor Brothers, whose trading expertise and numerous companies have built up a fortune worth an estimated half billion dollars.

Richard Dennis is an enigma to many. Probably Chicago's wealthiest individual speculator and certainly the world's largest individual trader, he doesn't seem to care much about material accoutrements or image. A philosophy major as an undergraduate, he considers himself a liberal Democrat on political issues. The enigmatic Dennis puts his money where his mind is, committing $5 million to support the Roosevelt Foundation—one of a few heavily endowed liberal think tanks in Washington. This is in sharp contrast to most exchange members who proclaim themselves to be working in the last bastion of free enterprise while kicking in more then $600,000 a year to conservative congressional political action committees to keep it that way.

He had inauspicious beginnings. After graduating from a Chicago South Side high school, Dennis took a summer job as a runner at the Chicago Mercantile Exchange. ("It paid $1.60 an hour. Whatever the minimum wage was, I kept getting it. That was my raise.") He continued at the exchange in the summers while studying at DePaul University and, after a brief stint studying *philosophy in graduate school, bought a seat at today's MidAmerica Exchange for $1600.*

In the next four years at the MidAmerica, and after at the Chicago Board of Trade, Dennis accumulated a large fortune trading. He said his strength was his ability to be unemotional about his craft and said that "trading futures markets is like playing a never-ending game of chess." Though he established a reputation as a wildly successful trader, he was never a dominantly aggressive physical force on the floor. Hence, few were surprised when in 1977 Dennis left the pits for the office to do "more longer-term trading."

But the transition was not at all smooth. He found out that while he knew how to trade successfully on the floor, this did not necessarily translate to automatic successful trading away from the floor. He lost a large percentage of his fortune in front of the quote machine before developing "something new."

At 35 years of age, Richard Dennis talks about markets calmly and with detachment. Dennis comments that "to follow good trading principles is tough. You're swimming upstream against human nature." Dennis asserts that most people do not have the courage to stick with their convictions. He believes that strong conviction only comes once a person has analyzed the market himself. "A flimsy 'everyone else tells me it's bullish' sort of attitude will tend to make a person a weak holder of a position — even if it's going his way." He recommends that traders should enter the market with 90% of their decisions already made. He is a contrarian, a rugged individualist in market terms. He has three basic rules on market analysis:

- *Figure out the market yourself.*
- *Try not to be influenced by news.*
- *Try not to be influenced by others' opinions.*

He says that, in a good year, "all the profits are in five percent of the trades." Dennis has had numerous good years and several "good trades," his best reaping a $20 million profit in bonds in 1982. "I made 10 or 12 basis points... and it only took three or four weeks."

It was in 1982 that Dennis decided to begin trading other people's money as well. The first year went relatively well with accounts up 95% in the second half, but trading other people's money in 1983 and 1984 has not gone well. Accounts have taken trememdous beatings.

But in good years, the managed account business should prove profitable to C & D: The partnership takes little or no management fee but a hefty 30% of profits, if any, as incentive. Hence, in the fall of 1984, the firm invested in training "trading surrogates." They have been hired not to raise equity, but only to manage it, and are paid a draw against 15% of profits. This investment in teaching trading technique none of the brokerage houses has been willing to make.

At 35, Dennis is successful, perhaps too much so. He raised the eyebrows of many well-heeled speculator friends when he publicly proposed a wealth tax which would go toward reducing the Federal deficit. He continues to speak out politically and back liberal candidates and causes not in vogue on La Salle Street. He sees himself edging out of trading and into the political world.

With so much financial success behind him, he faces a new decision about his own life: finding a new field to conquer. In his case, it involves politics. At this point, however, the esteem in which he is held by his trading associates begins to disappear. His political stance now makes him and his ideas a controversial topic, to say the least.

At the time of this interview, Dennis had been at the center of another controversy — this time about the markets. A farm state Republican senator, Roger Jepsen of Iowa, held informal, politically motivated hearings in Chicago and Washington, D.C., investigating the "efficiency of the markets" and questioning whether Dennis and others have pushed grain prices artificially lower.

INTERMARKET: Let's talk about the Jepsen inquiry into market manipulation. What is your relationship to those who clear through C&D as far as position limits and so on? Do you make all the decisions in trading or does your partner Mike O'Brien make some? What does the term "manipulate a market" mean to you?

DENNIS: You get into verbiage here. Any time you trade you could change the price. The more contracts you trade, the more you're going to change the price. If you trade with the intention of changing the price I suppose people would call that market manipulation, but there's no functional difference between that and trading to make profits.

INTERMARKET: If you and Mike O'Brien both look at the same computer, don't talk to each other and go and put on position limits ...?

DENNIS: Well, we don't ever do that. We're smart enough to realize that they (the CFTC) could misconstrue as improper anything that even had the appearance of impropriety. If we have a computer system, we make sure that only one person uses it. Or that all the people who use it, if they are in similar positions, stay under the position limit. That is not in fact what happens here really.

People imagine ... there's this myth of everything being a monolithic decision, which is a joke, because I sit up here and the partners come in and sometimes I'm on one line buying and they're on the other line selling. And that's no big surprise to either of us because if you trade in the pit for seven years, you get used to the guy next to you selling when you're buying and it makes perfect sense.

If you took a random sample of certain big speculators, I think you'd find that my trades track theirs a little bit, just as my trades track the people in here. But that is because all the speculators trade similarly. I understand they (the CFTC) have a rule and they don't want people to violate it. And I don't think people do.

Now what is the problem? Let's say everyone goes to his computer and winds up doing just about the same thing. That has happened in the past and it probably happened last year in soybeans. That does change the price, but you're committed to the idea that speculators are going to change the price if you're going to have speculators at all. Once you go past that point—that speculators should change the price because you want them in the market—I don't see that problem.

Speculators are all going to have to trade the same way in a trend. You just can't have 40% of them short when beans go up $4.00. They wouldn't be around very long if they're that stupid. So it's hard to see how they (the CFTC) are going to avoid this. There's a lot of this "they want speculators, but people don't want them to make a profit." They want people to trade, but they don't want them all to trade the same way. Well, you just can't get people into that box.

INTERMARKET: What is your reaction to the words squeeze and manipulate?
DENNIS: I'm somebody who knows nothing about spreads and nothing about expiration. (Thoughtful pause) No one gets squeezed—if there is such a thing as a squeeze or a manipulation. The only thing I can say is you can't squeeze or manipulate an honest man.

The person's got to be in there and think he has the right position and just be wrong. So I don't have any sympathy for people on the wrong side of a market to start. However, I suppose if there are situations where the price of something at some exchange is wildly at variance with the real price in the real world, they've got to come in line some way.

INTERMARKET: How does this relate to Jepsen's accusation that you made the price go down?
DENNIS: I wasn't even thinking of it in those terms. My view of the liquidity in the bean market is that if you put in an order for a million bushels, you might move the market a cent. So when you're talking about a price decline of $2.00, that means somebody would have had to sell 200 million bushels.

Well, there aren't 200 million bushels out there except what the farmers have. The fact that there wasn't 200 million bushels worth of demand at those prices meant the price sank. This idea that you can sell a few contracts and make the market do a humongous thing, in the absence of the market going that way anyway, is not right.

INTERMARKET: Do you enter markets like orange juice?
DENNIS: Well, I never—well, I don't know if I've never traded orange juice, but I'll never—that's below some of the liquidity thresholds.

INTERMARKET: What is that threshold, 10% of the open interest?
DENNIS: Well, it's not only open interest. The currencies may not

have a large open interest but there's a large real interest. So I don't have a rule, but I know that if I couldn't do 100 contracts without disrupting the market, it's not worth it.

INTERMARKET: Could I corner a market without being in the cash side or going into delivery?
DENNIS: You mean if you were in the deferred option all the time? Corner? You mean in theory?

INTERMARKET: In reality.
DENNIS: In theory, you could buy enough gold futures contracts to equal all the gold in the world, and eventually people would realize that they'd have to buy them back. But not in reality. The way people trade in any sensible amount that people would give you any credit to do, no.

INTERMARKET: Would you say that with less than $100 billion it would be impossible to corner a CBOT market?
DENNIS: Well, I try to think . . . the one obvious one that comes to mind is silver, because there's not a lot of supply relative to these other markets. And there's the historical experience. The Hunts had . . . well, how much silver did they have? I mean, did they corner it or not? Obviously they didn't. How much more would they need to have bought? Would it have done them any good? The answer is no. So you own every last bit of it? So what? (Laughs) You have to sell it to somebody.

The idea of cornering the market is kind of mythical. It has some kind of extra-sensible appeal. People think in their own mind of doing it or of others doing it. They like the idea or dislike it—they're attracted to it. And it's just not a sensible concept.

You could buy every last bit of everything, but then it's no good unless somebody buys it from you. And what are they going to buy it from you with? It's just not a sensible concept, much less possible.

INTERMARKET: How would you interpret the whole Hunt debacle, how they were treated and their intention to take delivery?
DENNIS: I don't know how they were treated. I know they think they were robbed. If they were, I'm surprised they didn't take stronger steps to protect their rights on the alleged breach of contracts. It's one thing to say you'll take delivery, it's another to say you'll take delivery with borrowed money. I don't know where it says anybody has to lend you money for that.

INTERMARKET: You've gone on record as a strict technician. Would you discuss the model for your system? Is it moving averages, oscillators, cycles, all of the above?

DENNIS: None of the above. (Pause) You know, I don't want to get down to specifics. That would be counter productive. If everyone knew, it would certainly diminish its usefulness to us. It's not a lot different in the end from some of those things you mentioned, but it is none of those. It works on the same principles that they do—trend following, cutting your losses, trying to identify trends, etc. I think that it just does it in a purer sense. It is as pure a price-trend following system as we could develop. It leaves out things like moving averages and cycles, which it seems to me were irrelevant, and systematically misleading in the quest to identify price trends.

INTERMARKET: How did you develop it? When you were trading on the floor?

DENNIS: No. I traded for seven years on the floor and came up to trade away from the floor. Since I knew—I thought I knew—what was happening on the floor, I thought that I must know how to trade away from the floor. It wasn't true.

I found that almost none of the ways I used to trade on the floor were translatable to off the floor. So really ... I didn't understand what I was doing. I'd be trying to systematize something. I had things that I'd watch out for—not mechanical trading rules, but sort of general guides of what to do.

I didn't have those guides anymore, and so I had to develop something new—something more objective, more systematic, but something I had never even thought of when on the floor. The cues are entirely different when you're on the floor. You learn to read people, and you learn to go with moment to moment short-term thinking and trading.

When you go off the floor, you increase your costs because you're not there to do the trade yourself. You lost the personal cues; there's no person associated with those numbers that are changing on the screen. You're forced to objectify it and trade systematically and more long-term.

INTERMARKET: Did you leave the floor because it's easier physically and due to the stress?

DENNIS: No, I needed the diversification, more than one or two markets. Even if you were real swift, you could only get around to one or two markets on the floor. And then, that would limit you to one exchange.

The center of gravity in the business has certainly changed from when I started, from the agricultural markets to the financial markets. And even back in 1977, it was pretty clear that the trader was probably better off diversifying, because the grains had developed into a trendless situation. I wanted to trade other markets instead of one or two.

INTERMARKET: Most people take a more aggressive trading strategy when young and are more interested in capital preservation at a later time. Has your money management technique remained as aggressive now, for your personal account, as it was when you first started out?

DENNIS: I understand why people say that—past a certain point, the marginal value of an extra dollar doesn't seem worth the risk. And certainly, in one way I've become less aggressive in that I risk less and less as a percentage of my total than when I first started.

I suppose most people in my position would have trailed off more and risked less. I certainly think that I risk less than I used to as a percentage of what I could lose. The risk of ruin is functionally zero. I never risk anything in a trade or a series of trades—if I have any sense—which could get me into serious trouble. So to start from that point, it isn't really a question of risking less than that. If your risk of ruin is zero, you don't feel you're at risk at all.

I suppose most people at some point stop, especially people who trade with the same intensity I do. To a large extent, I've been creating surrogates to trade for me in some way, shape or form. This makes me bear the risk without actually having to do the work. The computerized system does that.

INTERMARKET: Has that worked well for you? Creating surrogates? Since so many individuals lose money, it's interesting to see whether someone who's taken such a chunk out of the markets can transfer this talent.

DENNIS: Well, some people tell you "no," but I think it is transferable. That's one of the reasons I decided to do it. It seemed to me so clear that it is transferable, that there are no mysteries.

The single hardest thing I have to do to make people understand how I trade is to convince them how wrong I can be about things, how much of a guess it is—just as it is when they do it. They think that there's some magic involved and that it's not just trial and error. They might be right 50% of the time and I might be right 55%—they really don't think in those terms.

INTERMARKET: You're saying it's money management techniques that determine success?

DENNIS: I couldn't convince people of that, but I felt so much that it was true that it not only could be teachable, but that I could get someone to do it as well as I could. If it isn't a mystery, then I ought to be able to get people to do that. So I have set out to do that. Partially because I don't want to spend so much time working anymore and also because I want to prove to people that there's no great mystery to it.

Somebody asked me on a TV show why was I doing as well as I was and why weren't other people and what was the one thing that could explain it. One way is that there is a lot less to futures trading than meets the eye. Another way to say what I do that makes me better than other people is what I have fun with, what I don't pay attention to.

INTERMARKET: Is that other people?
DENNIS: No, it's mostly ideas about the market—if you went down and talked to traders and asked, "What's the most important idea about the market that you need to know?"

INTERMARKET: (Interjecting) The trend is your friend?
DENNIS: (Repeating to himself) The trend is your friend. (Pause) Some of those ideas might be true, though I think that of most things people pay attention to, at least half are categorically ignorable.

INTERMARKET: So you trade from principles as opposed to percentages?
DENNIS: When I traded on the floor in the beginning and then came to the rude awakening that I didn't understand it, I tried first to make explicit and test on the computer any idea on trading that had ever filtered by me. Just like what you said, you can take that and make it a rigid rule and test on what you have. I found that very few of the things people say work well enough to make a profit. I realized this in the process of searching through some ideas that did work.

  We created a bunch of numbers to spin through a computer, trades that had made a lot of money in the past. I went through that and tried to figure out what it was doing. Sometimes there were parts of that trading system I didn't understand; I tried to understand each part.

  So now, if I was to give you an explanation of what works in the market, what the numbers crunch out to mean, I would say that "the trend is your friend" is a generalization you could make from some of the computer studies.

INTERMARKET: If you were to put percentages on which is more important between the analysis of the market—Am I going to buy or sell today?—and on the other hand the money management technique— How much am I going to buy or sell and at what point am I going to add on?, etc.—would you say the former is 10% and the latter 90%?
DENNIS: Well, its tough to quantify in this sense. I suppose it's one-third knowing what to buy or sell and two-thirds money management.

INTERMARKET: To be able to go from 1977, when you were down quite a bit, to today, what percentage of your risk capital would you put on margin or be willing to lose?
DENNIS: Well, it was a lot more then than now.

INTERMARKET: How much would you put on one trade, and be willing to lose? And would you enter these trades knowing that you were going to get out at a dollar amount?

DENNIS: Any time I make a trade I do have a worst case scenario stop loss. One trade . . . Well, I had more than one trade on a day. I suppose it might be more realistic to talk about how much I'd be willing to lose in one day. I'd say in 1977 I was willing to lose, oh, say 10%.

INTERMARKET: Of your entire equity?

DENNIS: On one very bad day.

INTERMARKET: And was your entire net worth in the markets at that point?

DENNIS: Yes.

INTERMARKET: That's guts.

DENNIS: (Laughs) No, not if you don't come back and risk all that the second day. In other words, I wouldn't wake up in the morning and risk 10%. Perhaps you put on the first position the first day, the second position the second day, and all together you put on something that risks 10%. Let's say that over the week they make you 10%. When you come in the next day, the question is how much will you let all of these positions go against you from yesterday's close before you get out. And I would say 10%.

It would certainly be wrong to come in cold and put on enough positions to lose 10% in one day. And what would be worse would be to come in having lost 10% and risk 10% the next day. That should never be done.

INTERMARKET: Do you ever average a loss?

DENNIS: No, never.

INTERMARKET: What makes you add on? Do you add on to a position only when the market retraces yet holds above where you first entered?

DENNIS: Certainly when you have a position with a profit. Anytime the market goes up a reasonable amount—say a strong day's work—after you've put on a position, it's probably worth adding to that position. I wouldn't want to wait for a retracement. That is everyone's favorite technique—to buy something strong that retraces. I don't see any justification in the statistics for that.

When beans are at $8.00 and go to $9.00, if the choice is to buy them at $9.00 or buy them if they retrace to $8.80, I'd rather buy them at $9.00. They may never retrace to $8.80. Statistics would show that you make more money buying them and not waiting for a retracement.

INTERMARKET: When you add on, do you add on with what you have already made from that trade or do you add on with more money?
DENNIS: You know, I never do think in terms of margin.

INTERMARKET: Do you think of percentages then, when adding on?
DENNIS: Yes. Let's say for simplicity's sake I'm going to put on five contracts. Say you just put on your first one. You might need your equity to increase 3% to get to the second, and to get from the second to the third you might want it to go a total of a 9% increase. And then off the top of my head, 18% and then 30%.

INTERMARKET: And you're talking about margin equity already in the market for each position, not the aggregate.
DENNIS: Right.

INTERMARKET: Do you use buy-stops when adding on?
DENNIS: Sure.

INTERMARKET: Don't you give away the edge?
DENNIS: The stop order, well placed, can be the best kind of order. A random stop is probably a bad idea. If you don't have a decent idea of where to place the stop orders, you're better off with market orders.

INTERMARKET: Congress still is commissioning studies to find out "the economic function, if any" provided by the futures markets. Do you have any comments?
DENNIS: At the highest levels of the Fed there's a question in their mind about the function of the financials. In the history of all commodities that have been successful, as they come on, the people in the trade — the people who wind up using them the most — are opposed to it because they like their game of darts, which is the way prices would be made if there were no Board of Trade.

I know they (the Fed) have been complaining about the Standard and Poor's futures, but those things are going to be the biggest hedge market of all.

Anybody who manages money will hedge in these markets. And I trade enough stock to know that if you want to get rid of it, it's a total pain. You can pop 1000 contracts of Standard and Poor's in 15 minutes and you've dumped $70 million worth of stock without being a real big market factor. That's a very attractive alternative.

INTERMARKET: Could you tell me your reaction to how Mr. Mondale is doing so far? (Editor's note: The interview took place on March 14, 1984, the day after Super Tuesday, when Mondale began to turn the tide back in his favor over candidate Gary Hart.)

DENNIS: I'm not a good political prognosticator. If you asked three days ago I probably would have given you a more negative view of how he's doing than he's doing now. I think he carries some baggage that it should have been obvious would make it difficult for him to win the nomination.

I think that right now, it will be really hard to tell who is going to win between him and Gary Hart. So that's much worse than he was three weeks ago and much better than he was three days ago. Aside from that I can't really give a good prognostication.

I suppose all things being equal, he can't be too surprised—and I don't think he is—about where he is right now.

INTERMARKET: How do you think that Mondale's support in the economic policy sphere from Felix Rohaytn (the architect of New York City's fiscal bailout and a champion of a new U.S. industrial policy), yourself, and others will help? Hart really has no heavy-weights, no kitchen cabinet of noted people.

DENNIS: I think there is something to the idea that Mondale has more experience on all the issues than Hart, but I wouldn't go so far as to say that Gary Hart doesn't have some good people around him. I know some of the people who are alleged to be in his kitchen cabinet and they are not bad people.

INTERMARKET: How would you compare and contrast the Democratic Party to the Republican Party as far as the futures industry is concerned? FDR abolished some free markets.

DENNIS: That's an interesting question actually. There's no doubt that ideologically, the Republicans should be better for the futures industry. Their whole rap is free markets and self-regulation. The motif—most people here in Chicago would agree—has been that the Republicans have been just "promises, promises." When it gets down to brass tacks, this industry's had a better hearing from the Democrats than from the Republicans. That's probably because there's been some lessening in the anti-business attitude in the Democratic Party. A gradual lessening.

The prevailing point of view is that the Democrats have done a fair job. After all is said and done, the real ill to the industry is done by the Department of the Treasury and some leading Republican senators who I try not to name, who keep saying nasty things about the industry and keep trying to raise tax levels.

So I think the Democrats have done a better job than the Republicans. That's not what people expected, and I think there's a realization of that.

INTERMARKET: What's the sentiment out there against the futures markets?

DENNIS: First, there's farmers. Not all of them complain, probably not even half. The people I talk to, the only complaint I get is, "Hey, you may or may not have done anything wrong, but we've got a good thing going with the Board of Trade. Maybe you shouldn't, whatever you're doing, draw so much publicity." There is a certain percentage of the farmers out there who mix up the price dissemination function with prices. It's like killing the messenger because of the message.

Those people could have been educated better and really, nobody s been out to talk to them and try to explain what the Board of Trade does. It tells them the price. Without it, they'd be standing up against a pretty large economic interest without intervening speculators or price dissemination. So there are those who have the wrong opinion, but they need to get educated.

There's a problem of the idea of stocks and margins that bothers some people; that you could recreate 1929 with 10% margins on S & P futures or do the moral equivalent of getting the stock market up in a bubble like in 1929. I know that (Rep. John) Dingell and others are on that. It can be safeguarded against, but there has to be work with Congress. That's going to catch a lot of their attention. Again, it's a matter of somebody educating them.

INTERMARKET: What about government programs such as PIK (payment in kind) and other subsidies? What sort of role do they play in interfering with or allowing free prices?
DENNIS: Well, we shouldn't confuse the function of the Board of Trade with a political decision to support prices and intervene in the market. Traditionally, the markets are better when that's not done, but I don't think that's an argument against it.

Obviously the PIK program looks kind of silly because it pays people more money not to do something than the crops are worth.

Then there's the classic free market solution to an industry which constantly overproduces, which is to let it sort of dwindle until it produces the right amount. I don't think that's integral to the Board of Trade. The markets won't go anywhere under heavy government stocks, but the Board of Trade really shouldn't have a position on that at all.

INTERMARKET: If you look at the situation from an economic view, the government is subsidizing those less efficient farmers. Politically, are you in favor of that? You can go off the record.
DENNIS: That's a good question. I won't go off the record—I'll just meander around. Every Western country, including Japan, probably has a more serious problem with its farm lobby and its influence than the United States does. Consequently, they subsidize their production to the point of making a mockery out of exports to their country. This is especially true in Japan, where the farmers have a sort of strangle hold on the ruling party. I'm not sure that it's bad to subsidize farm produc-

tion to some extent.

I would rather have direct market intervention as the Fed does with the money supply: buy and sell grain as needed to create some stability in price. It may, over a period of time, reduce the number of farmers but it doesn't break them all at once.

INTERMARKET: But isn't the Board of Trade — futures — stabilizing the market? When you look at percentage price swings prior to 1948, seasonality and all that? Why doesn't the government guarantee you and me a profit? Or every other business, for that matter?

DENNIS: I guess because we don't control the electoral votes of enough states. (Laughs) Or the senatorial seats. Well, there are two ways production can go: either we can keep producing too much, in which case we will probably need some way to produce less over a period of time; or, we can go the other way, and run into some tough times, in which case a surplus wouldn't hurt.

It's probably wrong to just keep subsidizing people directly to produce. But it would make more sense to me to have a strategy which sort of held the prices up a little bit when they were down, and parcel that stuff out when there was a shortage.

INTERMARKET: Have you suggested anything like this direct market intervention to Rep. Paul Simon (nominated to run for the U.S. Senate), since he's a liberal Democrat from a farming region?

DENNIS: I haven't mentioned it to anyone. I guess it's my private idea, but I understand that the price mechanism doesn't always give the best result in the short, medium and long run. From year to year, some stabilization might be in order. If we're going to a scenario of overproduction, we can't just (eliminate PIK) all at once. On the other hand, these programs would not be political subsidies quite so much if there were intervention.

INTERMARKET: Who would determine when the price was "too low?" Isn't that the function of the marketplace?

DENNIS: I know, it sounds horrible, doesn't it? But whoever administers these programs like PIK would presumably have a lot of time on their hands. (Laughs) I don't know that I'd want those people to do it, but you might not just be adding to the bureaucracy. You might just be substituting one for another. It also would probably save a lot, actually, in terms of the cost to administer the programs. The government would probably make a profit.

INTERMARKET: Do you think 24-hour trading will take more of the highs and lows out of the markets — just like the introduction of futures trading did?

DENNIS: I think it will. We're going to get into that, to try to be a

dealer in the 24-hour markets. We'll trade with the other dealers for
ourselves. I know it makes a big difference, even in my own trading.

Before, if you had a position in metals and the close was coming up,
you were absolutely frantic because it was going to be eighteen and a
half hours before you got to do anything again. The idea now is, "Well,
it's going to reopen again in five or six hours," and you can get out
then. Those markets are getting liquid, even now, and I think they'll
get to be better in the future. It should make for less volatile trade.

INTERMARKET: What did you look for when you hired your
people?
DENNIS: Well, people who have high math aptitude, super achievers
in the ACT (American College Testing, a standardized entry examina-
tion) scores, people with some interest in computers or market meth-
ods or who worked in systematizing things. The last thing was that the
majority of people we wound up hiring had some interest in games.
They were chess players or backgammon players, enough so that they
would even mention it on a resume. That isn't a bad profile of a certain
type of trader. I can't say that all traders have that. It certainly fits the
people around here, though.

INTERMARKET: Does it fit you?
DENNIS: Yes. (Pause) Except the computers. (Laughs) I make up for it,
I hope, thinking systematically, although I couldn't program a com-
puter if it walked in and bit me.

INTERMARKET: How do you reconcile being the ultimate pragma-
tist when approaching the market, yet espousing what the cynics call
liberal ideology? What I suppose I'm asking is, exactly what are your
underlying assumptions when approaching the political arena? You've
gone on record as saying that your policy predilections are based on
how they affect the poorer 50% of the population.
DENNIS: You mean why don't I worry about the richer 50%?

INTERMARKET: Or what underlies that thought? We all feel for the
poor but realize that the people who create the means by which the
bottom 50% can get ahead are the top 50%. Wealth is created from
wealth and the ongoing parade of society sees that our bottom 50 % in
America is presumably better off than the bottom 50 % in India.
DENNIS: Okay, I have no problem with that. I agree with about half of
that. That's fine—you should have policies which incentivize the top
50% because that means that helps the bottom 50% the most. That's
certainly— if I bought what you said whole hog, and I buy about half
of it—that's the conclusion I'd draw.

That's my principal irritation with liberals in general: they don't
understand how it can possibly be true that you make the poor richer

by making everyone richer.

I can understand disagreeing with that. I don't understand that they don't even consider that possibility. It's kind of irritating. So I think there is a lot of cutting off the nose to spite the face.

You know, every program doesn't have to redistribute. It's an odd thing. What is going to make us richer? Probably somebody somewhere will discover something that nobody else thought of. So how do you make that happen? You can't do anything with the bottom 50% of the population to make that happen. But it's going to do them some good if it happens. Therefore you should do everything you can to incentivize that. In that narrow sense, you can help the poor people directly.

INTERMARKET: Who do you admire?
DENNIS: Foisted by my own question. (Long pause) You know, it's not like I haven't thought about this, either . . . I like David Hume. That's a pretty esoteric answer but he's as good as any. He was skeptical, kind of ruthlessly skeptical, actually. He took on the sacred cows of his generation. He came up with a philosophy which stands to this day, although there's some question as to its ultimate validity. He was a breath of fresh air in the period of time in which he lived.

INTERMARKET: What about Jesse Livermore?
DENNIS: No.

INTERMARKET: Bernard Baruch?
DENNIS: Hmm. I should know more about him than I do. Let me tell you about Livermore. I think that he's interesting. Fascinating. But I think you'd have to conclude that after all was said and done, he wasn't a very good trader. I mean, why else did he wind up with no money? There are no good traders who go broke. You can take that to the bank. There was something to those stories he never told. "I did this, I did this, I did this, and all of a sudden it didn't work and I was broke." And he'd have to go back and do it again. You get about one half of the greatest trader who ever lived and the other half who must have been pretty lousy.

INTERMARKET: Due to position limits, don't you have to keep your managed accounts out of the agriculturals?
DENNIS: We haven't had a trade—much to their dismay—in the agricultural market for about a year now. And that hurt. But I don't see what else we could have done. Clearly, the position limits, if you even believe in the concept, are far too low. They don't make sense internally; they're not internally consistent. Three million corn is not the same as three million beans. It should be nine million corn to three million beans or three million corn to one million beans.

Second, I'm led to believe there has been some problem of delivery when you have real large position limits and if that's the case, it seems to me still you could have a proposed system, much like some of the New York metals exchanges have, that has lower position limits for delivery months and unlimited or much larger limits for the deferred option.

There's no reason now that November beans couldn't have a position limit of 10 million bushels instead of three. December corn could have a position limit of 30 million bushels and not three. That would be just waking up to reality. That wouldn't be distorting anything.

INTERMARKET: Do the individual markets have their own personality or do they follow the same overarching principles?
DENNIS: (Laughs) Yes and no. They're all different but I trade them the same. There are differences that I could enumerate between corn and beans and bonds and currencies. None of them are functional in the sense of the huge general principles that people want to conduct their trading by—trend following, cutting losses, all that you have to do to get those differences. Corn starts to go up. It goes slower than beans, but you still have to do the same things.

INTERMARKET: The way you analyze, looking at high, low and close type of indicators, you don't look at them as different members of a family?
DENNIS: No, I try to look at it much more independently than most people. Yes, there's something to the idea of which one's strong and which one's weak, but I think that's an overrated idea. It worked a lot about seven or eight years ago, but hasn't worked too well since. Most ideas tend to get people knowing about them. I try to trade less on strength and weakness.

INTERMARKET: Do you trade by the seat of your pants, and if so, are the seats of your pants more experienced than when you first started?
DENNIS: If there are people who trade less by the seat of their pants than me, it is only those people who are trained to trade. Most don't even understand that idea. I try to convince people that intuition is overrated in commodities. Having a plan, a system, an approach, a concept of what's going on, and trying to institute that is much better than intuition.

Most people's emotions and intuitions will get them in trouble and I don't think I'm any exception. I'm not one of the one in a hundred people who can just do it intuitively; I don't believe it and I try to teach just the exact opposite.

INTERMARKET: When you took $20 million out of the market in bonds last year, how was your emotional pitch? What made you decide to add on and so forth?

DENNIS: What made me add on were pretty mechanical considerations, and I'm almost proud that I have another percent. I didn't get over-exuberant, that's not my style, in trading at least. (Laughs) Maybe if Mondale gets elected I'll get exuberant.

INTERMARKET: You don't act at all different when you do well?

DENNIS: I'd be surprised if you could tell the difference between after I took a $20 million profit or a corresponding loss. If you think about it, there's no way to be on that roller coaster for 15 years, you just can't do it. I don't wake up in the morning and say to myself, "Well, there's $200 million."

INTERMARKET: Do you look much at the time of day? For instance, will you trade any differently 15 minutes before the close than you would at another time?

DENNIS: Not substantially.

INTERMARKET: Do you think the opening and close are more efficient than any other time for the market?

DENNIS: More efficient?

INTERMARKET: Do you weight the closing price more heavily than inter-day?

DENNIS: The close might be a more efficient price to predict things from but it's hard to trade on because the price one minute before the close can be a lot different from where it closes. The close is the most important price but it is important in a semi-dysfunctional way, because you never really get to trade on it.

INTERMARKET: Let's say that you were in a position to give advice to the speculator who has less than $20,000. Should he stick only to MidAm contracts according to your principles or could he rationalize going a full contract?

DENNIS: Oh no, I think he could trade one contract of most things. He might get in trouble with one silver, but he could certainly handle one gold and probably one soybean. Below $20,000, I'd watch out.

INTERMARKET: If everything was taken away except your quote machine and $20,000, would you be able to build it back again?

DENNIS: Yeah, I think so. It would just take a lot of time.

INTERMARKET: How long before you could get a million?

DENNIS: How long would it take for a million? (Pause) Four or five years. What you're asking about is rates of return, what you can reasonably make. And I've found that my trading style with small amounts of money allows around a 300% return.

INTERMARKET: When you first started out, is that how you did?
DENNIS: Yeah. When you get up to $2 million, you might only be able to get 200% return.

INTERMARKET: Are you at all interested in rubbing shoulders with industry leaders like John Barkshire and Leo Melamed or are you just interested in governmental affairs?
DENNIS: More the governmental political thing. I'm not involved in luncheon commodity exchange politics. No one's ever asked me to become involved. If there's anything worse than Democratic politics, it's politics around here. Although I've gotten some unsolicited compliments for going out and talking to the farmers. Some people think that's been long overdue.

INTERMARKET: Getting back to your trading disciples, has your contention been borne out? Is trading acumen teachable?
DENNIS: It's at least as teachable as I imagined, maybe more so.

INTERMARKET: On the subject of change and prognostication, you are very innovative in that you stress a more meritocratic approach in your managed money program. You charge a higher incentive and little or no management fee. Do you think that's the way of the future?
DENNIS: Well, I think it should be. If it isn't, I could imagine why a lot of people wouldn't want to do that. Not many who are not profitable would want to rely on incentive.

INTERMARKET: How do you respond to those who "buy value?"
DENNIS: Well, there are those in stocks who are wildly successful. I have the feeling that they are the opposite side of the coin from me. Stocks are a different animal ... futures markets aren't very much a respecter of value. You trade them like that. Even if you're right most of the time, I'm not sure it's a viable strategy.

INTERMARKET: What do you think of the banks that trade currencies for the overnight move, not for the longer term? How easy would it be for you to be successful under these constraints?
DENNIS: How do they make their trading decisions? I have no idea how to do it, to tell you the truth. I know that if I were they, I'd try to guess what the large banks and governments are doing. That seems to be the main fact moving the currencies.

INTERMARKET: Can you give me a graphic example of what you might consider good trading technique?

DENNIS: I once knew a guy at the MidAm (MidAmerica Commodity Exchange) who wasn't all that good a trader, but he'd been around a long time. And I lent him money—everybody I knew lent money to him— until finally he made some money at the Board of Trade. I moved over there about a year later and the roles were reversed. He wasn't the biggest trader there but he was real successful and I was the new kid on the block.

Somebody who knew me took me around to the various pits and showed me the big traders. He mentioned two or three or four people and they said, "Oh, there's old so-and-so." And I thought, "Oh wow, so he's a big trader here. That's strange." And so he was one of the big traders.

About a week later, he came to me and said, "Can you lend me $20,000? I just busted out. And I'm going to have to sell my membership. But I can get out of it if someone will just lend me $20,000."

It sounds stupid, but I did it. And I said, "Hey, when I came here they told me you were good." He said, "Yeah, I made a profit every day here for a year, and I lost it all in two days. I got long 200 corn and they went limit against me and I just busted out."

It was clear to me that in his technique he had obviously done something that enabled him to make a profit most of the time. But he got killed, because in the long run, his was a bad strategy.

INTERMARKET: It must have involved averaging a loss.

DENNIS: Yes. (Pause) They say that people are overly attracted to strategies that get near a hundred percent success rate. You can come up with techniques that have close to that success rate and lose tons. And that's what he had done. It's a good object lesson. He had those people fooled. They thought that he was really good. But that's what adding to losing positions gets you. That's what he must have done every day he was in there. He must have added to losing positions until it came back. Until one time.

The question is—and I'm sure you'll say yes to this—would you have liked a strategy that lost most of the time but where you waited for those two days which would put you tremendously ahead? I'm sure you would say yes. Most people would. But you wouldn't have liked it. And the problem is that human nature doesn't like it for any of the days except those few when it works their way.

INTERMARKET: Does trading other people's money put more pressure on you?

DENNIS: No, I've given up having pressure. I realize people are not going to understand what I'm doing. They just want results. I imagine my trading as being the opposite to that of my friend at the Board of Trade. It means you're almost there but not quite: I can lose every day for a year and presto, I hope to make it up in one or two days.

But you have to wait a long time before the profits turn up. It used to bother me that people didn't understand that. Now I just do the trades and put them aside. I can let them (the investors in his managed accounts) decide if they like it, but I rarely change their mind over what type of distribution of trades they'd like.

INTERMARKET: Do you have any views on psychological makeup and its role in successful trading?
DENNIS: I might talk about outer-directedness: That's an interesting concept. Being inner-directed is a lot better for traders. Many people go home at the end of the day thinking, "It's nice to have made a profit." Even to the extent that is inner- or outer-directed, I try to tell people that's one of the worst things to try to judge yourself by.

The other thing — correct in my opinion — would be to go home every day and know exactly how you did. "Did I do everything I was supposed to do? Did I get out of losers?"

But whether the market accommodates your strategy on any one day is pretty irrelevant to whether or not you did the right thing. One should not miss the point of my friend at the Board of Trade — he did the wrong thing every day he was making money — it just took a while to catch up with him. And if he would have concentrated on his form, what he was doing, thinking about it, having a strategy, asking himself, "How is this all going to end?," he might not have blown out.

Instead, he was directed by the result. You cannot be directed by the result, it seems to me, and do the right thing. It's not a good guide. I don't think the results will tell you a hell of a lot. What it applies to is that you need an idea of what you're doing and some confidence before the results will tell you anything.

INTERMARKET: What about fulfillment? A person like yourself, when you're alone at night, how do you feel fulfilled? Certainly the job of a speculator can be financially rewarding, but is it fulfilling? Does money matter anymore to you?
DENNIS: Well, in the larger sense, I don't think the market does much for me anymore relative to what it used to. I would say early on in my trading I would really think about whether I did the right thing. Irrespective of what the results were, I couldn't feel good about it unless I felt I did my best every day. Or even if I could conclude I didn't, at least I understood what it was I did wrong. And I thought I understood how to rectify it. That kept me going even when the profits didn't, because I found it interesting. Other than that, when you've done it for 15 years, you've gotten whatever satisfaction you can get out of it.

INTERMARKET: What else is there for you, happiness and so on?
DENNIS: Is there life after trading? I mean, I'm taking a run at doing

something in politics in the wider sense. And I'm going to be interested to see if I can bring the same amount of understanding—at least to what there is in politics—as I have to trading. Right or wrong, if I somewhere along the way busted out in trading, at least I think I would have understood it real well.

It's going to be interesting to see if I come anywhere near as close to being as good at public policy in the wider sense as I am in trading. I write speeches, I write articles, I go out and give speeches at, I don't know, policy institutes. I try to support candidates that are good.

And I've kind of committed myself in the next four years—that I'll spend at least half my time, maybe more—in public policy, not trading. That's one of the other reasons I wanted to get surrogates—because I wanted to do this other stuff. I guess I don't—it would be kind of silly to say that I understand public policy as well as I do trading. But occasionally, a little glimmer of light comes through and I suppose that's somewhat satisfying.

INTERMARKET: How do you avoid what might be called "Cranston syndrome?" Everyone looked at (Sen. Alan) Cranston as the anti-nuke candidate and that's all. Doesn't everyone in the political arena look at you as the rich speculator?
DENNIS: I know. It's ... it's my ticket into the game and it's my albatross to carry around after I get in. Um, I think I just have to get around and show people that I'm not just another pretty wallet. That's what you have to do. Maybe it can't be done. I don't think it can't be done, but that's what the next four years are going to be about.

INTERMARKET: Some of the more cynical yet educated pragmatists say that it doesn't matter who's President, it doesn't matter which party is in power—especially for those who are at the bottom 50% in income.
DENNIS: It's hard for me to believe that in 1984, with the nukes out there waiting to go off, it doesn't matter who's President. He's the guy that's going to decide that. I don't believe that. Up and down the line, the person there makes a difference. And if he's the right person, he can make a big difference. I mean, would they have said that it didn't matter who was Germany's chancellor back in 1935? I doubt it.

INTERMARKET: But then that's the difference between a dictatorial and a pluralist system.
DENNIS: Well, sometimes pluralism becomes dictatorial.

INTERMARKET: As far as this overhanging (Federal) deficit, I suppose you wouldn't put much credence in George Gilder (author of "Wealth and Poverty") and friends: With recovery, receipts from taxes will eventually reduce the deficit.
DENNIS: (Pause) I characterize their policy as "With persistence, folly

becomes wise." I have a whole elaborate theory of what drives the economy and it would probably bore you to tears. But, it seems to me that you get high economic growth regardless of the major macroeconomic variables you have in effect.

You have huge things out there such as how educated the population is. How many natural resources there are. How many benefits there can be. At the marginal level, policy can make a difference. But those are largely uncontrollable variables and it seems to me that most of them are running in the wrong direction, and that's the major reason that we have less economic growth in the eighties than in the sixties, and a major reason why it's going to get worse and not better.

INTERMARKET: In something like this, where you are talking about major long-term movements which may need to be controlled, does the end justify the means?
DENNIS: What macroeconomics will do is either wreck the economy or else let us go the optimal path, mostly determined by variables it doesn't effect.

Strangely enough, I suppose, that's what Gilder thinks too. He's for laissez-faire and all that. I guess I think that the fundamentals analyses which I guess I shouldn't do—are so bad, that I don't see where the economic growth is going to come (from). And if you start from that premise, rather than the pie-in-the-sky premise that Gilder has, you're faced with the idea that the deficit is the uncontrolled solution to the question of who is going to suffer from the oncoming lack of economic growth.

My point, simply put, is that controlled, managed disaster—to put it in the worst possible terms—is still a lot better than an uncontrolled disaster. And that's what the deficit represents to me—an uncontrolled disaster. And I think that's a fantasy solution—that there are going to be high enough levels of economic growth to pay off the deficit. I mean, haven't we tried that experiment for the last two years? We got as close as you can get in the real world or in the laboratory. It was okay, but the deficits are just getting bigger and bigger at the end of it all. I sought out people at the University of Chicago who don't think the deficits are that great a problem, talked the thing through with them. I haven't found their explanation of the whole situation very sensible.

INTERMARKET: Where are you putting your assets? Treasury bills, gold, real estate, or what?
DENNIS: If someone can figure out what is going to be the equivalent of gold over the next 20 years, I think people should be in that. I say that because gold specifically, and to a lesser degree silver, are yesterday's inflation hedge.

Real estate certainly won't be as good because of adjustable rate mortgages. Some real asset will be the best thing, I just don't think it will be gold. I guess I'd say anything but the things that have gone up. What has gold gone up? 850% since 1965? It seems to me that gold has anticipated inflation until Armageddon. There must be a lot of things out there that haven't built that in.

INTERMARKET: Would you rather hold beans than gold now?
DENNIS: Sure. No doubt about it. I'm as sure about that as I am about anything. That if you want a hedge against inflation, anything is better than gold. It's just last year's song. What's going to happen is that we're going to get some real inflation if these deficits aren't cut. Gold's going to go up 50% and everything else is going to go up 500% and everybody holding gold will say, "What the hell happened?"

INTERMARKET: Getting back to your trading "surrogates," has your contention been borne out. Is trading acumen teachable?
DENNIS: Yes, I think that it's at least as teachable as I imagined, maybe more.

INTERMARKET: You stress a more meritocratic approach in your managed money program. You charge a higher incentive (30% of all profits) and little or no management fee. Do you think that's the way of the future?
DENNIS: I think it should be, if it isn't. I could imagine why a lot of people wouldn't want to do that. Not many who are not profitable would want to rely on incentive.

INTERMARKET: How do you respond to those who "buy value?"
DENNIS: Well, there are those in stocks who are wildly successful. I have the feeling that they are the opposite side of the coin from me. Stocks are a different animal ... futures markets aren't very much a respecter of value. You trade them like that. Even if you're right most of the time, I'm not sure buying value in futures is a viable strategy.

INTERMARKET: Have you ever considered doing what some other successful traders do, and involving yourself some way in cash markets in order to become a legitimate hedger and boost the limits you are allowed to trade?
DENNIS: In the grains?

INTERMARKET: In the grains or the meats?
DENNIS: Well, I don't trade the meats, so it wouldn't do me much good there. I wouldn't want to trade that much more than the limits. It wouldn't be worth my while to do.

INTERMARKET: You said that 95% of your profits come from 5% of your trades.

DENNIS: Yes, that's about right.

INTERMARKET: What makes you get out of a trade that is making you a profit? On a bull move, do you wait for it to go past the top or do you try to get out before the top?
DENNIS: I don't try to get out right at the top. But I'm not averse to making a stab at a counter technical consolidation if the position is right. I'm not paying attention to it—it has to sort of come up and bite me. That happened last summer in beans. That was a classic total correction. But that doesn't happen as much as the other kind where I just wait until it goes against me a certain amount before I get out.

INTERMARKET: Do you have a set amount you let the market go against you when you have a profit? A percentage?
DENNIS: No, it has to do with more than just how much it's going down after how much it has gone up. What's the structure? I look a lot at structural consideration in terms of charting where the tops and bottoms are.

INTERMARKET: Do you ever think that at certain key chart points your entry or exit, or others' entry or exit in a big way, pushes the market?
DENNIS: Temporarily. But I guess I think that whatever I or anyone else might do, given 24 hours in the market at most, the price is right where it would've been had we not acted.

INTERMARKET: Did you catch the yen on, I believe, March 14th, when it was in that consolidation channel and exploded?
DENNIS: That was interesting. We came in that day short. And we got out, and got out a little bit long—at that point it was 10 points higher on the day. And 10 minutes later it was 100 points higher. But in fact we didn't buy as many as we would have if it hadn't moved so quickly, so it was not an unmitigated triumph. That move in the yen was as quick a change in pace as I've ever seen.

INTERMARKET: Do you pay much attention to the so-called "bible" of technical analysis?
DENNIS: I've read it. But I think that most of the patterns are outdated.

INTERMARKET: You're always traveling. Is it all for political work?
DENNIS: No, I come and go. My upcoming travel schedule is typical. I'm going to Washington for three weeks to see what they're doing at the Roosevelt Center (a liberal Democratic think tank supported in large part by his contributions). I come here for three weeks and will then go to Europe for a vacation.

INTERMARKET: Is there anything you would like to be remembered for when you're dead?
DENNIS: (Laughs) God ... I don't think I'm old enough for that question. Umm, I should put this on my questions for next year's recruits. Umm, (Long pause, with seriousness) I guess I'd just like my friends to smile when they think about me. (Pause) I don't really care about other people.

INTERMARKET: Could you talk about success and what it feels like?
DENNIS: I don't know what other people say or if they give an honest answer, but I have a feeling that if everyone gave an honest answer, it probably feels like less to me than anyone I've ever talked to about it. Everybody has a host of things in their life that they're interested in. I suspect that there's no one who feels they're successful in all. Just because a lot of other people rate being a successful commodity trader as real important, I don't think of my life as a trader as all that important.

INTERMARKET: Don't you feel somewhat depressed thinking that had you not gone into trading, people wouldn't be coming to you, asking your opinions?
DENNIS: I don't know if that would depress me. (Laughs) I always used to say—you know I try to be quotable—(Laughs) when you trade, you shouldn't confuse your net worth with your self worth. And I really do think that's true. I don't think that anyone gets self worth out of net worth. And I think actually, almost everyone who tries to, fails to trade well. It's common. You get your ego all wrapped up in your position ...

The biggest strength I've had in trading—and probably in life, if I succeed in politics or whatever—is at some level that I could stand to fail. That the sun would come up in the morning, the birds would chirp, or whatever the hell they say is supposed to happen, and I wouldn't just feel crushed. I know that's true. And it's helped me immensely trading, because it puts it in perspective.

It doesn't make failing as bad as other people in this business think it is. If it would have depressed me not to do this, I probably wouldn't have gotten to this position. That's the paradox, I suppose.

Like a lot of things in this life, it wouldn't have killed me to get a job. It would be a major factor in my life, I suppose—to go get a job—but that's what everyone else does so it's not a big deal.

INTERMARKET: No plans to run?
DENNIS: No. (Laughs)

INTERMARKET: How could you succeed in politics and how could you fail?

DENNIS: (Pause) Well, subjectively, I suppose that I couldn't fail if I gave it my best effort and it doesn't work. Objectively, if, (Pause) see, it's harder to know than in trading. It's a lot harder. And maybe that's why there's nothing to quantify.

I remember Walter Mondale told me once that it isn't like the markets— you never know how the hell it's going. You can be doing this for three and a half years and not know if you're up or down or what people think. And he was right. That's the tough part. If I know the answer to that maybe I'd know more strongly what direction I'd want to go in. I know the kind of things I'd like to have happen—better policies, a better political system ...

INTERMARKET: Will you succeed if you give your view, people don't listen, and after it all, they say, "You know, we should have listened to him."
DENNIS: If they implement it and it works, sure.

INTERMARKET: Do you see an Armageddon type of scenario—a credit collapse and a destruction and redistribution of wealth? A 1929 type of thing?
DENNIS: The depression was the only time in recent history where you had a distribution where the rich got poorer than the poor got. And I suppose any economic calamity makes both poorer, but the poor more slowly, because they have less to lose.

There's a large chance, in the absence of some fundamental rethinking of our political system, how it works and how disciplined it is, that this will happen. Everyone will get poorer but the rich will get poorer faster.

INTERMARKET: How will you prevent this in your own case?
DENNIS: (Laughs) Primarily the wipeout will come in paper financial instruments and people who hold them will be the ones at risk, it seems to me. If you've got a million dollars worth of farmland, you probably will still have a million worth of farmland.

I don't understand farmland anyway. I go out and talk to farmers and they say, "Oh yeah, we get 3% or 4% return on our money."

I ask them, "Couldn't you get 8% to 12% at the bank?" "Yeah, we could do that, but then we wouldn't be able to farm."

INTERMARKET: But they're getting 3% to 4% on someone else's money—the bank's. The farmer is mostly affected by interest rates.
DENNIS: Well, that's what I keep telling them. The interest rate rise will be the death of the farmer. They lose on what they owe and they lose on what they sell. They ought to be up in arms when someone like (Sen. Roger) Jepsen goes out and tries to bamboozle them and support policies that wind up putting the interest rate where it is. He ought to

be accountable for that.

INTERMARKET: What is your most asked question?
DENNIS: I generally get pulled aside at the end of the interview and the reporter says, "I'd like to learn to buy and sell and make a profit." (Laughs) Unfortunately, it's true. I've had more than one person interviewing me immediately want to throw away his press card and want to begin trading. The first guy who ever did an interview with me did that.

INTERMARKET: Perhaps that's because you're not the stereotypical floor trader.
DENNIS: Yeah. I'm different from most of the people down there, there's no doubt about that. Maybe I'm more like them (the locals) than it shows but I'm at least more cerebral about it.

INTERMARKET: Who do you respect as a trader?
DENNIS: The O'Connor Brothers are very good ... What I really expect is that the people who are working with me will be among the best traders in three to five years. They are going to be real top-notch.

INTERMARKET: What was the number of people you had to draw from?
DENNIS: 1100 applications, 40-some interviews, and we picked 13 or 14 people.

INTERMARKET: How would you have reacted to the ad your company placed? Would you have applied or would you have thought about it and forgotten it?
DENNIS: I guess I would've applied. I have no doubt that for the people who got the job, it was the best job that has ever come along for them.

But on the other hand, there is some synergy (allowing C & D the potential incentive on funds Dennis does not manage on a daily basis) and in that, it would be a good deal.

Obviously not all 14 are going to be the greatest traders who ever lived, but I think there are two or three who could be really excellent.

INTERMARKET: If you would throw yourself into the camps of either the "doer" or the "thinker and planner," which would you be? Is there a conflict between the speculator as pragmatic doer and policy analyst and ideological thinker?
DENNIS: I suspect I'm more a thinker. And that's very contrary to what most people think. Somebody said that to me the other day, a computer analyst. He didn't trade, he just made up the system and he said, "I'm the thinker and you're the doer." That's not right.

I'm actually out of my element here in the real world doing it. I really prefer the theoretical approach to the market. And that does hurt in policy where a lot of it is how much you get out, how many hands you shake, and how many people you get by the lapel and say, "Here's what I'm doing." I'm not interactive like that. Definitely not a doer. The object of all action is contemplation; that was one of my favorite lines in philosophy—I think that's Aristotle.

INTERMARKET: Do you think under differing circumstances you could have become a Marxist?

DENNIS: No, I'm an empiricist, through and through. David Hume and Bertrand Russell. I'm solidly in the English tradition.

2

Clayton Yeutter

O n May 16, 1972, the Chicago Mercantile Exchange introduced foreign currencies as the first financial futures. Trading on a division of the Merc then known (almost pompously) as the International Monetary Market, the currency futures concept applied the same leverage principles used for almost 125 years in agricultural futures to finance. The introduction of currencies was the industry's revolutionary step up from the egg, butter, and pork belly markets.

The Merc's bold move proved viable and the world's second largest futures exchange extended its reach over the next nine years to include debt instruments such as U.S. Treasury bills, Eurodollars, and Certificates of Deposit. However, the Chicago Board of Trade ended up with the world's largest volume futures contract, U.S. Treasury bonds. Regardless, the Merc has the world's most substantial currency futures market, a broad range of the short-term debt instrument market, and it dominates stock index futures with the Standard and Poor's 500.

Industry observers attribute the Merc's meteoric rise to a disciplined floor membership, revolutionary marketing effort, but most of all, tremendous leadership. This has been leadership both within the exchange and within the industry. It has been leadership in the cigar-filled backroom of Washington, where friendliness with lawmakers and regulators has made life easier for the Merc in particular and the industry as a whole. And, it has been leadership abroad, where financial deregulation has spelled opportunity and growth for European and Asian capital markets.

Dr. Clayton Yeutter was, at the time of this interview, one of the Merc's high profile leaders. He was President and CEO of the Mercantile exchange for six years, and mysteriously announced his intention to step down in early 1985.

Clayton Yeutter is not a man of controversy. He is an accomplished man, a man respected in all quarters — by traders, regulators, politicians and the financial industry as a whole. In six short years he has become one of the most influential men in the world of futures. Yet he is surprisingly affable.

A gentleman farmer from Nebraska, Yeutter holds a Ph.D. in agricultural economics as well as a law degree. As Assistant Secretary of Agriculture, he was largely responsible for the way the Commodity Futures Trading Commission (CFTC) was structured. Because of his experience and popularity on Capitol Hill, Yeutter has been a tremendously successful industry spokesman. His approach while at the Merc has been to "educate" Capitol Hill rather than batten down the hatches and square off in an adversarial relationship.

When the Carter administration came into power, he left government and joined a law firm, from which he was offered the Merc presidency.

Prior to giving this interview, Yeutter surprised industry observers by announcing his intentions to leave the Merc and remove himself from industry involvement altogether. His reasons are based on his need "to explore other areas." His options were wide open and indeed, some speculated openly that he was in the running for a high-level government position assuming President Reagan was reelected. Several months after this interview first appeared in Intermarket, *Dr. Yeutter was nominated for a position in President Reagan's cabinet as Trade Secretary and was subsequently confirmed by the Senate.*

INTERMARKET: So you're interested in leaving the industry?
YEUTTER: Yes, I am. It's just time to move on. There are a whole host of other possibilities.

One is corporate management — it would have to be the number one post. I'm not interested in being number two to anybody, because I don't have to go that route. It would have to be a chief executive officer of a major corporate entity or financial institution. Or else, something totally unrelated — the presidency of a university, for instance. I've turned down three of those in the last several months. Because of my agricultural background, the only type of institution I would be interested in is a land-grant university.

There are all kinds of opportunities. One recent offer involved what would have been the world's largest agricultural development organization ...

I'm not in any big hurry to make any decision. I've had an exhausting several years. If I had my druthers, it would be to continue here (at the exchange), probably through 1985. It could well be a little earlier. After that, I wouldn't mind giving myself a sabbatical.

My job here is very heavy and very physically demanding because of all the airline travel.

INTERMARKET: Could you comment on the difference in styles between the Board and the Merc?
YEUTTER: Well, it's difficult to comment on that subject, obviously,

because that involves commenting on an individual competitor and we really don't pay a lot of attention to what the competition is doing. We just try to do it right and do it well. But I suppose there have been a couple of factors. I will not put it on a level of the Merc versus the Board of Trade—you can do that editorially if you wish—but I will simply put it on a "me versus everybody else in the world" level.

We've had several advantages. One is that we've been first with almost everything—that makes a big difference. We've been a year or two ahead of our competition in marketing endeavors and in product design, just to use the S&P 500s as an example. Everyone assumes the Kansas City Board of Trade was first with stock indexes.

We were there probably as early as or earlier than they were in terms of the work that went into that product. So very few people understand that. We were heavily involved in working on those stock index contracts immediately after I came, six years ago today. (It was his anniversary at the exchange.) There was even some work that had been done prior to my arrival six years ago. The difference was that we weren't announcing it. Kansas City was announcing to the world that they had this beautiful idea, but we were quietly working away on the research, determining which was the logical product to use. We determined the S&P 500 was it.

We've been very successful in our new products. One exception to that was energy futures. We should have gone into them sooner, but we didn't have the space on the floor in the old building. If we had had the space, we probably would have been first in the energy area as well. But that's one area that we lost out on simply because we had no place to put it. I regret that we can't do anything about that.

INTERMARKET: Do you think there will come a day when the Mercantile Exchange will have the highest volume?
YEUTTER: Well, let's put it this way—we're postured very well in that regard in terms of a number of successful contracts that we have.

It will not happen overnight, because the Board of Trade happens to have some successful products. It has some very outstanding ones. The grains area is still a big success and they are going to continue to do very well on the agricultural side. And of course Treasury bonds is an incredible contract; it takes two or three other more successful contracts to match the enormous success of T-bonds. But the S&P 500 should move into that category in time as more and more volume is generated from pension funds and the like.

INTERMARKET: Just from a theoretical standpoint it seems it would be so unstoppable if the Merc and the Board joined forces. Is that inconceivable because of exchange politics? What about from the government regulator's point of view?
YEUTTER: I really don't think it's inconceivable from any point of

view. The principal roadblock is the enormous financial investment both institutions have made in their respective sites within the city. And we well recognized these possibilities at the time both of us were contemplating expansion a few years ago. We had discussions about combining the two institutions — physically, in the same structure — not in terms of joining the two from a management standpoint.

INTERMARKET: Was Les Rosenthal chairman at that time?
YEUTTER: Yes, he was chairman at that time and Larry Rosenberg was chairman here. We actually had a joint committee evaluating those prospects and it is my personal judgment as well as that of everyone here at the Merc that it should have been done at that time. The resistance came on the other side for a variety of reasons, and I wouldn't second-guess those. They (the Chicago Board of Trade) were by then well on the way with their own expansion plans and it was difficult to back off.

But whatever my personal judgment, looking from a standpoint of the industry as a whole, it was a mistake not to put those institutions in the same physical location at that particular point in time. Now that both of us are in huge physical facilities — both are new and modern and state of the art — that makes it much more difficult to pull them together. I suspect that now we're both committed for the next 10 or 15 years.

Conceptually, though, there's no reason for them not to be combined. It could be done and it could save a lot of money for the industry. Even combining them in the same physical locations could save an immense amount of money in terms of ...

INTERMARKET: Communication?
YEUTTER: Sure, communication, staffing by brokerage houses and all of that would save immense, immense amounts. It's not likely to happen soon, though. We'll undoubtedly go our separate ways, although there are many ways you can realize economies of scale. Clearing processes — there's no reason why we can't have a lot more combinations in clearing systems in this country or elsewhere around the world that internationalization of each market is bound to enforce in time anyway. There will be a savings in audit programs and a whole host of things, a good many of which are already underway.

INTERMARKET: Could you talk a little about what you've done in your travels and where you've spoken and what you've said?
YEUTTER: Well, travels ... I've traveled so much that I get so many free tickets I can hardly use them all.

We have a concern about opening up options trading on currencies, and it looks like it's going to fall into place very nicely now, too ... The CFTC will have to change the elements of their pilot program because it only provides for a maximum of two per exchange. Our options are on the S&P 500 and the Deutsche mark.

INTERMARKET: After options on the currencies, where else would the Merc be going?
YEUTTER: Options on Eurodollars, probably, I'm not sure how we would get prepared priorities between Euros and some of the currencies. We'd probably launch a couple of the options on Euros. Yet, at the same time, we'd likely launch options on Euros ahead of a couple of the other currencies that are of less importance.

INTERMARKET: To what do you attribute the success of the Deutsche mark option, and how do you contrast that to Philadelphia's efforts?
YEUTTER: Basic liquidity, coupled with the presence of the underlying futures contract. Those are the two major market advantages we have over Philadelphia. They do not have the underlying futures on any of their currencies, as you know, so they have to compete against that.

They also just don't have a floor membership of any mass proportion. We've got 3000 people or so out on the floor each day, which Philadelphia simply cannot match.

There is also a lot of interest in Europe and clearly more interest here than in Philadelphia because we've had more of a presence in Europe. As you remember, we launched our London office about four years ago—no, I suppose, a little longer than that. No other exchange has that kind of presence in Europe. Plus we've had a very extensive marketing effort in Europe ever since the office opened, and a very successful one.

The Swiss banks are now buying memberships here. We think some of the other European banks will do the same thing. So we just had a much higher level of marketing activity over there, and that's unusual. A lot of that business is coming from Europe. Our Eurodollar volume, for example, is very heavily European volume. The growth there has really been impressive.

INTERMARKET: How would you describe your particular job role? Where do you spend more time, the floor membership, Congress, the industry as a whole?
YEUTTER: My role within the exchange and within the industry is somewhat different from anyone else's because of my experience in Washington. So it's important to the industry and to the exchange that I use that background for the benefit of the industry.

That's why I spend more time in Washington than probably anyone else does in the industry. That's also a comparative advantage I have over anyone else among the exchange presidents, simply because of the exposure. I was there for six and a half years and a lot of the people who are in power in Washington either in the Executive branch or in Congress are longtime friends, many close personal friends. That's very helpful to the industry as well as the exchange.

My role in speech making and seminars is much heavier and more intense than anyone else's. I did 67 presentations of one kind or another around the world last year. This gives the industry and the Merc exposure—positive exposure to the financial institutions and agricultural communities and all other user groups.

Between those two major functions, a lot of my time is taken up, and so I simply cannot devote the time to day-to-day management that other exchange presidents can. So what we have to have here at this exchange is more of a Mr. Outside, Mr. Inside relationship. Mr. Inside functions on day-to-day management responsibilities. I simply love corporate management or management of anything. That's really been my long-term, lifetime interest. But I can't afford to spend the time on that here.

INTERMARKET: It seems that before the Merc took the initiative, there was really no interplay with Washington, no real dialogue other than what seemed like an adversarial relationship.
YEUTTER: That's exactly right. It was very adversarial, combative. The industry was exceptionally defensive back in those years. The attitude was, "Why don't you keep off our backs and let us do our thing." And life isn't like that anymore. The industry cannot function like that, and it was evidently an impossible objective. Completely unrealistic. It wasn't practical and the industry simply had to change.

I did a speech in New York back about that time that people now call my "goldfish speech." This was before the New York exchanges were even regulated.

I made the point that they were now operating in a "goldfish bowl," that the industry had grown to a point where it simply could not continue to operate in a country club atmosphere. They were and they would forevermore be in a "goldfish bowl" and they would have to conduct themselves accordingly.

Well, you can imagine the consternation that provoked, but it was an accurate estimate—100% accurate. Everything that I prognosticated at that time would occur under regulation has since occurred. The CFTC was formed, and those exchanges were brought under the jurisdiction of the CFTC.

The industry has had enormous exposure since then, some positive and some negative, so it was important to turn that around.

Well, we're not doing everything right yet, but as an industry we've made enormous changes over the years, and at the moment, our relationships with the Congress overall are excellent. They're outstanding with the Senate and House agriculture committees, which are the two key committees with which we work. We still have more work to do with related committees like energy and commerce, banking and others. But we've come a long way in the last six years, and that's demonstrated by how well the CFTC reauthorization was handled about three years ago—much, much better than was true four years earlier or eight years earlier when the initial act was passed.

The members of Congress themselves know much more because we helped educate them over the last few years. They have experience in dealing with the industry and they understand its function in the American and the international economy, and that helps. That gives them a sense of policy direction that simply wasn't there 10 years ago. Basically, the level of understanding of Congress today is much higher than that of the general public on this issue.

INTERMARKET: Well, on that note, let's talk about you. Your reputation on the one hand is that of the exemplary diplomat and on the other the guy who really knows that happens on the floor.
YEUTTER: Yes, that helps. You really need to have both to sustain credibility because if you're just a human signpost, people begin to ask you questions about, "Are you just trying to turn us into supporters of your industry? Is there anything really behind all of this?"

That's particularly true with user groups. You have to be able to talk to those user groups on their level and be able to debate with them on an issue. The cattle groups are an example of that. We've had a lot of problems with cattle groups, but we've gradually been able to overcome the myths. That requires being able to answer every one of their questions, to take on every one of their negative arguments one by one and beat them into the ground. It's important to have the substance.

I was a hedger back in my own department of cattle operations in Nebraska. It's very useful to be able to say, "Now don't tell me that you can't hedge cattle successfully, because I did it."

INTERMARKET: When you hedged, would you hedge in percentages or would you hedge all at once?
YEUTTER: Well, I would never hedge in everything because all farmers, I suppose, have a little gambling blood in them. Very few of them will hedge all of their cattle or wheat or whatever it is, simply because they want to take a chance on prices becoming more attractive.

INTERMARKET: Were you doing it with technical analysis or just fundamentals?
YEUTTER: Primarily fundamentals. If I were buying cattle, it would be close to the bottom of the curve and if I were selling cattle, of course, close to the top of the curve. Fortunately, I was able to do that rather successfully. At the time I was hedging, I only closed out one hedge at a loss. And this was through a number of years of hedging, so hedging worked out very well for me.

INTERMARKET: Did you sell the farm or do you still own it?

YEUTTER: Still own it. It's all cash leased now. One reason why it's cash leased — I'm prevented by the rules of the exchange from hedging and so rather than take that risk of having a crop share lease where I could keep my share of the crop — which I would prefer to do — I just put it all under a cash lease, and that also takes less management time.

And of course, having been a regulator helps too. As you may know, my staff and I did most of the work on the creation of the CFTC.

INTERMARKET: About a year ago you made some interesting remarks about third-world nations and how they could boost themselves to the level of the developed nations, instead of asking for subsidies and artificial price supports.

YEUTTER: Yes, I have felt strongly about that for a long time and I've made that point in a lot of speeches around the world in third-world nations. I've done a whole host of seminars over the last few years for the U.S. Information Agency, primarily in third-world countries. That kind of issue has come up in a number of those seminars. I did some in Mexico, Venezuela, Costa Rica, Colombia, Ecuador, and a lot of other Latin nations because I speak Spanish. That's why the U.S.I.A. had me down in Latin America.

I keep trying to make the point that they ought to use futures to protect themselves, particularly on input costs in imports. They could do it in some cases as exporters too, like the Colombians on coffee, but every time they tried they used inadequate strategy and got themselves into trouble.

If you remember the coffee scandal a few years ago, what they were really trying to do was manipulate the market. LDCs seem to be intent, somehow, to get the price higher than supply/demand fundamentals will provide — and that's a loser. And they just keep trying to do that through international commodity agreements and then through this effort to manipulate futures markets and any other scheme that they can devise that will overcome the basic fundamentals.

I told them over and over again that that's a fruitless and losing proposition and they ought to abandon it. LDCs ought to start becoming a lot more pragmatic about their international trading endeavors, both in terms of controlling input costs and taking the risk out of their export endeavors.

INTERMARKET: Do you know any countries that are doing it very skillfully now?

YEUTTER: I doubt it. There are a number of countries that are seriously examining the possibility and in fact, the World Bank now has a small group, as you may know, attempting to generate their interest in this area. People are working on some potential seminars for Southeast Asia, and a number of other activities, so it's good to see the World Bank has some interest. There may be some hedging going on, but I suspect it's very limited.

Take Brazil, for example, a major wheat importer. Look at the international debt burden they have, and the risk they have in not paying those debts.

Now why in the world didn't they use futures markets to lock in wheat imports when they were down at that price level? The wise thing to have done at that point in time was lock in wheat imports for as far as they could lock them, because there was no way that wheat could have gone very much lower. It was banging on the bottom of our price support level and that's essentially the bottom, in terms of world price levels. The downside risk of hedging at that point was essentially zero and the upside potential in terms of cost — added cost — was very great. Yet I doubt very much that Brazil or any other wheat importer around the world locked in its needs.

Their follow-through is very poor. You see, the LDCs are determined somehow to get the developed world to give them something in this area. They'd really rather not earn it on their own efforts, their own commitment to marketing endeavors. They really would rather have a gift somehow. And they'd rather do it by negotiations than by operating in the price system. I told them over and over again that they're never going to get it done by negotiation, that they are being unrealistic in their expectations. The developed world isn't going to offer them all of these . . .

INTERMARKET: Free lunches?

YEUTTER: (Laughs) Yes, all of these free lunches. It's just not going to happen! And I think that for several years they were convinced that it was going to happen. They thought that if they were obstreperous and cantankerous enough the developed world would finally say, "Let's get these guys off our backs. Let's just give them all of this money and all of these things and let's pay them 25 percent more for all our goods."

INTERMARKET: Could you give me your feelings on the significance of the recent tax changes, both on a micro view and a macro view — the significance for the industry in Washington and the significance for the user in the market?

YEUTTER: If you define macro view as being national or international, I'm not sure how you would use macro in this context. It probably is not a major factor in terms of the total dollars that are involved in a multi-trillion dollar economy.

The area in which it is significant from the macro viewpoint: it will help create substantially more liquidity in all of these markets and make it easier for everyone around the world to use them. To the degree that members of all of these exchanges have held back somewhat in their trading activities because of the unknown tax elements in their personal trading pictures, it will be beneficial to now have that burden removed.

From a micro standpoint, of course, it's enormously helpful to traders. In my judgment, harassment is not too strong a word. The IRS clearly ignored the intent of Congress in 1981 on this piece of legislation. The arrogance of that institution is simply indefensible in a democratic society. But there seems to be little anyone can do about it, other than legislate their arrogance out of existence—which was what occurred in this case.

INTERMARKET: How does this piece of legislation effectively stop them?

YEUTTER: Well, it may be premature to conclude that it has stopped it, but I would hope it will. The principal benefit of this legislation is that it creates a presumption that the professional traders have had a profit motive in their straddle transactions. It now shifts the burden to the IRS to show that that assumption is not applicable on a case-by-case basis.

There is a great deal of money involved. This goes back to several years of tax returns prior to 1983, at what was intended, on the part of the IRS, to be 70% tax rate with interest compounded since then. So, to go to a totally different situation will be exceedingly beneficial on a microeconomic basis to all of those traders. It lifts an enormous burden off their shoulders.

INTERMARKET: Can you comment a bit on how far the industry has to go?

YEUTTER: It has a long way to go in a lot of respects. In terms of volume growth, we are not likely to repeat the performance of the last decade in the next decade—in percentage terms. The curve has been so steep that there is no way to continue with that kind of percentile growth rate.

We're just beginning to develop the options and I see that area as having potential that would be at least equivalent to that of futures and may be even greater. We could have a very steep curve in options coupled with a flattening curve in futures over the next decade. As a combination, those two could be very helpful to the industry as a whole.

We have further to go also on the issue of image. Even though we've come a long, long way, the image problems have not yet disappeared and are not likely to do so over the next decade or so.

INTERMARKET: This is more in the public as opposed to Capitol Hill.

YEUTTER: The NFA (National Futures Association, an industry self-regulating association) will help in that regard because most of the image problems are off-exchange. Perhaps 90 to 95% of them are off-exchange problems relating to bucket shop operations and some of the leverage institutions and others. In time, it will come under control. But the general public does not differentiate between off-exchange and on-exchange transactions, nor does it differentiate between exchanges.

INTERMARKET: How well are you coordinated with John Damgard (president of the Futures Industry Association) and the NFA in terms of, let's say, this recent straddle piece of legislation?
YEUTTER: Well, in this particular case, we did this one essentially as a Chicago Mercantile Exchange, Chicago Board of Trade activity. And that was strategy, because we wanted to keep a very low profile. Tax straddles are a difficult issue to handle politically and we wanted to keep the profile as low as possible, and the more fingers that get in the pie, the higher the profile becomes. So, to some degree, we kind of excluded everyone from this one. Ordinarily, though, we would coordinate quite well.

INTERMARKET: Could you talk about some of the fortunes that you've seen made and lost in the business?
YEUTTER: Well, I can give you one or two maybe, and I hope this one is supportable in terms of the facts. One never knows for sure how much these things get embellished. But I don't think this one was embellished at all.

It's probably the most spectacular of all — it involves gold futures here at the exchange shortly after I came — it must have been five years ago.

It was just as gold took that big rise. There was a Kansas farmer who took a very substantial position in gold futures, when they were still down. I'm not sure where he came in but it was way below $100, probably somewhere around $50 or $60 or something. When they got to $300, the brokerage firm from which he was trading — which is in Chicago — was sufficiently interested in his economic welfare that one of the top people made a trip to Kansas to suggest that perhaps it was a good time to liquidate these contracts. He had a very substantial profit by that point and was told that "gold futures can go down as well as up. Why not take the profit and run?"

But as you know, some farmers can be very difficult to persuade. He was in that category. He was determined that the high had not been reached and he was willing to take the chance and so he said, "Thanks for the advice, gentlemen, but no thanks. I'll just sit awhile."

He turned out to be exactly right. He held until $700 and then he began to liquidate at $700 and above. Some of them as high as $800, as I recall. I am told that he netted $100 million on that set of transactions.

INTERMARKET: I wonder if he stopped trading after that?
YEUTTER: I have no idea. I heard nothing about that one after that. That was a spectacular one.

Fortunes lost? I suppose the one that comes to mind was a poignant case from a few years ago. I can't remember the name of the clearing firm, but it was established in New York, primarily to deal in interest rate futures.

It was a partnership of three or four people who put in a relatively small amount of money to trade interest rate contracts on behalf of customers. Those were the early days of interest rate contracts.

They were consistently right on their advice for a period of between one and two years. They were tremendously successful. The value of their partnership just skyrocketed. And they began to generate additional clients among the major banks.

When their troubles began they were on the floor trading on behalf of six or eight major banks. And they began to accelerate their own trading activity in their house account. They made the classic mistake of believing that they would always be right . . .

Finally, the roof fell in. But they were determined that they were correct in their assessment of the market. They thought that if they'd just hold on long enough—for their own house account and for their customers—they'd be proven right. Unfortunately, they were wrong. Within three months they were on the verge of going under. All of a sudden we all got calls over the weekend in essence saying "help."

All of us in the top leadership got involved then. We had to work out the arrangements to liquidate all their contracts on behalf of themselves and their customers. Fortunately, they left soon enough to have $100,000 left over. There were no losses for anybody that couldn't be covered. Everyone got out whole. The exchange did not have to cover losses. But the partners, they lost between $15 and $20 million in a period of three months.

3

Tom Willis and Bob Jenkins

*A*bout $500 million is currently being managed in public or private commodity funds. Yet the overall performance of these funds has been anything but stellar since the end of the uptrending markets in the inflationary late '70s and early '80s. Publicly issued funds were down an average 3.3% in the last 12 months ending July 1, while private placement funds declined 6.6% during the same timeframe. The best performance turned in either by public or by private funds was that of the pools managed by Willis & Jenkins, Inc. — up 92%.

Who are the world's most successful fund traders of the mid-1980s? How do they trade and where do they come from? Not from an engineering program or financial background, the usual origins of fund managers. Tom Willis and Bob Jenkins became money managers the hard way, fighting and trading their way out of the pits.

Tom Willis entered the financial world humbly, as a runner and card counter for his uncles at the Chicago Mercantile Exchange. He broke from the career path his uncles planned out for him and temporarily severed the family relationship when he bought his own seat at the Open Board, now the MidAmerica Exchange.

As a MidAm floor trader, Willis experienced a lackluster first year, barely breaking even. Despondent, he received trading advice and encouragement from a fellow MidAm floor trader, Richard Dennis. Willis was strongly influenced by Dennis' approach to trading, and cleared $125,000 during his second year on the floor. Each year he honed his skills and grew wealthier. Today, although he only occasionally makes an appearance in the pit, Tom Willis is known as one of the fastest and toughest pit traders in Chicago. He is in his early 30s and is rumored by his colleagues to have a net worth "greater than

$10 million."

"Getting out of losers is no problem — it's getting out of winners," he says, "that makes the difference between survival and prosperity."

After meeting with success, Willis encouraged Bob Jenkins, a boyhood buddy and Yale graduate, to try floor trading. Jenkins bought a MidAm seat and, after a frustrating year-long stint as a concert promoter, went into floor trading full time.

The two teamed up to manage other people's money in 1982, incorporated, and had lawyers draw up a private placement. They raised $1 million, mostly from Chicago floor traders, friends and family, solely on their reputation as savvy traders.

They set out to prove that success trading from the floor for their own account would translate into success trading other people's money. They started out managing money from the floor but within three months moved off the floor, to "more profitable opportunities." Thus far they have succeeded. At the time of this interview, Willis and Jenkins are managing some $17 million, including three private placements, several managed accounts, and their own account. At the end of June those accounts were up 92.4%.

Managing money as a CTA is somewhat similar to structuring a venture capital or leveraged buyout deal. The person who puts the deal (or trading system) together has upside but no downside (unless he puts in money). He takes a percentage of the investors' profits and is not exposed.

As a money manager in the futures markets, the CTA gets his cut in two ways: a management fee which is enough to put food on the table (usually 6%), and an incentive fee — a cut of the profits, if any. As with venture capital and leveraged buyouts, the incentive fee — usually 20% of profits for the CTA — is where the big money is made.

Yet Willis and Jenkins have renounced the passive money management style of traditional system traders who develop a computerized (usually moving average-based) model which generates buy and sell signals for the various contracts. They do use a model, but mix in their trading savvy earned from "a combined 20 years of cutting our teeth on the exchange floors."

Despite their trading record — one of the best in the industry — the broker- age community has been slow to welcome them, or raise cash for them. While the CTA makes money by making the customer money, the brokerage firm makes money only on the commission charges per trade. Willis and Jenkins have strong opinions about the brokerage community in general, which they believe avoids them because they insist on low commissions, something that helps them and the customers while lowering the brokerage's bottom margin.

Both were in good spirits on the day of the interview in early July of 1984. Their marked-to-market positions from Friday's close until Monday's close yielded their personal and customer accounts $822,000.

INTERMARKET: How did both of you get into the business?
WILLIS: I started first, so I'll answer first. I had two uncles who were members of the Merc. They brought me down to be a board marker as a

summer job. I'd run [between the trading desk with orders to the pit], count cards [keeping track of the trades for the floor trader who bought and sold too quickly to calculate the net position], everything. This was in the late '60s, and my uncles were trading pork bellies and eggs. I didn't have any idea what they were doing.

My first job was to count cards for my uncle. I'd stand next to the pit, he'd give me his cards, I'd total them up and tell him, "You bought 100 and sold 90." It's pretty clear that since he was long 10, he was supposed to sell 10 and get even.

Of course, that being the only thing I had to do, I did it wrong. (Laughs) In one instance, I told him that he bought 90 and sold 100. When he went in to even himself up, he actually doubled the problem. I didn't catch my mistake until 10 minutes later. He would never have caught it.

I went up and said, "When I told you you sold 10 more than you bought, it was really the other way around." He grabbed me, gave me a cuff on the head and said, "Your little mistake just cost me $5000!"

Then and there I thought to myself, "If a little mistake like that can cost $5000, I want to find out what's going on around here."

This was my junior year in high school—18 years ago. I went to Valparaiso University with only one thing in mind—to trade futures. But how was I going to get started? Even then, a seat at $30,000 was way out of my range.

I saw an article about Rich [Dennis]. I had never even heard of the MidAm—or the Chicago Open Board, as it was then called. They were selling memberships for a couple of thousand dollars. I thought they left off a zero on the seat price. I called and asked if they meant $20,000. "No, $2,000. Why don't you come down and take a look at us?" I did.

I was shocked. It was rough. Old men all over the place. There was Rich Dennis, two or three fellows maybe around age 30 and then everyone 70 or more—nothing in between.

I bought the seat when I was at Valparaiso, so my summer job was trading. The only goal I had was to trade. So my last two years I set up my schedule so that I had Monday, Wednesday and Friday classes and could commute and trade on Tuesday and Thursday, Christmas vacations, Easter. I stayed home at the folk's place and commuted.

INTERMARKET: Didn't that make school seem rather mundane?
JENKINS: It put it in its proper perspective.
WILLIS: I couldn't wait to get out, that's for sure. I had a chance to do some independent study—that helped. But I wanted to get out quickly.

I was anxious to trade because I wanted to hold the ball myself. I come from a Greek family and my uncle is very much the family patriarch. He had a grand plan for my life. I was supposed to come up through the rank and file at the Mercantile Exchange. I went out against his will by buying this membership on my own. He didn't talk

to me for a year.
JENKINS: He wanted you to be a board marker, then a runner, then an assistant deck holder. Maybe when you're 30 you might get a membership.
WILLIS: Yes. And I was watching the price of the seat go from $30,000 when I started to $65,000 by the time I was board marker. I estimated that it would be $250,000 by the time I was 25. And it was. I'd still be a board marker if I'd waited around.

INTERMARKET: How did you start?
JENKINS: I was just a capitalist and wanted to make money. Tom and I had known each other since seventh grade. I took my time in school. I took a fifth year in high school in England and I worked after my sophomore year in college.

INTERMARKET: Where did you go?
JENKINS: I went to Yale—"jail," as I called it. After two years there I thought the place was totally useless, so I thought I'd go out and work for a year and see if I could decide on some course of study which I might enjoy. Here I was, supposedly in one of the world's great academic institutions and I couldn't see anything germane to the real world.

I was a very directed person—I wanted to make money. But the courses at Yale were intentionally impractical. I couldn't sink my teeth into them. I kept thinking, "How is anything I'm studying going to help me in any way when I get out of this place?"

I was extremely depressed all four years at Yale. I kept telling myself, "If you can get out of here with any ambition left, you'll probably become successful." The whole place was so anticapitalist—God forbid you should want to make money.

This was 1969-74. To give you an idea of how "uncool," to use a word from the '60s, it was to be a capitalist, we started a group my junior year called the Yale Business Forum. It was designed to get people on campus together who were interested in business. Also, we wanted to bring in some speakers. Most of the Yale alums were disgusted that there was no one like the old Yalies on campus. We thought, "If we just let them know that we're here, maybe they'll come and discover us."

So we ran an ad in the Yale Alumni Magazine, which must have a readership of 50,000. We got two responses, both of whom thought we were some crackpot organization making fun of the business community. Out of a class of 5000 undergraduates, we got only about five people to admit they were interested in business per se. Everyone else wanted to be a doctor or lawyer and help humanity. I said, "Well, I'll see you guys in 10 years, see the fees you're charging, and let you know who you're helping."

The guys who wanted to be doctors were very directed in what they wanted to do, but they were also very phony in terms of their real reason for becoming a doctor. Most of those people were not going off to the Third World nations to make up for the shortage of doctors. Or even into Appalachia.

No! They went right to New York or Los Angeles, wherever they could charge the highest fee to remove cataracts. The hypocrisy that pervaded Yale was rampant even among the administrators who, on the one hand, went and criticized capitalism and the business world in general, and on the other, asked all the rich Yale graduates for tens of millions of dollars. Frankly, I'll never give them a dime.

I decided to major in economics, which is somewhat business-oriented. But in fact, after introductory economics, nobody agrees about anything anyway. Galbraith on one side, Friedman on the other. If those guys can't make sense of it, how the hell was I as an undergraduate going to make sense of it?

The bottom line is that I don't think I learned anything at Yale that helped me when I got out of there.

INTERMARKET: What about the argument that liberal education teaches you to think and analyze?
JENKINS: My theory on that is: if you don't know how to think by the time you're 18, you've got a major problem.

I think the whole notion of a liberal arts education is a load of malarky, myself. I'm being slightly facetious. I think there is some value to a liberal arts education, but I think it's highly overrated. When I think of the amount of money it takes to send a kid to a private school—it's absurd. I would rather have been given the $40,000 to go start a business.

Anyway, I was in my junior year when Tom began trading. When I was a senior he told me he was making six figures a year. I thought that wasn't a bad thing to do. I went down to the floor and said, "What gives down here?" He showed me around and said, "A lot of guys are making a decent living who aren't any smarter than you are."

Tom helped me buy my first membership in November 1974 and I started trading in November 1975.

The thing I like about this business is, to whatever extent you're in control in any business, you're in control here.
WILLIS: We're in control. We take three weeks off if we're tired of it. We don't have to ask anybody, we just take three weeks off.
JENKINS: You can't blame anybody if you lose money. And you don't have to thank anyone when you make it.

INTERMARKET: How long did it take for you to catch on? Was your uncle your mentor?
WILLIS: No, he wasn't—not that he wouldn't have been, had I asked. I cut loose and was going to do it alone if I could. My first year I was

floundering, making just about every mistake possible. It was good. Now that I look back, that's basically what I tell people when they come in.

INTERMARKET: What mistakes did you make? Taking home losers?
WILLIS: All kinds. Adding to losers, which is even worse. I went through a time of adding to losers and averaging down. I cut my profits short: I'd make ten trades, eight of them winners, and make $55. I hung on to losers. I was very one-dimensional in my trading. When I first started I traded just wheat. What are soybeans? What is silver? Why would you want to trade silver? When I came into the business, futures trading was basically meats and grains.

I was making every mistake possible. Luckily, it was at the beginning of a boom and the mistakes weren't too costly. Also, I was at the Open Board of Trade, trading smaller, so the mistakes were 1/5th as bad.

And I have to give credit where credit is due. Rich Dennis spotted me — probably because I was the only guy in the place remotely close in age. He said, "Hello, how's it going?" I said, "It's going pretty lousy. I'm lucky I'm not broke. I'm basically breaking even. Any tips?" He said, "Yeah, I've got a lot of tips. When the beans are strong and the wheat's weak, why don't you sell the wheat instead of selling the beans?"

I said, "Well, I don't understand that, but I'll try it." It worked. It worked as well as anything works — maybe 55% of the time.

But it still gets down to discipline, basically just discipline. You can do a lot of things wrong and one thing right — that being cutting your losses — and you can make a lot of money in this business.

By the second year I had what I would call at the time a very good year. It was six figures.

INTERMARKET: Low six figures or high six figures?
WILLIS: It was low — about $125,000. It was very consistent. It was made up of a lot of $500 days.

INTERMARKET: I was told that you're one of the fastest and loudest traders in the pit.
WILLIS: Well, I am quick and loud. But screaming in the pit is a terribly inefficient way of doing things. If the rest haven't figured this out, I have. When someone screams, "I wanna sell a million!" what they really want to do in the back of their head is buy it. Nobody will really tell you what they want to do. Whenever I'm doing my screaming and shouting, it's a smokescreen. The real trades are very fast with the hands as acknowledgment: "I'll take yours and yours."

INTERMARKET: So you give away the edge on your big trades?
WILLIS: Well, to an extent. You have to give away a little bit of

something. The edge is just the most apparent thing. After my second year in the business, Rich told me, "When it's $6.00 last on the board and someone wants to sell you soybeans, you bid $5.99. When someone wants to buy them, you offer it at $6.01." That's the edge that's most apparent.

JENKINS: I trade on the floor too—probably not as much as Tom does—and I always sell at the bid and buy at the offer. Our concept is that if you're buying what's strong and selling what's weak, you're getting the edge. The guy who's taking the half cent from you is getting an edge because he can probably scalp a half cent out of it, but he isn't going to want those trades 60% of the time by the end of the day. If he just stood there and made those trades with us, he'd be a loser.

INTERMARKET: What about what has happened in gold lately? For a strength-weakness trader, the chart of silver seems very weak. Gold, meanwhile, was holding up well and did not break until a few days ago. The currencies also were telling the technician that gold should be selling off, but it wasn't. Why didn't you buy the gold in that situation?

JENKINS: Well, by looking at the chart, we never would've bought gold anyhow. We don't buy what happens to be the least weak. We buy strength. In the case of gold, it was the least weak, but we wouldn't have bought weakness.

INTERMARKET: So you don't compare the various groups against each other?

JENKINS: We try to compare what people think is supposed to be happening with what's really happening. Everybody thinks that the fact that currencies are diving means interest rates are going up, that T-bills and such should drop. In fact, what was really happening all last week was that currencies fell and everyday T-bills, bonds, Euros and CDs were higher on the day. What we look for is the divergence between what everyone thinks is happening and what's really happening.

INTERMARKET: How do you quantify that and where does judgment come in?

WILLIS: The judgment? I think it's based on fact, actually. It's not really a function of my getting up on one side of the bed versus the other or whether my wife screamed at me this morning.

Look at the bond market last week. When every market was lower, bonds in the last two minutes moved up and closed higher on the day. That's a fact.

INTERMARKET: In that case, would you want to buy them on the close or wait until the opening the next day?

WILLIS: Actually, I bought a little bit on the close—enough to insure that it would open lower. (Laughs) It opened five lower, made the lows on the opening, and came out of the opening range on the upside. Now I'm ready.

The nice thing about closing at or near your highs is that on the next day, unless it's sharply lower, you're always playing around with the previous day's high, which to me is an edge, a buy signal.

On my bond example, the bonds opened lower, made the low and came out of the opening range on the upside, after a decent close the previous day. Being the only contract higher in the world, plus, being over the previous day's high, I knew we were in a loaded situation. Risk? Reward? If I was wrong, could I get out quickly? Yes. Would I lose much? Not very much.

INTERMARKET: So you have no problem buying a gapped market [a major move between the previous trading level and the current one in which there are no trades executed]?
WILLIS: No.
JENKINS: That's one reason why we're up 92% in the last 12 months. Many of our competitors, CTA's, came from numbers backgrounds. They were physicists, chemists, statisticians, mathematicians, engineers. They all want to quantify these markets under the B.F. Skinner type of assumption that these markets are in fact predictable and that things occurring in the pricing in the past will occur in the future.

That's fine in the static world, but the point is that we're in a dynamic world. Not only are the markets changing, we're getting new products. Look at the open interest in the beans. It's half of what it was when people were excited about soybeans. Why? Because there are new products getting everybody's attention.

And the markets themselves have changed because of the so-called computer trend trading. There's no doubt.

INTERMARKET: You've evolved considerably from Richard's approach — a trading strategy which looks for certain spots. Now he's a computer trader.
JENKINS: He said in your interview that 90% to 95% of his trades were numbers-oriented. I don't believe that, frankly. I have a managed account with Rich and I've stood in the soybean pit and have seen trades made recently which were not pure system trades. There are many trades he makes which — I'd like to ask him why he sold wheat at $3.71 ...
WILLIS: (Interjecting) I asked him.
JENKINS: We were still long and it was making six-month highs and he pitched them ...
WILLIS: (Interjecting) Well, do you want to know the answer? I was at his house over the weekend and asked, "You know something, Rich, there's something I really have to ask you — how come you sold wheat?"

It happened to be the high.

JENKINS: It wasn't making contract highs. It was making highs for six months, the kind of place you'd *expect* him to be buying.

WILLIS: For all intents and purposes they are contract highs, as far as I'm concerned. Anyway, he said, "Oh, I was getting on the airplane going to Europe. I didn't feel like looking at it." (Laughs) Another great trade by design.

JENKINS: I disagree with Rich's whole trading premise which he discussed in his interview—frankly, I disagree with a lot of what he said and with what I know about him. Yes, I think there are certain parameters which can be developed to make money in the long run, but there are vicious swings in the interim.

We try to control the downside. Making 92% in 12 months is meaningless if you're going to turn around and lose 50% next month—we'd be back to zero. We try to be consistent. The only way you can be consistent and control the risk of the downside is to have hands-on decision making. Defensive trading. Tom taught me—and basically anyone who's been within his sphere of influence—that the most important thing is to conserve your equity and defend yourself.

This is not an offensive game. You do not attack the markets. You try to be like Sugar Ray Leonard and wait for Tommy Hearns in the 15th round to drop his hands so you can knock him out. The key thing here is not whether or not you're losing at 10:30 or 12:00, but how you're looking on the close. Basically, we look at trading as a defensive enterprise. You just keep your guard up and look for the openings. You don't make openings in this business—they happen. The computer traders are round-house punchers. We prefer to sit and wait until the fat kid drops his guard.

This is a battle. This is war, make no mistake about it. That's how I view trading—them against us. We view each day as a separate day. If we smell smoke, we'll use our trading judgment—if 24 contracts on the board are higher and the one we're long is lower—even though it might look good on the charts and all the numbers and systems would be saying, "Go, be long," if it's the only thing that's lower, we know we have a problem *today*.

Maybe we'll sell half of our position. Maybe a third, maybe all of it if it gets below two or three days of lows. Then if it turns out that it might have been as good a trade as we thought it was, we'll probably get back in, but we save ourselves a lot of grief. The guy who just has a system doesn't know, if it closes below three days' worth of lows, whether it's good or bad or indifferent. All he's got is a number here that says, "Well, if it closes above $6.56, it's okay."

That's why CTA's get so much blood on their sheets—they don't have front-line experience, time in the trenches. Tom's been down there for nine. This adds a dimension to our off-the-floor trading indicators which no guy who's just sat in front of a screen can ever have.

The only other guys I've ever invested money with—[Jim] Hickey and Rich Dennis—are guys who cut their teeth on the floor.

We don't like to lose money and we don't want to lose money. The way you make money is to take lots of small losses.

INTERMARKET: The second year you made $125,000 and were heavily influenced by Dennis. Did you become unafraid of giving up the edge?

WILLIS: No, at that point I was still afraid of giving up the edge. I was a one-dimensional edge trader who knew enough to let the bad ones go. I'd stand there and take the edge.

INTERMARKET: Did you pull money out of your trading account?

WILLIS: We tended not to spend money and we paid cash for everything. I don't remember when the turn came, when I knew I was not trading by the seat of my pants and could depend on it. It was about my third or fourth year.

My third year I made $500,000, something like that. Even at that point I was waiting for the shoe to drop. By my fifth or sixth year, I began to feel comfortable.

As Rich said, there is no mystery to it. It's a matter of actually just doing it. Just performing the simple function of disciplining yourself. You stand in the pit and continuously take small losses. It's like learning to type—you can't ever forget it.

It becomes very much second nature. And also becomes very much like a job, which I never bargained for. It got to be: stand there and wait for the broker to open his big mouth, fade him [take the other side of the trade] and trade as much as possible. Generally go against the order and get out on the subsequent stop-loss orders [a pre-determined level at which a trader cuts his losses].

INTERMARKET: To summarize how you traded at this period: You were getting the edge on the orders, cutting losses, using strength-weakness. Would you take positions home?

WILLIS: Yes. I was taking positions home right off the bat. The first thing Rich told me was to take edges; if you have nothing better to do, stand there and call everyone else wrong, since they don't know anything either. The second thing was that the hardest money made was between 9:30 and 1:15; the easy money's made overnight.

At the close, it's very unlikely that I'm going to sit there thinking the same things as most of the guys. I think I have a lot more bullets than most: What does this rally really mean? Is it rallying up to three days' worth of lows? Am I supposed to buy it here? Obviously not. In my opinion, this type of move is probably just a short-covering rally. This kind of analysis keeps me out of a lot of bad trades.

I was still not beating a lot of locals in the pit out of anything meaningful. I could scalp out whatever I scalped out, but that was not the point. The point was to make more. Really, the way you do that is with overnights. The thing Rich told me that helped me my second year was that money overnight is your best friend. Keep it, don't sell it. Unless they're paying plenty for it.

INTERMARKET: On the close?
WILLIS: Right. But why sell something at the close that has made you money? Keep it! When it opens five higher in the morning, it'll be the easiest five points you ever made. You can't beat those people out during the day. They're not dummies. They're giving you the edge when it's starting to look lousy. Always. They never give you the edge when it looks good. Maybe two times a year.

I always take overnights. I haven't been flat since he told me that.

INTERMARKET: Do you view a position differently when it has moved your way, or do you view a position that has already made you $1 million the same as the one you just put on?
WILLIS: No, I view it as my money. If the bonds close a point and a half higher tonight and if they open half a point lower tomorrow, I say I'm losing 16 points on it. You look at the statement, you look at the bottom line, and that's yours. You don't look at it as "$100,000 here and I've got $25,000 open equity."

No. You look at it as "I've got $125,000 open equity." I do; everybody should. I really consider what I have at the close as mine. To do otherwise would be generally to hang on to something that might not be as good today as it was yesterday.

But there is a transition period. This is my learning curve. To answer your question: when the bonds open a half a point lower tomorrow, I'll ask, "What does this really mean? Should I get out? How close are yesterday's lows to today's lows?"

If I were standing in the pit, they'd have to go at the opening or on the first rally. I'd get them back again when they got higher, and if they didn't work out or they got lower, I'd get out of them again.

If you're in the pit and long bonds, and they close strongly and they open half a point lower, you've got a problem. When you're off the floor managing money, it's a different game.

INTERMARKET: That's because you put a lot lower percentage of your entire equity on that one trade.
WILLIS: Yes, and I think you're looking more long-term. When you manage money, the bottom line is: if you start with $100,000 and the move took you at one point to $160,000, but once the smoke clears you're out at $140,000, that's considered a good trade.

When you're in the pit, you can make $60,000 on the move from $100,000, get short, and make $20,000 on the short side. But you can't do that with $20 million.

You can stand in the pit at a certain level, but after a certain amount of money, it becomes unlikely that you can do anything in the pit that you couldn't do from a desk.

INTERMARKET: Would both of you describe your first big trade?
JENKINS: Most of the money that Tom and I have has not been made on big trades per se.
WILLIS: Mine was in the wheat market, after the Soviets had gone in and bought up all the wheat. At this time, I knew enough to buy something that was limit up, but that was about all. It was a situation where the front end of wheat had never gone over the back end. I don't remember the contract months at this point, but this was one situation that had never happened before at the Board of Trade. This was before the news had hit the wires, but every day the front month was gaining on the back. It was still discounted, though.

The spread slowly but surely got to even, and slowly the front months went over [to a premium]. They said it could never happen. The point was, no one knew why it was happening. And of course, the tout was, "Boy, you better sell the front end, because this has never happened before." They were wrong.

It's history now, but there were times when the front end would open limit up and the back end would open limit down on the same day! This was my first big trade in my $125,000 year.

INTERMARKET: How much size would you trade with $125,000 in the account? 20 lots? 30 lots?
WILLIS: Back then I was willing to trade one mini [the MidAmerica contract] for every $1,000.
JENKINS: In these markets, you'd be risking more than 10% of your equity with that equation, which you really shouldn't do.

INTERMARKET: How much were you willing to lose on a trade or on the day?
WILLIS: I hope I never see the day when I lose 10% of what I have. I'm thankful I never got to that. I'm a classic undertrader, so that's a bad question for me. Frankly, if I have a trading flaw, it's that I trade too small. It's not *if* I have a trading flaw—that's the trading flaw.

INTERMARKET: What about you, Bob?
JENKINS: I'm probably the other side of the Ying-Yang thing—if anything, I trade too big. That's why we complement each other very well. He designs the race car and I step on the gas.

There were many days when I lost 10% of my equity.
WILLIS: It should never be any more than that.
JENKINS: As far as my "greatest coup" was concerned, it was in orange

juice. I sold them and watched them go up as I lost my [expletive deleted] on them. That happens when you're new to the business. You make a little money and you think you can suddenly beat everybody at everything.

I started trading markets that I had no business trading. I started picking tops. I did all these stupid things—probably times five. They say the average kid learns when he's burned his hand two or three times. I had to do it four or five times. [Laughs] All over! [Laughs] If stupid losses were burns, I probably would look like the Elephant Man. [More laughter.] Internally, I probably look like Dorian Gray. Our guts have been torn and burned by this business for 10 years.

My biggest trade was my stupidest, orange juice. I lost my entire net worth on one trade. I had the misfortune of making money my first year. I call it misfortune because, although I had a good teacher [motions to Tom], after I had done well my first year—I thought now that I'd made X dollars doing this, I could trade 10 times bigger and make 10 times as much money. I was violating a capital rule.

I was risking too much money—more than I could afford to lose—and I started making bad decisions because of it. I hesitated. As soon as you start to hesitate, you're in over your head. You're in the deep end and you'd better get the hell out.

It took me a couple of years to recover from some of the stupid things I did. Actually, it was a tremendous growth period for me.

INTERMARKET: You tapped out?
JENKINS: I lost all the money in my trading account. I started filling orders. In retrospect, it's probably the best thing that ever happened to me.

Part of the problem was that I thought I was smart when I came in the door so that when I made a little money, I thought, "This is easy. I made $30,000 my first year, so if I trade 10 times as big I'll make $300,000." When I started to lose a couple of thousand, I choked. I said, "Gee, I really don't want to lose $4,000 or $5,000." Next thing you know, it's $10,000.

Then I made my goofy trade in orange juice. I sold orange juice after the freeze. It was limit down one day and then I thought, "Now I'm really going to get them." I just couldn't believe the strength of the subsequent rally. You remember that Bill Cosby song? He's sitting on the railroad tracks as the train rumbles toward him and he sings, "I can't believe this is happening to me?"

I think this was the most constructive thing that could have happened to me. I didn't enjoy the process while it was happening, but it made me appreciate what the business was all about. The name of this game is, don't lose money. It's not how much you make, but how little you lose when you're wrong.

INTERMARKET: Why was getting wiped out so constructive? What did you learn?
JENKINS: If there are 100 things you can do to be a great trader, there's only one thing you have to do in order to stay in business, and that is take your losses. The corollary of that is that you can do 99 things right, but if you do this one thing wrong, you're going to bust out eventually. If you don't take your losses, you will tap out.

INTERMARKET: So you made your first million within four years?
WILLIS: You mean if you added it all up? Yes. I actually paid taxes. But that was left after my first five years.

INTERMARKET: If you were still on the floor, assuming you had twice as much money today as you did last year, would you be trading twice as large a position?
WILLIS: Now I would. I wouldn't back then.

INTERMARKET: Then why did you make so much more on your second, third and fourth years?
WILLIS: I think particular trades would have been bigger. If we're talking edge trades, if I got a tremendous edge, I might have done 25 or 30. In a particular instance, I might have bought 150 or something crazy like that, fallen on my face on 75 and kept 75. Particular trades were two or three times bigger in the next year, but I didn't sit down and calculate return on investment.

INTERMARKET: Would you take something like that home in your third or fourth year, a 75 lot?
WILLIS: Sure.

INTERMARKET: But on a limit move, you'd have been risking more than 10%.
WILLIS: I'd never take it home when it was limit against me. I'd take it home when it already had 15 cents with me. Maybe it was limit bid with me. I guess in the '76 bean market, it was not unlikely that I'd take home 100 beans. They'd open 30 higher and boom, $30,000. Not unlikely at all.

INTERMARKET: You'd start off the day, you'd buy 20, buy 20, and by the end of the day you'd take home 100. You wouldn't start the day saying, "I'm going to buy 100 today and take them home."
WILLIS: No. As a pit trader, I always used to let the pit dictate to me what would happen. I wouldn't go home with any game plan. Toward the late '70s I got an idea what ought to happen. By then, if I'd had a game plan, I'd know what I wouldn't want to do, not what I'd want to do.

If something closes limit up and it had a chance of opening limit up the next day, I wouldn't come in and say, "Well, I'm going to sell it if it opens limit up, because it's done this three days in a row and it's got to react." I would eliminate that silly kind of trade.

Do they offer more and how much do I buy? That is the question! If I came in with 100, I certainly wouldn't add more than 50, and the next time, given the chance, I wouldn't add more than 25. And then the fourth time 12, and so on. I wouldn't add 100, 100, 100, because once it breaks, you're all even.

INTERMARKET: Your net worth is pretty substantial. How do you view diversifying your wealth?

WILLIS: There are all kinds of investments in this world, and futures are a portion of what we look at. It's obviously what I do best, but we're not silly enough to think that there aren't people out there who know just as much as I do in futures, but are instead doing real estate.

I used to be interested just in futures. As long as the bottom line got bigger, I didn't worry. That kind of thinking is wrong. I believe you have to diversify and keep active. Bob's been more of a businessman.

JENKINS: Although it was his idea to start trading for customers.

WILLIS: Well, I can come up with good ideas, but let's face it. Bob did all the grunt work, got the lawyers facing each other, and actually raised the money, which is the gruntiest.

JENKINS: But it was an easy sell. 99% of our investors are other traders or people who know Tom's reputation. And of course the main thing they were in is the knowledge that Tom wouldn't lose the money for them. Our investors really know the product.

There are some people in the business—including some of the C&D partners—who think that, dollar for dollar risked, Tom probably makes more money than anybody in the business. For the size of position that he takes, there probably isn't anybody who takes more out of the market. That's a pretty big compliment coming from people who know probably the greatest trader of the 20th century.

WILLIS: But the biggest thing this guy brings to the party is how big the position should be to get a commensurate rate of return.

JENKINS: It's extremely unlikely that we would look at a market and he would say buy it and I would say sell it. Usually we want to do the same thing, but it's a question of timing and the size of the position. Today we bought the D-Mark and made 30 points on it by the close. There was a 40 point range, so we did rather well.

The question is, do you wait for it to get higher on the day? The answer is yes. We made our first buy there. Do you wait for it to get above yesterday's high before you make your second buy? The intelligent answer is yes—although I don't think I did.

I'm a little less risk-averse than Tom is. We have a very synergistic relationship, in that sense.

I've suggested, only semi-facetiously, that Tom should say what he likes and rate it on a scale of 1 to 10, step out of the room, and let me decide what size position to put on.

You're able to think more objectively. The primary definition of overtrading, to my way of thinking, is when you begin to think of money instead of quality of position. The moment you think, "I'm losing X number of dollars per tic," you're in over your head. That way, if Tom didn't even know what the size of the positions were, he could be totally objective about the quality of the position.

One of the big transitions we had as a money management team, coming off the floor in August 1982, was learning how to trade the big positions. While Tom had a large net worth, he didn't keep it all in his trading account. It was a big mental transition to go from buying 10 bonds for yourself to buying 50 bonds for the fund. Fifty bonds for us now is a small position.

Another transition was to get the numbers into their proper perspective. Markets are markets, numbers are numbers and we've all made a lot of money trading things we've never seen. [For example,] we have an account with $5 million in it. Your first order for them might be 200 bonds. It was a big transition to stand the pressure mentally.

There is a tremendous sense of responsibility to go from trading your own account to trading someone else's hard-earned money. It hurts much more to lose money for someone else than for yourself, irrespective of the fact that these people are friends and family. These people have given us a tremendous vote of confidence to take their money and put it to work for them. We accept losing our own money as part of the turf of being a trader. But that's not what people gave us money for.

We consider it our primary responsibility to *not* lose the money. Secondly, we try to get an above-average rate of return without the roller coaster effect that typifies the record of most other trading advisors.

INTERMARKET: How is the business structured?
JENKINS: We trade three private placements. We are the general partners for two of them as well as the CTAs. We probably have five or six managed accounts—minimum $100,000.

INTERMARKET: Isn't that a pain keeping track of $100,000?
JENKINS: No, $100,000 is a number you can do something with.

INTERMARKET: Do you lump all the accounts together?
JENKINS: Nope, individual orders for each account. We enter orders all at the same time. We have to enter them in order. C&D is on the top today. For the next order they are on the bottom. Lind-Waldock's on the top, then Conti, and so on. Our personal account, unfortunately,

has to go on the end of the stack, but we're having our lawyers examine whether we can go on a rotation as well. Right now, our personal orders are last.

So we go on a rotation. But with the more money we're getting, we're realizing that we have to scale our way into these orders. We can buy 500 bonds or currencies, that's not a problem. But with sugar, you'd better start out with 150 or 200 at most.

This serves two purposes. First, you don't hurt yourself with slippage [failing to get all the intended volume executed at one price]. Second, you only put on the second wave if the first one's a winner.

So there has to be some kind of sophistication as far as order entry goes. In my opinion, the best brokers in Chicago work with us. Not for us, like Rich's brokers.

We're not just a faceless order and they know that we won't have any qualms about calling up and screaming if it's a lousy fill. We don't want them to play with orders, we just want them to fill them at the market. I don't want to sell it at 5 when it's 6 bid. But I also don't want to sell it at 3 because he thought he could get a better price. That's not what we're paying them for. We're calling the shots, they're filling the orders.

INTERMARKET: How much did it cost in legal bills to set the fund up?
JENKINS: It cost about $20,000. We raised $1 million in our first fund, $2 million in our second.

INTERMARKET: No sales commissions?
JENKINS: No. We sold them ourselves. There was no front end load, no trailing commissions, etc. Part of this performance, although a small percentage, was due to the fact that we didn't have a front end load, and the commissions were low.

Our commissions on the private placements might average $10, which most of our investors think is outrageous, since they're floor traders used to paying $1.50 per throw. $10 to any retail customer would be great. The main thing that accounts for our performance is not our low commissions and lack of front end load but rather our trading ability. Sure, we fought for our investors. Tom's dad's one, my mom's one; they include family and long-time friends.

The thing we do that these guys don't is get out of the trade when the smoke first is coming under the door. We don't have to open the door, burn our hand on the handle, plus have the fire leap on top of us. If we smell a little smoke, we get out of them. If the building is not on fire, we'll get back in. Like a sinking ship: the two or three guys nearest the lifeboats get out and everyone else goes down. We want to be by those lifeboats. If the ship isn't sinking or the building isn't burning, we'll get back on again.

INTERMARKET: Exactly what will make you "smell smoke?"

JENKINS: Things like consistently bad action for several days, like the beans a few months ago. Things have to act right. Beans would close on their highs three out of five days and they'd never open higher. They'd always open 10 lower.

When something closes on its highs and is making new high ground for a six-week period, you should expect some follow-through once in a while. You don't have to have it every day. But in a good bull market, if you see consistent bad action . . . like when the corn looks good, up 3 or 4 cents while the beans are only up a penny. Or they're lower, or the deferreds are stronger than the nearbys, which means that nobody wants the cash.

What we look for in exiting a long position is either consistently bad action or something dramatic, like being long the only thing in the world of 25 futures that's lower on the day.

INTERMARKET: But when you're putting on a position, you can't really wait for several days of bad action. You put on Deutschemarks today. What will make you get out of them?

JENKINS: First of all, we didn't make that trade for our customers because it's not a strong enough trade. We'll make counter-system trades for our customers when we have more things going for them than the D-Mark had today. All it had was that it was only down a tic on Friday, and when it got higher on the day, one tick higher, it was actually unchanged over two days.

They were proclaiming the ascension of the dollar on all three networks this morning and in the *Wall Street Journal*. It's only been going up for 10 weeks now. You can't read the newspaper and/or watch TV and make money trading futures contracts.

We would have gotten out of the D-Mark on a lousy close, or if it had gotten higher on the day and then made a new low close for the move, or if it had gotten back below the previous day's low. We would be gone immediately. That was a trade where we came in and risked 10 points.

INTERMARKET: Do you use stops in that case?

JENKINS: We hardly ever use stops. We use market orders. Stops can be triggered off by a five lot [order]. Lowball it or highball it. We sometimes use stop-close-only on entering and exiting a position, because obviously the close is the single most important thing that happens in the trading day.

We use stops more to get into the market than to get out. We know we want to add at certain points. Today we wanted to add to our D-Mark if it got above the previous day's high at 83. We might have put a buy stop at 84. I'd rather see it hit 84 and see what happens than just buy it there, because it might be a one tic highball and back off to 78, which is in fact what happened. So I bought them at the market at 80 and 81.

Order entry technique is something that we're especially good at: we know how these guys in the pits think.

WILLIS: You're not fooling anyone in the D-Mark pit. They know what yesterday's high was. Friday's high was virtually the same, 82. Yesterday's was 81. They know what you're thinking.

When I was on the floor, I knew what the guy on the outside was thinking: "If it gets over 84, buy it." Given half a chance on the floor, you pay 84 to see what's there. A couple of buy stops, maybe?

INTERMARKET: You don't charge a management fee but a decent incentive fee?

JENKINS: We started out charging just a straight 20%. The reason we did that was to make it an extremely low-cost vehicle. We wanted our investors to know that we're not going to make money off it unless they do. I wanted to make it easy to sell. As it turned out, we were oversubscribed for it, as we were for the second one.

But that's changed. We have changed that concept for two reasons. From running a simple business, we started to take on more expenses, and we needed a little cash flow since we were getting paid only at the end of each quarter. If, God forbid, it was an unprofitable quarter— this only happened once in two years—we wouldn't get paid anything. The other side of the coin which we discovered is that there is an awful lot of pain and suffering for which we felt we should be compensated. It sounds ironic—why should you compensate the guy if he's not doing well?

If we come in long 425 bonds and the market opens up 16 tics lower, I've got my own 75 bonds I'm hurting on and I've got 350 customer bonds I'm long. That hurts. It doesn't matter that we've got 64 tics on them. The point is, there's aggravation involved here.

Others call the 6% a management fee. I call it an aggravation fee. It's there to compensate us for trying to do our best. Since we're doing the same thing for our customers as we do for ourselves, and our customers include our family and friends, we feel like we deserve a management fee.

INTERMARKET: Some arrangements take the money out in commissions, which you don't seem to be interested in doing.

JENKINS: We might ultimately, but we're not now. We think that funds should be performance-oriented. Frankly, two years ago, if I thought I could have sold a 6% [management fee] and 20% [incentive fee], I probably would have done it. We're entitled to that 6%; we're also entitled to an incentive fee. Virtually all of our accounts are structured that way. The only way we would forget a management fee is if someone wants to throw us $1 million on a no-fee, 33% incentive. That we would take.

INTERMARKET: You said that you turned down $10 million be-
cause the commission house wanted to charge between $70 and $100
per round-turn.
WILLIS: This was a subsidiary of a wirehouse that was talking $100
per contract. We don't have to name any names, but I can be very frank.
I said, "How do you have the $10 million? 10 guys? 20 guys? 100 guys?"
He had 1000 $10,000 accounts. I said, "$100 at the Board?"

He said defensively that it could be $60 at the MidAmerica. He
meant $60 for one, or $300 for a full size contract. I said, "Let me get this
straight." I knew the answer as soon as he said it but I wanted to walk
him through it so that he'd know why I'd hang up on him for his $10
million.

He probably doesn't get too many CTAs that hang up on him. Every
time I make a trade, that's $100 for a $10,000 account? That sounds like
1% commission per trade. That's ridiculous. I'm happy if I'm up 5%
per month and I have to give up 1% per trade? Plus what I give away to
the pit? My job is not to make you a multimillionaire. I said good-bye.
JENKINS: We have a lot of guys come in here, put their arms around
us and say that they are going to make us millionaires. Fortunately, we
can say, "We're already millionaires, thanks."

INTERMARKET: Enumerate for me how you trade your account
differently from the fund.
JENKINS: We trade our own accounts more heavily than we trade the
fund. If we ever lost 5% in a day for the fund, I would consider that a
disaster. I don't consider it a disaster if I lose 5% in a day. Well ...
there's a lot of money in my account, so maybe I would consider it a
disaster. [Laughs]

Off the floor, there's no difference at all except on how we weight our
account.

INTERMARKET: More aggressively?
JENKINS: Yes, more aggressively. Everybody gets the same trade at
the same time. Today, we bought the D-Mark for ourselves but not for
the funds. This is not that strong a trade. Something coming off the
contract low like the D-Mark is not something you put your customers
in. It might be a buy on a pullback tomorrow.

So we might make trades that are of a higher risk for ourselves.
WILLIS: If the fund has it, we have it. It's not necessarily true that if
we have it, the fund has it.

We have also sworn off the meats. If we trade them twice a year, that's
a lot.
JENKINS: The only other situation that we might trade differently
from the funds is if we're on the floor scalping. I'm not much of a
scalper; I never have been. Tom is a scalper par excellence. I don't
think there's anybody better down there. If all of us are long beans and
Tom's down there and somebody bids three cents over, which they do
in a volatile market, he's going to sell that to him.

We have it very clearly disclosed in our operational and disclosure documents that we can and will sometimes have positions opposite to the funds when we're on the floor. We're trading our customers from a medium to long-term perspective. When we're on the floor, we're trading from an extremely short-term perspective, which is why you pay $300,000 to walk on the floor in the first place. You can buy at the bid and sell at the offer, which you can't do sitting up here in videoland.

INTERMARKET: Tell me about your computer system.
JENKINS: We refer to it only as a guideline. It gives us parameters. We could follow it and make some decent money doing it. But we use our judgment to fine-tune everything.

INTERMARKET: Is it moving averages, cycles?
WILLIS: It has a nine-day moving average, and we look at closes within a time frame.
JENKINS: Closes are the single most important thing that we watch. We compare today's close to closes X, Y, and Z days ago.

INTERMARKET: So you look at today's close and high and low versus yesterday's close, high and low? Or today's close versus yesterday's close, with the high and low being secondary?
JENKINS: The high and low are more daytrading techniques. The close is the thing to really look at.
WILLIS: Our computer system looks at closes. The problem with this system is the problem with all of them: the time lag. I've tried to factor in some things that reduce the lag.

INTERMARKET: An exponential or weighted moving average?
WILLIS: I try not to be so mathematical.
JENKINS: You can fool with computers, but you'll never be able to be that successful with them until they can think. Let me give you the classic example of how a computer fails you. It was about three months ago. The bonds closed on their highs up around 66.28. Everyone was looking for a money supply decrease of $3 billion. They got one of $5 billion.

The cash market rallied up half a point [16 tics] and everyone was expecting the futures market to open sharply higher. Instead, it opened up 3 or 4 tics higher, made its high in the opening range and got lower on the day within three minutes of the opening. Within 10 minutes, it was below the previous day's low. Now you've got an outside down day going, within ten minutes, and everybody's long. At this point, no computer in the world would have gotten you out, probably for three or four closes. Needless to say, the market closed a point and a half [48 tics] lower.

The difference with our 20 years experience in the trenches is that, were we long on that opening, not only would we have gotten out, we would have gotten short. No computer in the world has that program written. It's an analysis of expectations versus reality. How can you program in the expectations of the call? We put a lot of weight on how the market is called and how it opens.

WILLIS: Our system by itself will make money. But it sits through a lot of terrible action which we don't like to sit through. A good part of making money in the office is a function of being able to make the trade because you're not worn out. If you have to go through five bad days because you're short and you know you shouldn't be and wouldn't be but you're following the system, you get worn out. Then, when you get the legitimate signal, you don't move because you're worn out. Don't wear yourself out. Use common sense.

JENKINS: There was a time when we made every systems trade that came down the pike—and sat with it as long as we could. We were ready to jump out the window in two days. It was crazy. So we now blend our judgment and common sense with our system and can live with it. We've eliminated a number of markets. Now we only trade 14.

INTERMARKET: Which ones have you eliminated?

JENKINS: All the meats . . . First let me tell you some of the criteria we use. Since we trade in such large size, we don't want any part of any market that has a daily volume equal to the open interest. There's not enough hedge participation. Most of the meats fall into this category. Also, any market with a low open interest, which is almost a subset of my first point.

We don't trade markets like cocoa or lumber. Our orders are for hundreds of contracts, so any market with less than 25,000 open interest we try to avoid. We can't enter markets being 1 or 2% [of the] open interest.

Much of many markets' open interest is spread positions anyway, so what's the outright speculative open interest?

We've eliminated all the meats, we've eliminated the Canadian dollar—too illiquid—and we rarely trade the S&P.

INTERMARKET: Really?

JENKINS: It's a very aggravating market. By the daily volume versus open interest criteria—they are the S&P bellies. They are up and down like a yo-yo. They'll trend, but there's a tremendous amount of aggravation. We know we're being aggravated when a market that closes well opens 100 points lower. A system trader can sit through it because he doesn't know that he's being aggravated.

We don't trade coffee. And we've given up on cocoa—there's not a market more likely to open sharply lower after closing on a six-month high or a six-week high or a six-day high. Conversely, it can open sharply higher after closing below a major support area or six-month lows.

We've given up orange juice for the same reason. Cotton we don't trade anymore. We obviously don't trade oats, 10-year notes or the Ginnie Maes.

INTERMARKET: Are you trading Eurodollars?
JENKINS: We're long 200 Eurodollars right now. Euros have the biggest open interest of anything at the Merc. You'd be surprised— almost three times as much open interest as the S&P. I'll tell you what we do trade. The five grains: beans, meal, oil, corn, and wheat. We trade bonds and the short rates. CDs and Euros track each other pretty closely and T-bills move in the same direction at a reduced velocity. In fact, we're long all three of those right now.

INTERMARKET: Did you enter them all on the same day?
JENKINS: Yes, we did. And I'll tell you why. We had what we consid- ered a legitimate system buy signal in the bills, but we also bought CDs and Euros because there have been times where the bills would be up five and CDs and Euros would be up 25. We try and spread it around a bit. The nature of the instruments is not that different, but market perceptions are.

INTERMARKET: Do you trade the TED [T-bill to Eurodollar] spread?
JENKINS: No. We'll do a July-November, old crop-new crop spread once in a while, but we're generally not interested in spreading.
WILLIS: That's like two different positions, anyway.
JENKINS: We'll trade gold and silver; we don't trade platinum, we don't trade palladium. We'll infrequently trade copper—another very frustrating market from a technical point of view. We trade the D-Mark and the Swiss franc very actively; less frequently, we'll trade the yen and the British pound. We trade sugar—we like sugar very much. And in season, so to speak, we trade heating oil. We'll also trade crude oil. Those are very volatile but trending markets.

We're down to 12 or 14 commodities which are the most trending commodities and, not coincidentally, are very international in charac- ter. They therefore have a greater open interest and greater liquidity, so the costs of getting in and out with a large position are not that great.
WILLIS: These markets are exceptional in their liquidity. Bonds, currencies—
JENKINS: [Interrupting] Currencies—You want to buy 1000 D-Marks? It will cost you two points, although the other day they ripped me for four points on an order for 130.

INTERMARKET: You were probably right on the move.
JENKINS: Yes. I knew that I was right when they took me for four points; nobody could afford to sell me any. They were all short.

But most of these other CTAs trade 25 commodities, and some of them, actually two successful guys, Booth and Dunn, much to my surprise, have reversal systems.

WILLIS: Well, I don't think that anyone can follow it better than you or I, and we have headaches with more than seven positions on at once.

JENKINS: If you told me I had to have positions on in 25 markets, I'd shut up shop tomorrow. First of all, there probably aren't more than seven good trades to put on at one time anyway.

This is another thing we do differently from other people. It harkens back to strength-weakness trading: You may have all the metals in an uptrend, yet you always have a clear leader and usually a weakling, a tag-along.

There was an excellent example in last summer's grain market. Soybean oil and corn were really the leaders in 1983. Meal was a pig the entire way. You could have made a career selling meal last year — and I think we did. We were short meal nine months out of the last 12.

Here's another trade which we would never make, but the typical systems guy would. By the time beans rallied two and a half dollars, which is eight limits, [calculates aloud] eight times 30 cents, $2.40, wheat was dragged up 50 cents, which is two and a half limits. Everybody got a buy signal at $4.00 in July wheat last summer and loaded up. And because there was enough bad buying, they actually got the price up to $4.30 and then dropped it 25 cents the same day. We would never have accepted the buy signal which everyone else got —

WILLIS: [Interrupting] Which we got, too.

JENKINS: We got it too, but we ignored it; we were actively waiting to sell it. It was clearly the weakness in the complex. We always look to sell weakness and buy strength, and we look for bad buying, as in this wheat example. That's something that we're always on the lookout for — that weak sister who's been dragged along by the kind of guy who thinks, "Gee, I missed the move in beans so I'll jump on the wheat bandwagon."

The metaphor I use is driving on the expressway. If people traded the way they drive, they'd be a lot more effective. In rush hour, if you're in the middle lane and the right lane's going slower and the left lane's going faster, you're going to try to get into the left lane.

The typical customer or unsophisticated trader — which is a lot of our competition, in our opinion — will want to be in three lanes at once, which is the approach of the systems trader. Since he can't, the CTA or customer will look at the slowest lane and think, "Well, I'm going to get in that, because that's going to catch up. I'm going to get in the slowest moving commodity, which is the wheat, and it'll catch up. It's *undervalued.*" They jump in the wheat, and there's enough bad buying to force it up.

People would never drive that way, and they shouldn't trade that way either. What they should do is get in the fastest moving contract month

of the fastest moving commodity—whether it's going up or down.
That's where all the money's made.

INTERMARKET: Other than avoiding the aggravating markets, do
you trade them differently? Do bonds trade any differently from corn?
JENKINS: No. We don't trade them any differently.

INTERMARKET: So you just put blindfolds on?
WILLIS: Well, there are some personality differences. In the last
couple of years corn has made a little bit more sense; when it closes
well, it continues to move.

Bonds are a good trade, but sometimes they do strange things.
JENKINS: What Tom's saying is that the bonds, in the course of a
general trend, will very frequently open counter to the trend. Bonds
closed well on Thursday, on the high of the day. Then they [the
government] came out with a goofy unemployment number and bonds
opened 20 lower. Conversely, if you're short and they're going down,
there'll be a lot of ferocious rallies.

There are markets that trend in a very predictable fashion, and
markets that trend in a very erratic fashion. Corn is relatively predictable. The currencies also trend in a very predictable fashion. Now there
are some markets ...

INTERMARKET: Cocoa?
JENKINS: Cocoa? Yes. That's why we don't trade it. The ultimate
profitability does not justify the exposure and aggravation. It's not
that you can't make money trading cocoa, any more than you can't
make money trading bellies. But for the aggravation involved, there
are better markets to be trading. [To Willis] What's your great quote on
technicals? You've made millions of dollars trading soybeans and
you've never seen a soybean in your life. That's a technical statement—
the fundamentalists go out and look at how big the beans are.

INTERMARKET: It seems to me that you are fundamentalists insofar
as you look at the fundamentalists and make fun of them ...
JENKINS: We totally subscribe to the philosophy of technical analysis:
Everything known is reflected in the price. It makes inherent sense. I
could never hope to compete with Cargill that has soybean agents
scouring the globe knowing everything there is to know about soybeans and funneling the information up to Lake Minnetonka, their
trading headquarters.

Unless I have a friend at Cargill, I can only get this information one
way: I can infer it technically. We have friends who have made millions
trading fundamentally, but their problems are (a) they can rarely know
as much as the major commercials; and (b) they are limited to trading
their speciality. They don't know anything about bonds; they don't

know anything about the currencies. I don't either, but I've made a lot of money trading them. Every picture's worth a thousand words.

WILLIS: They're just numbers. Corn is a little different from bonds, but not different enough that I'd have to trade them differently — not different enough that I would have to have a different system.

JENKINS: Some of these guys I read about have a different system for each commodity. That's absurd. We're trading mob psychology. We're trading numbers. We're not trading corn, soybeans or S&Ps.

INTERMARKET: When you're in the pit, you must add on when you have winners.

JENKINS: Sure. That's the whole point.

INTERMARKET: And when you trade upstairs, you must do so as well. Is that when you use stops?

JENKINS: We've discovered that adding [to a profitable trade] is one of the hardest things to do properly. Where do you add when you get a trade that's good?

We bought when it was above 10 days worth of highs. Now it's above 20. Is that a buy? Or do we wait for 30 or 40?

We've learned from doing it ourselves and from seeing the way that Rich [Dennis] adds; he's probably one of the best adders there is. Good adds are put on so close to each other that they're almost part of the initial trade.

INTERMARKET: You said that when trading sugar, you put on the position and if it keeps going your way, you keep adding.

JENKINS: Yes. And it's partially a function of not being able to put on the maximum position at once. Actually, for my own account I put on as big a position as I can stand, right from the start, because I've never found a great way to add. Adding is an extremely fine art.

We found that it's impossible to make three sales or purchases in the same day [in equal time increments] and have the third one work out. We'll do 15 minute or 30 minute buys — anything — but no matter what the time frame, the results are the same.

Say we buy some gold at 9:30 and can add on only if it's a winner. We buy another one at 10:00 and wait until 10:30, where obviously they both have to be winners to buy again. If we are able to buy at the third increment, guaranteed, you'll never see the price of the third one again.

We used to joke that we should hire ourselves out as consultants to countries that wish to arrest the decline of their currencies. We could call them after the third sale and tell them to buy, because it definitely isn't going lower today. It's obvious that if you are able to make three adds, the move is over for the day, though certainly not for the duration of the swing.

INTERMARKET: You'd never add 100 contracts to a 100 contract position?

JENKINS: No! Never! Rich does that, though it wasn't his school of thought 10 years ago. Now he's decided the next signal is as good as the previous signal.

A move has both a time and a price function. You enter a trade as a function of price. What you have to consider about your add is the function of time. To be really effective, you have to add on to your profitable position early in the move. It's real hard to do. Like these D-Marks. I'd like to have some more, but I'm not going to buy on a 20 higher opening tomorrow.

INTERMARKET: Wouldn't you like to see a retracement of this move where you hope you're picking the low?

JENKINS: Well, your interview with Rich was interesting in that he made the point that, given the choice between buying continued strength and waiting for a retracement, statistically you're better off buying strength.

The pain theory—the harder it is to make a trade, the better it probably is to make—goes back to our observation that the trade that you least want to make is usually the best.

When you're on the floor and everyone is bidding, 350 bulls all screaming bids, it takes a lot of confidence to contemplate selling it, let alone *actually* selling it.

In September last year, we made $1.3 million for our customers and ourselves being short beans and meal on the day the beans made their contract highs.

INTERMARKET: That was the famous $9.68 day, wasn't it?

JENKINS: Yes. $9.68 1/2 actually. Then it broke about 50 cents.

A couple of astonishing things happened that day. First of all, the USDA figures came out, similar numbers having first been released by Sparks of Refco and then by Conrad Leslie at least two weeks before. I was flabbergasted because the USDA's confirmation of the previous numbers made the front page of the [Chicago] Tribune. "Beans going at least to $10, maybe into the teens."

I was shocked—not that they opened 10 higher, which was caused by all the hoopla—but that they went limit. Richard's buying made them go up the limit. That surprised us. We sold 500 at the opening, because we knew this was it. It was as if Rome was burning.

Good friends of ours, intelligent people, were calling up saying, "This is it, man. Beans are going to $12." Traders from the Merc whom I hadn't seen in years were over in the [Chicago Board of Trade] pit buying beans.

All everyone was talking about was beans. It was no secret that they were going up. We knew as traders that we didn't want to be long when the market turned. Instead, we were looking for a place to get short. It was a time to sit on the sidelines.

The guys on the floor of the Board of Trade are just like the customers. They love a bull market because it brings in paper and that's how they make all their money.

WILLIS: This bean swing is a great example of bad action. Beans, in our opinion, acted badly for two weeks prior to the top. Specifically, you'd walk into the pit at 10:30 and it would be limit bid. There were legitimately 20 million bushels bid on paper a couple of days. Then the market would come off limit and let all these guys come in.

If the market is still going up $2.00, it is not going to let 20 million longs in. That's absurd. It would come off, close limit [up] and open higher the next day. Talk about distribution! The market let everybody in! We sold prematurely several times and took small losses. But when it finally came, we creamed 'em.

INTERMARKET: Did you add on?

JENKINS: We sold so many that we couldn't! We were short the position limit of meal—which is 720—and we sold a couple million bushels of beans. We sold the equivalent of three million bushels and ended up making 1.3 million that day, and we took 80 cents out of it. That money materialized quickly.

INTERMARKET: Did you put that position on in staggers?

JENKINS: We sold the meal early in the day, because the meal was clearly weaker.

WILLIS: I had sold some beans and they ran me in. I no sooner paid the limit to take the small loss than they broke 10 cents. I looked at Bobby and I said, "Are we crazy or what?" I knew everybody in the world was bullish so I sold them back out.

INTERMARKET: How often do you do that—take the small loss and then put the position back on again?

WILLIS: Well, at reduced rates, the customer doesn't get that tremendous a break because we trade more. But he gets the break because it gives me more flexibility: "I think they're going down. Oops, I was wrong, I'm out. No, I was right. Sell them again." There is no way you can do that with $60 commissions.

JENKINS: I would like to make a point here. Obviously, we would love a system where we could come in and put our feet up on the desk and look at the screen once in a while and smoke a cigar and say, "Hey, Mary, if the beans close below $7.50, get us out." Go to the health club with a little beeper on and do push-ups and sit back like we've got the game figured out and it's over.

The problem is, this game is always changing. People who think they can develop a computer system that does everything for them make a spurious assumption. All a computer does is read yesterday's newspaper and try to trade off it. It's a business of the now and the future, not of the past.

INTERMARKET: But systems traders would argue that you don't have systematic indicators that can be shown viable over time.
JENKINS: Some wirehouses have been afraid of bringing people to do business with us—aside from their aversion to working with people who insist upon low commissions, which we do—because the way we trade is not strictly quantifiable. They want to be able to say that if the fund manager blows out, they've done their due diligence.

We've a two-year track record and a system which shows a 10-year record. But we'll be the first to admit that our system's only as good as yesterday's markets.

The bulk of the heros in this Managed Accounts Report [newsletter which reviews public and private commodity fund managers] are guys who are living off their laurels from the '79 and '80 bull and who have been losing their collective asses ever since. Some of them made 80 to 90% of their entire profits as CTAs in '79 and '80. And some of these on simulated paper trades!

We in the last 24 months have made $4.8 million real dollars for our customers, not to mention what we've done for ourselves. We've made big money, not paper trades. We don't have tweed suits on. I went to Yale, but that's not part of my sales pitch.

Let me show you how these statistics can mislead. Let's look at Charles Curran's record. Now if you're the casual observer you might say about Harvest II, "Wow, a 118% gain in the last 12 months. Let's get in on this guy." And in fact they are taking Curran out and marketing a new fund on him. But what does your 118% gain really mean? In terms of net asset value, the $970 you invested four and a half years ago is now worth $937. He had to make 100% just to get even. [In 1982, Curran's fund lost almost half its equity.] Nobody with any brains is still invested in the fund. They all should've bailed out years ago.

And his other fund [Harvest I] is only good if you invested in the beginning, probably a compounded annual of 25%. But they sold Fund II, which obviously hasn't done very well, on the basis of Fund I. And based on his performance of last year—he made back most of the money he lost—they will sell Fund III. It's ludicrous. What you have to look at is what your net asset value was when you started. What is it now? What's your compounded annual rate of return? And what was the largest drawdown?

Our goal is to be as consistent as the Hickey brothers [Bob and Joe]. We probably won't be. We're not arbitrageurs; we're speculators. I've invested in other fund managers and I look to invest in others because I know that people can outperform the market. We do it, Dennis can do it, and I'd like to find some others who do it. I, like any other investor, want an above-average return. There are two things I use to eliminate someone immediately. First, have they had a losing 12-month period? If so, I don't want any part of them. I don't care how well they've done over the last 10 years.

INTERMARKET: Do you care about a losing month?
JENKINS: No, but I care about the magnitude of the losing month. If in a winning year, the guy had a losing month that could have wiped out the whole year, then he's a no-no. One guy has a pretty good record but was ahead 8% and lost that in one month. What happens if you put two of these months together? You're a loser.

My second criterion for pinpointing a good fund manager: I would never invest with someone who's had a drawdown of 20% in a month. God forbid we should ever do that after going on record — our worst drawdown was 11%. If you lose 20% in a month, that's one thing, but what happens when you do that back to back?

I usually pick this up [picks up Managed Account Reports] with a glove on. The tone of it is so dry — they never praise anybody, nor do they ever criticize anybody. The thing is, nobody buys any ads in there. I could understand it if they accepted paid ads and they didn't want to piss the advertisers off — if Charles Curran were going to buy the back cover for $5000 or something. Yes, you can buy a booth at one of their conventions, but even then, that's only a couple of hundred dollars. Editorially, Managed Accounts Reports is like lukewarm water, or toast that you cooked up two hours ago — there's just no taste to it.

How about a little praise? We had the best performing fund in the country last year and hardly got a mention. Praise us when we do well, because you're sure going to damn us when we don't.

The bottom line is not that we're so good, but rather that the competition is so bad.

INTERMARKET: Are you jaded?
JENKINS: Well, perhaps a bit. We're not members of the club. One of the great frustrations we've had — though actually, we're not naive people, so it shouldn't have been a surprise to us — was the cold reception we've gotten from some of the Wall Street wirehouses. They don't seem to want to go out and sell our product. Obviously we have a winning product. But we will only work with a low round-turn commission.

The wirehouses don't understand — and they hardly give us a chance to tell them once they've heard the low commissions we want to charge — that we trade about two or three times more actively than most CTAs, so in fact a $20 commission from us is like a $60 commission in terms of the commission to equity ratio.

When we insist on a low commission, it's real hard to get through the front door. We went to the MAR [convention, January 1984] in Las

Vegas, thinking that since we were the number one fund in 1983, perhaps someone would want to seek us out.

WILLIS: It was like we had leprosy.

JENKINS: The bottom line is that there is an inherent conflict of interest between our goals and those of the majority of commission houses in this industry. The goal of the traditional brokerage house is to make money for the brokerage house. That means the house comes first, the broker selling the product comes second, and the customer, well, what can I say? It is not for the customer first. If it were, the whole cost and fee structure would be more performance-oriented.

WILLIS: It's worse than that. We've actually come across wirehouses where the thought of making money for the customer hasn't occurred to them. There literally has never been such a thing. "How much can we charge?" and "Let's get it going for each of us."

JENKINS: Everybody's losing money, so it you can lose less than most of the people, chances are you can still find warm bodies. Their approach is, "Let's go out and kill the guy in 12 months with high commissions and an inferior product, and then go out and get a new warm body." Our emphasis is on longevity. We've never had a losing account in two years of doing this. We don't intend to, to whatever extent we can keep that under control — probably someday we're going to have one. We believe that it's better to make a little money off a guy and keep him alive.

Two things will happen: He'll be there and you won't have to replace him, plus, he'll bring his friends in. The word-of-mouth effect. We're on the verge of doing our third $2 million fund and we've gotten between half and two-thirds of it informally sold to people who've called us up, saying their friends — current investors — recommended us.

We've got some heavy hitters: The heads of five major commodity brokerage firms and over 27 Board of Trade members are among our investors. We have members of every major commodities exchange in the country as investors. We call ourselves "the Traders' Traders." Most of our investors are friends, family or exchange members.

We're starting to get more customers who are not referrals. There are a few houses that understand why charging low commissions is ultimately a better deal for the house as well as the customer. This understanding is a prerequisite for raising money for us.

We don't have any business where we charge over $30 per round-turn, and very little at $30.

What we predicted six months to a year ago is coming to pass. We said to some of these guys, "If you don't get with a lower commission rate, you're going to be a dinosaur in the tar pit." Those of us charging commissions and marketing products which allow investors to make money will stay in business. Of course, they laughed in our faces. We were the young kids. There's $500 million sitting there [in public commodities funds]—or there was—which lost 3.3% over the last 12 months, which is an improvement over where they were six months ago.

WILLIS: The rate structures which charge $70 per round-turn are destined to lose the customer money.

INTERMARKET: Any thoughts on general partners who promote funds while refusing to invest in them?

JENKINS: We like the concept of the promoter investing in its funds. We invest in our own funds. Furthermore, we trade our own money the same way. Tom's dad is in [their first private placement fund]; my mom's in. When I'm putting on a trade, I'm making that trade for my mother, so I'm not going to go haywire and deep-six the thing. She can't afford it and I don't need the aggravation. Frankly, I don't think you can sell a fund with conviction unless you have your own money in it.

We had a guy who was interested in taking us as a replacement advisor to a fund, even before it started trading. The CTA bombed out during the registration period. The promoter called us down to his office. To give you an idea how some people think in this business, when he found out that it would cost another $10,000 or $20,000 in legal and accounting fees to bring our track record up to an SEC format—versus a private placement format—he refused to pay it, and decided to sell the inferior product. This CTA had lost 50% for his customers in 1984, while we had made 30%. Even so, the promoter went ahead and marketed the loser to save himself $20,000—the customers be damned.

That's the problem with some of the guys running this business; they're former refrigerator salesmen and they don't have any sense of integrity.

I guess there's the question, "How badly do you need the money?" That's the good thing about Tom and myself—we don't *need* the money. We're comfortable.

Which probably brings you to the question, "Why are we doing this?" At a certain point, we'll have a large enough net worth that there won't be any point in taking any more risk. I have a figure in mind, at which point I'll stop trading my own account. I don't need more money than that—I can live comfortably off my investments and through doing this. We'll be making without risking what we have, and I'll still have the thrill of trading. And by the way, trading is thrilling. I can't imagine anything more stimulating in business.

Greed kills in any business, and especially in this one. When I first started in this business, I was greedy. I quickly learned the merits of not being greedy. It's a killer.

That's one of the things that's so unique about Rich. He doesn't care about material things. His personal life reflects that. This isn't money to him. It's a chess game and he wants to be the best chessmaster—Bobby Fisher times 10. And he certainly is.

You can't think about money when you're trading, but it does represent reality for me. I still care about it.

So, if we can take on more customers and do a good job for them, feel good about the product that we're selling on the streets, and have happy customers — which we do have — that's what I want to do.

WILLIS: And there's a lot of money in it.

JENKINS: We can ultimately trade $50 million. We've already weeded out the markets which are structurally ineffecent for us in the sense of lack of volume or open interest. We're trading $18 to $19 million and we could easily trade two and a half times bigger in the currencies, the bonds, the grains and the metals. Our first trade in the currencies will be 400 or 500 and we could easily do 1200. In bonds we open with 400 or 500 and could easily do 1500.

INTERMARKET: What do you think about the corn versus soybean limits [a controversial rule which limits the total amount of soybeans and corn a trader may buy or sell to three million bushels in each contract]?

JENKINS: It's rediculous. The [corn] crop is three or four times as big. The exchange tacitly acknowledges the proper proportion in that the bean price limit is three times the corn limit. [The bean crop is one-third smaller and hence three times as volatile with a 30 cents daily price limit versus 10 cents for corn.] For the spreader, if you buy a million beans, you're short three million corn against it. That's just the three to one ratio.

Of course it's absurd. But will it be changed? Probably not. But we can go to the MidAmerica.

INTERMARKET: What's the difference between trading a primary market versus a secondary market — the Board versus the MidAm, for instance?

WILLIS: Trading the primary, the quality of trade is a little less clear. When it's all said and done, there really isn't much of a difference. An edge is an edge is an edge. They'll give you the same edge at the Board as they will at the MidAmerica. It all boils down to the same dollar amounts.

INTERMARKET: You mean that you don't find it any harder to trade from the office at the MidAm than at the Board?

WILLIS: I asked Rich this. I sometimes floor trade at the MidAmerica to have fun. I was doing this a few weeks back. It turned out that he was trading [from the desk] heavily. He was giving a penny or a penny and a half edge to the last known price at the Board. So I said, "Sold! 500." I was interested about what he thought about his fills.

Certainly at the Board of Trade you can bid for a million at the wrong time and pay five cents over the last price. At no point will you ever pay five cents for a million at the MidAmerica. They are stymied because they don't make their own market. Instead of five cents over, if paper bids one and a half cents over, everybody's selling it to him.

The first 500,000 bushels are basically the same. For a half a cent, you can buy 500,000 at the Mid, and it costs the same half cent at the Board. After that, it gets sticky. Last week, Rich thought he was getting better fills than he would have gotten at the Board. At the Board, the last price is the last price. It's a much easier market to read at the MidAmerica.

JENKINS: At the MidAm, if a fund trader comes in with a million-bushel order, that's it — except for the ones and twos.

But at the Board, there are millions trading all the time. You don't have any real idea of the quality of the edge.

WILLIS: The floor trader has to have a better idea of what he wants to do at the Board. At the MidAm, you can come in and let it happen.

INTERMARKET: If you had it to do all over again, would you start on the floor?
WILLIS: Yes.

INTERMARKET: How much do you need to start trading, assuming you already own the seat?
WILLIS: $10,000 is a bare minimum. I know people who are doing it for less, but that's what I'd want.

INTERMARKET: Did you attribute your first year's success to your quickness as opposed to —
JENKINS: [Interrupting] As opposed to having any brains? (Laughs)

INTERMARKET: As opposed to applying technical analysis and strength-weakness perceptions — buying a rally above three days' worth of highs, for instance.
WILLIS: I didn't have any knowledge of what was going on. Floor trading is very narrow in scope. The reason we left the floor was to diversify. If markets really are just numbers, let's look at as many of them as we can.

But my first three or four years were really just grinding them out.
JENKINS: Being quick is of no value unless you know what to react to. Tom is very quick, but he also knows what's worth being quick for.
WILLIS: Even on the floor, the money's made on the position, not by clipping some order. That kind of money is very limited.

Take the best floor traders at the Board. A few made a million dollars a year just trading — just pounding it out. Those guys are the top guys. The next best guy might make $500,000. There are only two or three guys who are really good, two or three more who make decent money, and then you're down to the rest, who are groveling for $50,000 to

$100,000. That sounds like big money, but let me tell you, it's rough: no paid vacations, no benefits, no guarantees, no nothing.

JENKINS: You could make $30,000 in interest off the money tied up in your seat alone, or you could rent it out. You have a big opportunity cost just to come down there [to the exchange floor].

If you could rent out your seat for $4000 per month, that's $48,000 a year. If you're only making $100,000 a year, is that $52,000 worth it to take all that risk, and the jostling?

Coming from the MidAm to the Board of Trade, you think you're walking through St. Peter's and everyone's going to be real sophisticated and smart. The bottom line is — if anything — they have a smaller perspective than traders at the MidAmerica because they don't *need* to have a bigger perspective. You can think in smaller terms because there's a huge volume. You can be K-Mart in the lead option of the bonds. There isn't any K-Mart franchise at the MidAmerica — you have to trade everything. You better get out there and use your imagination.

INTERMARKET: So what are your tips to the beginning trader at the MidAm?

WILLIS: Trade as many different commodities as you can stand. If they [the locals] did this at the Board of Trade, they'd make five times the money.

At the MidAm, there are no deep markets. You can't stand next to your friendly neighborhood broker and go up and down the scale and expect to make a lot of money. You can make some money, yes. What you have to do at the MidAm is expand your latitude, be willing to trade wheat against beans and gold against silver and bonds against corn. Since you're forced to do that, you find you can make more money with less risk. I'll argue it with any econ professor: You can minimize risk and maximize profit. They'll disagree, but I'll prove it. Trade as much as you can, don't have any preconceived notions about yourself or the markets, believe in what you're doing, and if you're wrong, get out. Your opinion is only worth what the market thinks of it.

JENKINS: Tom is making the point that Rich believes: You can teach someone to do this either trading on the floor or away from it. There are simple principles. There are no great secrets or mysteries. Sometimes people will sit in our office — or even drop in uninvited — waiting for us to pull the magic wand out of the closet that we hit the markets with to make money. There's just no substitute for discipline and for knowing what you want to do.

There are no secrets. Tom told you what is sort of a secret but really isn't: When everything in the world is higher except for one thing, sell it. Tom was speaking at a seminar and said that everything was higher except for bean oil, which made us sell a couple hundred contracts. We made $60,000 on that trade that day. Tom told the audience about the trade. A guy raised his hand and said, "Come on. You mean that you sold the only thing that was lower?" [He was thinking that you should *buy* the only thing that was lower because it would catch up.] He didn't believe it.

And that's how most people think. To be a success in this business, you've got to screw your head around 180 degrees. Whether you're of average intelligence or above-average intelligence, you've been raised on the same media as the rest of the world, taught to react as everyone else reacts. And you can't make money doing what everyone else does when trading. Common knowledge is not knowledge which is going to enrich you.

INTERMARKET: If you were suddenly wiped out and had but $10,000 to trade at the MidAm, how would you trade differently?
WILLIS: So I've lost everything?

INTERMARKET: Yes.
JENKINS: His wife would probably kill him to collect the life insurance. (Laughs)
WILLIS: At this point it would be hard to unlearn everything. I would make the same kind of trades. I'd buy the D-Mark, for instance. I may only buy one or two, but I'd still take a strong trade.

INTERMARKET: Why is it that today you're not making the same percentage return that you were during your second through fifth years?
WILLIS: It's harder to make a great rate of return on a large amount of money.
JENKINS: You can't do it scalping. Tom was never just a scalper in the sense that he bought something at five and sold it at five and a half. He was a scalp-position trader. He let the pit put him into a position. If he bought some at five and they went to seven, he might buy some more at six if they were selling under, then buy some more at nine. When he put the trade on initially, he may have liked it, but he probably had no idea of what to expect from it.

But since he's been down there a couple of years, he knows what to look for. If the market's over two days' worth of highs, he may be in there for five, 10, 15, 20 cents. Who knows what the day has in store for him? A scalper, by definition, never makes more than a few tics on a trade and a good one never loses more than a couple. Tom was never a scalper, except for maybe the first year he was down there. He was always a position trader who was in the pit and scalped around his position.

INTERMARKET: You've said you were willing to lose 10% on a scalp?
WILLIS: I'd trade a position small enough that if I were dead wrong, I'd still only lose 10%. In D-Marks, the risk is 20 points.

I think the big difference between my trading now versus when I started out was in risk-reward potential. I wouldn't take any trade which didn't offer three or four to one in my favor. In reality, all trades are even. You are either going to win or lose. They will be up or down, 50-50. the difference is, a good trade can lose 10 points or make 30 to 40.

What's different about me now is, if I have a good trade going, I'll probably squeeze the $3000 out of it, whereas years ago, I might cut it loose after $1500 or so of profit. Now I'll get every ounce out of it or it'll be a scratch [a breakeven trade].

INTERMARKET: Tell me about openings and closes. How will you respond if, say, the D-Mark opens 10 lower?
JENKINS: I'll be upset. Actually, I won't be upset — because I expect it. If it opens 10 or 15 lower, I wouldn't get out of the position right away, because it might still have some potential. If it opens 30 lower, gets below the contract low-close, as it did yesterday, *that* would get me out immediately. If it opens five or 10 lower, I'll wait. Chances are it will trade higher at some point in the day. We're not married to any of these positions. We don't get opinionated.

But we bought it because it acted well yesterday when everything else acted poorly and it didn't act bad today.
WILLIS: It was a technical trade with a bit of contrarianism.
JENKINS: We don't have absolute fixed points, we know in a rough area where we want to buy things, sell them. We don't sit down and figure out, "I'm going to risk 1% on this trade and 3% on that trade." We look at the quality of the trade.
WILLIS: You see, we've been taking small losses for so long, it really is second nature. It feels good to take a small loss.
JENKINS: It's like when you have a mosquito on your arm, you slap it. You got bit, but you're not going to let it feast on you.

INTERMARKET: How would holding a loser too long affect someone's trading?
WILLIS: Not taking the quick, small loss is costly. That's very true. But the opportunity costs are probably more costly — holding on to a loser effectively takes you out of the market.
JENKINS: You get fixated on the loser, and you miss all the other good trades. You bought it at six and it's now at two. If you had been a disciplined trader, you would have sold it at no less than four. Now you're hoping that it comes back to four, where you should have gotten out. In fact, it goes from two to even. So now you're four tics lower than where you should have gotten out and you think, "God, I can't affort that big a loss." Meanwhile, had you taken the quick loss, you might have been able to make four good trades which would have covered the small loss and then some. You could have had a profit instead of the six tic mess you got yourself into.

WILLIS: The hardest thing—and this gets back to "What do you do when your D-Mark [a profitable position] opens lower?"—depending on how low it is, taking a loss becomes automatic.
JENKINS: And you look at it in relation to the rest of the group.
WILLIS: Sure. If the Swiss opens 30 lower and the D-Mark opens five lower, I have to ask myself, "Do I really want to run out of the D-Mark?"
JENKINS: We'd be waiting for the D-Mark to get higher to buy more, probably.

INTERMARKET: So if it has to open lower, you like to have it open less weakly than any of the other currencies?
WILLIS: Absolutely. Say the Swiss opens five higher and the D-Mark opens two lower. Two lower—how much can that hurt? A lot. I think you've got a problem. It's not so much how many points, but what it looks like in relation to something else. The most important thing is not that sort of thing, because that has to become second nature—taking small losses. If you can't do that, you're gone. That's the fatal flaw. But really, the hardest thing in trading successfully is, what do you do with the D-Mark when it opens higher? How do you handle your winners?
JENKINS: Once you've learned to handle your losses—which becomes second nature to all successful traders—the next crucial lesson to be learned is how to handle your winners. Do you take 50 points out of the move or 300 points out of it? Everyone always pays so much attention to trade initiation. But it's much more important how you get out of a trade versus how you get into it.
WILLIS: I don't think entry trades are any secret. "The chart looks like this; you get into a trade here."
JENKINS: Last year's bean market is the example that keeps cropping up in my mind. The question isn't, "Did you get in at $6.75 or $7.00?" I don't think C&D even bought until $7.25. The question is, "Did you get out at $9.00? $9.25? or $9.50? Or did you hold on too long and end up where you're sitting there puking them at $8.00 like Refco? Or were you selling them at $7.00 like the farmers and then calling up your senator saying that it was C&D and Refco's fault that they came down, even though they didn't give the major longs [C&D and Refco] credit for the market's rise?"

That's the real key. We not only got out of our longs in the $9.00 area, we became major shorts within a few cents of the season's high because of poor action the market exhibited over several weeks. We think that's one of the key things we do that separates us from the other guys—getting *out* of trades.

INTERMARKET: Do you use the rule of taking a position on whatever side of the opening range the market breaks out of first?
WILLIS: That's a daytrader's rule. That's the first part of the ballgame,

the opening innings. Surprisingly, what you'll find is that the highs and lows are frequently made in the opening range. That's significant. Why? Because it tells you where the low is. What it does is eliminate one side of the market, if you're smart.

JENKINS: If you're asking Tom as a daytrader, obviously that's important. But if you're asking him from up here, it's not as important.

INTERMARKET: So if the lows are made on the opening range, you'll get long and probably take them home?

WILLIS: What I know I'm not going to do is sell them. If the low is made on the opening range and the low is still up there half an hour into the session, I'm not going to sell them in general unless I already have them.

INTERMARKET: So we're coming up to the close and they're breaking through nine-day highs. Are you going to take them home?

WILLIS: Definitely! You can make a lot of money buying things that are closing on their highs—not to mention closing over nine-day highs—and selling them the next opening. That will work six times out of 10.

INTERMARKET: Do you have a good idea as to what the public thinks about, when moving average signals are generated, and so on?

JENKINS: You don't see huge orders coming in, or stacks of orders. You don't look over the broker's shoulders. You just know they're coming in.

WILLIS: We have a pretty good idea what people think about because we are systems traders.

INTERMARKET: Do most locals?

JENKINS: Most locals don't even know what yesterday's highs and lows were. That's a fact. I've gone into any number of pits and asked, "Does anyone know what yesterday's high was?," only because I was too lazy to pull the card I'd written it down on out of my pocket. They don't know!

WILLIS: I sometimes wonder if they know whether they're higher or lower on the day. Of course spread traders don't need to know. Neither do brokers. To the guys who are clipping the orders—getting the edge—it doesn't matter.

INTERMARKET: Are the locals smarter than we think they are?

JENKINS: No! [Laughs]

WILLIS: No! Unequivocally. [Laughs] They are the lowest men on the totem pole. As a matter of fact, as bad as the fund managers are, the locals are worse. The fund managers are going to lose most of the time. But you can never convince me that any of those locals are really winning. I'm factoring in days out of our lives that we are going to lose, everything.

The floor traders have the least idea of what they want to do. They'll take a bad trade and try and make a half a cent off it.

INTERMARKET: How do you view a trade differently when you have a profit in it?
JENKINS: It's your money, whether you've just put the position on or whether you've already made a million from the position.

INTERMARKET: Any interesting war stories?
WILLIS: The stories about Rich in general are true. He really does live it the way he says he'd like to see it done. What's so beautiful about that guy is that the whole world is trying to get what he has. And the reason he has it is because he doesn't really want it all that badly.

The whole world's trying to get his millions — how many zeros it is. They'd do almost anything to get it; most people would stop at very little to get it. They'd do a lot. Yet I don't think he'd ever change one thing he's done — the way he's treated anybody. Richard Dennis really is a good success story because he hasn't sold himself out and he hasn't changed a bit. In all the millions of dollars he's made in the time that I've known him, he hasn't changed at all.

That's tough. I've gone through periods where I've made some fast money and have gotten uglier. I've said things I wish I could retract.

INTERMARKET: Has success changed you? Has it changed your friends?
JENKINS: Well, we've never really had any friends to begin with. [Laughs]
WILLIS: We hate people. [Laughs]
JENKINS: No, I think that draws back to being able to judge character. Sure, we've had people chummy up to us for ulterior motives, but usually we can tell.

Contrary to the commonly held belief that this is an ugly business, that it's a zero sum game and that if I win, he loses, the beauty of this business is that you're competing only against yourself. You're trying to fulfill your own potential as a trader.

That's what's exciting about it — your potential is limited only by your own imagination, your ability to think creatively, and your discipline. You're not limited by a bottleneck in some corporate hierarchy, where you won't get promoted until there's an opening in your division.

This business is pure capitalism — it allows the cream to rise.

4

Richard Sandor

*R*ichard Sandor, at age 43, has seen the financial industry from many angles. He has seen it from a theoretical standpoint, having been a Ph.D. teaching during the rebellious days of the mid 1960's at the University of California at Berkeley. As a Board of Trade economist and principal architect of the first interest rate contract, he has seen it from the angle of a growth industry needing pioneers. And, as a floor trader speculating for his own account, he has seen it broken down to its basic element — the fluctuation of price over time.

Richard Sandor left the ivory tower to journey out into a growth industry. He came to the Board of Trade at a time of immense flux in the financial system, saw the opportunity for a futures contract based on cash Ginnie Maes, and gained recognition once the importance of the concept became apparent. He then turned to selling his expertise in the proper usage of the interest rates for financial institutions. He has been tremendously successful, some estimate to the extent of seven figures per year in earnings.

Some would say Richard Sandor has been in the right place at the right time. And he would smile and not disagree. But others, himself included, wonder what could have been ... what could have been had he run for chairman of the Chicago Board of Trade (where he mysteriously pulled out of the running in 1983) ... what could have been had he spent his energies in founding his own firm rather that building up ContiFinancial and later joining the Drexel Burnham Lambert partnership.

INTERMARKET: What did you get out of *The Art of War* (a book prominently displayed on his bookshelf)?
SANDOR: It is not only a book on military strategy. It's really far more

than that. It's a book about strategy in business and strategy in life, in terms of discipline, attitudes, conducting oneself. It gives you principles that can be established not only in your business life but in your personal life, your intellectual life. Within lie the secrets of good trading, leadership, etc.

INTERMARKET: How did a Ph.D. in economics end up in this industry?
SANDOR: It really all began at the University of California-Berkeley's campus in the 1960's.

INTERMARKET: Were you a radical?
SANDOR: No. At that point, not at all. I was very much trained as a professional economist. I believed in free markets and was teaching at the university. One of my colleagues there got me interested in futures markets and I basically started speculating in futures while a teacher.

INTERMARKET: Paper trading or the real thing?
SANDOR: The real thing. It was fun and very enjoyable. After doing that, Bank of America was interested in establishing—or helping to establish—a Pacific exchange. I did a very thorough study of brokers when I was opening my account and I met some of the people whom I thought were very capable. I subsequently started working with one of them, a forward-thinking guy who was interested in establishing the exchange in San Francisco.

INTERMARKET: The INTEX concept.
SANDOR: Exactly. I started consulting and set up the project at the university. I got somebody from the electrical engineering and computer science departments. We did the study. I had to fly out to Chicago to learn how the markets trade from a mechanical point of view, how they function and whether a computer program could be developed to simulate the auction process, and so on. I was involved in this for some time. I started teaching a course on futures markets at the university.

INTERMARKET: Were there any others at this time?
SANDOR: To my knowledge, at that time, mine was the only one solely devoted to futures in any graduate school of business. It was a big departure.

INTERMARKET: It must have taken some lobbying to get the administration to approve.
SANDOR: Well, at Berkeley in the sixties, experimentation was looked upon favorably. Getting the course approved was relatively easy.

What I did was bring in many speakers from the industry. It was a very small business then. Most of my guest speakers were local traders or people who had practical experience that I wanted to impart to the students.

One of the speakers I had out there was Warren Lebeck, at that time the secretary of the Board of Trade.

We got into a conversation to the effect that it would be interesting to actually be involved in the real world. A year or two later, Warren called up and said, "Do you think you'd like to leave the university and come to Chicago and be the economist for the Board? We don't have an economist." This was in late 1971 or early 1972.

INTERMARKET: (Interrupting) Were you thinking about tenure and how you might lose it?

SANDOR: Yes. I had been teaching six years, and I was going to take the traditional leave of absence and hopefully come back a tenured associate professor.

The Board of Trade was a new alternative. I had an offer to go to the Chinese University of Hong Kong, one to go to the Helsinki School of Economics, and another to Iran's Abadan, the oil university. I was searching for something to do on my sabbatical, so I came to Chicago and interviewed.

In 1969 I had thought about the feasibility of a futures market on financial instruments. In the next year, I got a grant from the Center for Real Estate and Urban Economics to study the feasibility of a futures market in mortgages.

INTERMARKET: What year was that?

SANDOR: That was 1970 or 1971. I had started analyzing a portfolio of 18,000 loans that an S&L in San Francisco had given to me to see if we could develop a homogeneous product. This was before the cash Ginnie Maes were developed. It became clear once you understood futures markets that it could be done. And as an economist, if you understood mortgages, it was very simple as well.

INTERMARKET: So you applied what the farmer could do to the S&L's situation?

SANDOR: It slowly progressed. The production pattern and the distribution of mortgages was in theory identical to the production, origination and distribution patterns of grain.

During 1969, we had the first real credit crunch. And it became clear that if interest rates became volatile, a futures market would become very necessary. I got a grant from the university center and was in the midst of studying it when the Board of Trade called. They invited me to come, but I said, "Yes, I'd like to, but I'm working on two very exciting products. One is a futures market on interest rates."

They said no. They didn't want somebody for a sabbatical; they wanted somebody full-time.

INTERMARKET: So you had to make your career decision?

SANDOR: They finally agreed that I could come on a one-year sabbatical. I almost didn't come because of that. I had tenure coming and thought I would go back. I came on in the spring of 1972.

INTERMARKET: When currencies were about to be launched.

SANDOR: They were launched subsequently, if my memory serves me. That summer was the beginning of the volatile grain markets with the Russian purchases. After that the IMM (The Chicago Mercantile Exchange's subsidiary, the International Monetary Market) was launched, as was the CBOE. In the spring of 1973, I had to go back to the university. But I was getting to the point where I had to make another decision.

At that time, I also worked on the existing agricultural products, and also the other duties an economist would have: planning, representing the exchange before governmental bodies, etc.

Also at that time the whole economic system was cracking. We had another credit crunch in the making and the new exchanges were growing—the people whom I talked to on financial markets were laughing less when I walked in the door. The receptions and the open-mindedness toward the concept were growing. I requested a second year of sabbatical. They said, "Okay, but this is it. Either come back or cut loose."

By the spring of 1974, the interest rates had come full circle, and people were getting excited about the possibility of this market. It was a very timely and a very exciting market.

INTERMARKET: Did they have to up the ante to encourage you to stay another year?

SANDOR: Not really. Most of the first year was spent in the agricultural end. I wrote a hard red winter wheat contact which failed miserably. But I learned more from writing that contract that helped me with the Ginnie Maes, the bonds, the options, the 10-year notes than I ever could have learned from a success.

INTERMARKET: In terms of dealing with the CFTC or constructing a contract?

SANDOR: Both. The first one was not really a CFTC question but really the art of designing a contract. The economics of it: how it had to be balanced so that giving something to the long meant giving something to the short. How you had to provide the ability to develop a hedging vehicle as well as an arbitrage vehicle. The fact that it couldn't be just a cash market instrument, but had to be a futures instrument.

All of those things became critical in the design of the Ginnie Mae contract. It took 26 separate drafts. The first draft was a 6-1/2% coupon on a $250,000 contract—interest rates were not volatile enough. By the time we ended the process it went to an 8% coupon and a $100,000 contract.

INTERMARKET: How was this revolutionary concept received by CFTC and by the agricultural people at the Board?
SANDOR: I think this was the first new contract that the CFTC looked at. The CFTC came into existence during the spring of 1975. Virtually the day they came into existence, this contract to trade interest rate futures came about, their first confrontation with a new contract. The agency at that time was staffed by predominantly agricultural people and it was a very arduous education process.

There were also a number of people we had worked with over the years in the academic world and the real world who understood the economic role these markets could perform. And of course, Les Rosenthal, as Chairman of the Board, was instrumental in convincing the people at the Board that these markets would succeed.

It is interesting to note that the CFTC subsequently approved the contract, and the seeds for the jurisdictional dispute were sown. The day before the Ginnie Maes were scheduled to begin trading, the SEC sought an injunction to stop them because they were a registered security. It was thrown out by the court. So the interest rate contracts were almost killed 24 hours before they were to open, all for a jurisdictional dispute.

INTERMARKET: Did you ever write a thank-you note to the judge?
SANDOR: No. (Laughs) I don't remember his name but I thank him to this day. The concept of Ginnie Maes was still viewed with a good deal of skepticism. I had a good deal of my professional career in the balance, working on this idea for six years, so if it didn't succeed —

INTERMARKET: (Interrupting) You didn't succeed?
SANDOR: Yes, if it didn't succeed, then I didn't succeed. So I decided to go into the business of advising people on how to use these markets. There was obviously a lack of talent, both on the user's side and on the brokerage side. It was a new (futures) product, and the underlying product itself was complicated. As in any infant industry, it suffered from a lack of human capital. It was necessary not only to develop credible hedging knowledge, but credible sales knowledge.

A wide variety of talents has to be created to develop any industry. It was clear that that would have to happen in this industry. I had been fortunate to do a thesis on the economics of inventive activity. I really wasn't a financial economist to start with. Although I had studied finance, my interests were in the psychology and economics of inventors and inventions. Having been a student of growth industries, it was easy to see things that were required for the industry to succeed and for a new product that had to be used by a lot of different people, few of whom had any knowledge. The dissemination of the knowledge would be critical.

It's interesting that the financial futures industry had developed much like any industry. The product cycles are almost identical. Every time a *Wall Street Journal* or *New York Times* story comes out, some of the concerns expressed by people who are either writing or being interviewed are the same things expressed by people in the early days of the computer, the automobile.

I found enormous educational problems, enormous lethargy, resistance to change. You see that among users in the business.

If you take a look at the names of those who used financial futures initially, it looks like a list of Who's Who in finance. Not because they used futures, but because the initial users of a new market tend to be divergent thinkers, people who would not necessarily be bound by old ways, who have the creativity and the imagination to try out another product, and those are typically the people you would expect to advance to greater planes.

What's happened over the decade is that those initial users have moved up in the banking, investment banking and corporate worlds and the next generation of people who are both on the user's, side and the sales side are a generation of individuals who've learned about it at the university level.

INTERMARKET: Did you have a seat at the Board?
SANDOR: Yes. I made the move almost simultaneously with the introduction of the futures markets, and I felt — and Continental Grain agreed — that this particular product needed a professional and specialized sales force. I got a seat on the exchange and went down to the floor and sold concepts and ideas — arbitrages also. And I tried to learn how to speculate. I spent the quiet hours — and there were a lot of quiet hours in the beginning — in the corn pit, trying to learn how to become a trader.

INTERMARKET: I see a three step movement from the theoretical to the real — from the university theoretical level, to the exchange political/economic level, then finally down to the bottom, the exchange floor. What was that like?
SANDOR: There was a lot of culture shock to try to — well, some of it was culture shock, some of it wasn't. I basically went into a business where education was critical. I was trying to teach people about the product and how to use it. I had to communicate and make complex things simple.

INTERMARKET: But on the floor, education is not at all an asset.
SANDOR: I think to a great extent, that's true. The education was valuable in the selling. The education was not that valuable — and

possibly even a liability—in the trading.

Trading requires a whole different set of skills, not necessarily forecasting skills, either. It requires physical and mental agility. Basically, doing things which professional traders do is not necessarily intellectually the best thing to do.

INTERMARKET: For example?
SANDOR: For example, a local will buy breaks and sell rallies. That's not something that the academic would advocate. He might not go contrary to the market. The discipline also is very important.

INTERMARKET: So you were very schizophrenic at that point?
SANDOR: I was very schizoid at that point. I got teased a lot in the pit. I basically would walk into the pit and I would bid when I was trying to offer and offer when I was trying to bid. They'd yell, "Hey doc, waddya doin'?" So now my badge reads "DOC," a tribute to the mercilessness of the floor traders. It was a lot of fun, a lot of discipline, and I learned a lot, too.

INTERMARKET: What did you learn (on the floor) that helped your trading (off the floor)?
SANDOR: Essentially discipline, which I think is the most critical factor in profitable trading. To understand how to take losses and how to be a good loser, which, I think, runs hand-in-hand with discipline.

It's easy to be a winner. Almost everyone can win easily. In many respects, it is more difficult to be able to lose in the right way.

INTERMARKET: Do you think success in trading, either from the desk or on the floor, requires the same skills as running any business?
SANDOR: That's an interesting question. I think that to some degree there's an overlap. There is a wide variety of traders or trading patterns and I think you have to distinguish between them. There's a scalper, there's a spreader, there's a position trader, and all of them are different.

Scalping has a much different orientation—it tends to be more mechanical. It requires the same psychological discipline that it takes to run a successful business, but it doesn't necessarily require the analytical skills. In fact, the analytical skills can get in the way of good scalping.

The position trader, as well as the spreader—who, in the parlance of financial futures, is more akin to the arbitrageur—requires a very, very different set of analytical tools. The talents found in a spread trader who is disciplined could easily benefit someone running a business. In fact, some of the most successful people around the exchange have made the transition from traders to successful businessmen. They are analytical, and either they lost interest in trading or it became too physically demanding. They took what they learned as traders and applied that to businesses.

INTERMARKET: Tell some war stories about some companies that because of their hedging with you, changed their bottom line.
SANDOR: Those people who have hedged against adverse moves in the market have been able to change their entire structure. A recent client made a statement to me that if last year he had had the net interest cost on his liabilities that he has today, then he would have thought someone was crazy.

A lot of people mature in the way they think about their own businesses as a result of getting involved in a risk management program involving the futures markets. People who've been involved in bond options have created either liability products or asset products with optional features. Using the market not only helps hedging, but they took what they learned in these markets, and designed new products in their day-to-day business that they never would have thought of had they not been involved.

Businesses can change dramatically when they get consulting on (1) how to measure risk; (2) how to transfer unwanted risk; (3) how to restructure that risk, given the risk tools that they have; and (4) how they can use what they've learned in these markets to create additional business opportunity. Much of the trend in the financial futures brokerage industry is a trend toward looking at these markets from the investment banking point of view, as opposed to the futures brokerage point of view.

INTERMARKET: What are the specific questions you ask me when I come to you and say, "I'm a president of an S&L; I borrow money for 90 days and lend it out over 30 years. Help."
SANDOR: I would start by asking you if you can identify your interest rate risk. This tends to be a far bigger problem than you could ever imagine. Obviously, hedging is out of the question if you can't identify where your risk is.

INTERMARKET: Let's say each month, 200 Brits subscribe to a certain magazine, but there is a three-week lag between when I calculate their bill and when they pay. What do I do?
SANDOR: If you're billing in dollars, there's no problem. If you're billing in pounds, you have a certain amount of pounds which you will receive in the future. It will be X amount of pounds at today's dollar rate. The question then becomes, what is your risk? Your risk clearly comes from the fact that the pound may drop in value, and if it does, you will have a dollar value of receivables which is less than you have billed at today's prevailing exchange rates. We would first measure that. In the case of your magazine, it's a straightforward, simple calcu-

lation. In the case of a financial institution, it would become much more difficult.

The second thing we must know in order to hedge a risk exposure is what the available alternatives are. One solution might be to sell your magazine only in terms of dollars. You might reply that that's not good business and that you couldn't sell any magazines that way.

A second alternative might be to hedge by going to the interbank market. A third alternative might be to hedge using a futures contract. A fourth alternative might be to purchase a currency option on the pound. A fifth alternative might be to purchase an asset that gains in value when the pound goes down. In the case of your magazine there's nothing that comes to mind, but in the case of an S&L, it might be a variable rate type of interest bearing investment.

INTERMARKET: So to compare and contrast each one of these, I would look at the dollars out of my pocket, both now and at delivery; the risk reward ratio; and what else?
SANDOR: The first thing I would look at is, what is the price of all of these? In the case of a forward, is it cheaper or more expensive than a future?

INTERMARKET: Both today and when I take delivery.
SANDOR: Right. With an option, do I want to pay a premium to have limited risk? That would depend on your risk profile. Can you afford to purchase an asset which would move inversely with the pound? Then I would compare what flexibility I have with each.

For instance, I might have more flexibility with a futures contract than with the forward with a bank. Say that some of those subscriptions get cancelled. How could you go back to the bank and get a decent bid/offer spread on the forward as opposed to reversing the futures position?

INTERMARKET: So you measure the likelihood that my cash position may change?
SANDOR: Sure. And for that reason you might find that you bill for the subcriptions but only 75% of them come through. You might want an option because it wouldn't matter if the option expires worthless. If I purchased an asset—let's say a theoretical asset where if the pound went up in value, the coupon payments to you would increase—if someone could issue such an asset, how readily could you buy and sell that asset?

INTERMARKET: How liquid it is?
SANDOR: Yes. Liquidity. So the question of the use of futures becomes a question of (1) price; (2) flexibility; and (3) credit—that is, is there a likelihood of a default in the forward contract? Is there a likelihood

that if I were to default, I'd be stuck? And how does that default compare with the risk of daily mark-to-market that I have in the futures market, and the clearing corporation?

INTERMARKET: Can a troubled S&L still be saved?
SANDOR: I think that it is possible to restructure an S&L in such a way that it is much less sensitive to interest rate movement, and still profitable. I have a client who has a $500 million S&L that's totally insulated, via futures markets and investment banking tools, so that which way interest rates move is almost totally irrelevant.

INTERMARKET: He has a perfectly matched portfolio?
SANDOR: Yes. It is very possible to save any S&L. The problem is not in doing it; it's the management commitment to doing it that's critical. It has to have the creativity and the ability to accept new tools, and the ability to understand that the world is changing. One has to change one's management's attitude and the skills required to run the institution, in order to benefit from change.

After World War II, interest rate expense was just a fraction of corporate profits. Today it's grown to be 50% or 100% of corporate profits. If this is the magnitude that exists, it clearly is important that one manage it the same way one manages a manufacturing plant or a marketing department. The treasury in effect has got to be viewed as a place to minimize interest rate cost, as well as interest rate risk.

INTERMARKET: How do you convince a CFO who doesn't understand marked-to-market that he should examine them and compare them to the traditional forward commitment?
SANDOR: I think that this is one of the limitations of futures markets: The cashflows go back and forth. I'm not convinced that's a bad limitation. By that I mean that somehow people who don't mark-to-market get diluted into a position of comfort that they otherwise wouldn't have. For instance, portfolio managers who don't have to mark-to-market are much more risk-prone than those who face up to the risk element every single day.

As a matter of fact, I often wonder how many people take much greater losses — individual investors in the equity market — by not writing the check out for the losses on that particular day. How many people would continue to hold a stock if every day that it went down, they'd have to deposit extra money with the broker? It might force a realization.

Going back to being a trader with personal discipline, I try to evaluate what my assets are worth on a liquidation basis and I visualize my losses. It gives me a better idea. I might at a particular point write a check to a brokerage account, even though I don't have to come up with the cash, to reflect the losses I incurred. Once you do that, the pain of what you've lost becomes very apparent. It becomes easy to recognize that these losses have occurred as opposed to saying, "Oh, the stock will come back. The value of this property will come back. The value of this piece of art will come back."

INTERMARKET: Would you ever consider taking on a top position at a financial intermediary?
SANDOR: Oh, I'm so involved in what are still the adolescent stages of this industry that I really have no interest. I like being a problem solver in my current situation.

I don't know where I'll be in 10 or 20 years, but right now, there's still so much to be done in these markets. A major accounting firm did a study which suggests that 95% of the potential users of financial futures are not involved in these markets.

INTERMARKET: What will happen when they are? And why aren't farmers?
SANDOR: Well, farmers haven't had to—

INTERMARKET: Because they pay their grain elevator to do it?
SANDOR: Exactly. And I think you'll see the same trend in the financial futures community.

INTERMARKET: With interest rate swaps?
SANDOR: With interest rate swaps, exactly. With interest rate guarantees, with caps, people will develop expertise in repackaging futures and selling them as forwards and options. People will get paid for doing your hedging. And it probably is a very good set of resources for a small entity which doesn't have either the physical capital or the human capital. It is wise for them to pay somebody in the form of a markup to do their hedging. It's the theory of comparative advantage — you do what you're comparatively best at.

INTERMARKET: Is this what the bank FCMs will take on as their goal?
SANDOR: I'm not knowledgeable enough about their goals, but I doubt you'll see this develop from the brokerage side. I think it is more the general rubric for commercial and investment banking rather than brokerage. It goes back to our discussion: There may be five ways to solve a problem, one of which is futures. I think a firm has to be able to deliver the other four. The correct solution is not always futures, and it's very difficult to be in the risk management business and have only one product.

INTERMARKET: If you had applied yourself, could you have become a major speculator and made a tremendous amount of money?

SANDOR: It's harder to speculate on whether one will succeed or fail at an effort like that than it is actually to speculate on the markets. It's a very hard question to answer. It's only a question of comfort. Everyone has the ability to learn a wide variety of things, and those particular activities which we pursue are a function of the things we are comfortable with, and we use the tools we learn. That, together with native abilities and dispositions, determines the course we take in our lives.

INTERMARKET: Wouldn't you say that to be a great hedger you need some of the traits of a good trader?

SANDOR: To some extent, there's an overlap. I think to be a great hedger, one has to be a student of relative values. And I emphasize relative values. You are choosing among many alternatives.

A great trader does that too. If he thinks the grain markets are going up, he has to determine which one is the most undervalued. To the extent that great traders are students of relative values, the talents of the hedger and trader overlap.

A relative value trader might think exactly the way an arbitrageur thinks. For example, when a sale of corn is extended to China, one might buy corn. But the student of the market might say, "Soybean meal moves in sympathy with corn, and is more undervalued — maybe I ought to buy that."

The ultimate student of the markets might reason that the Chinese might have to sell gold to finance the purchase of corn, and therefore the best trade of all on a relative basis is shorting gold.

That is the kind of relative mentality that would apply to figuring out the best way to raise funds and to hedge the cost of raising those funds, be it in the domestic instruments of five-year maturity, be it in Eurobonds of a similar maturity, be it in Swiss franc borrowing with the currency hedged, be it in one-year borrowings at a commercial bank with the next 12 months unhedged, and a forward contracting mechanism thereafter. The analytical part of that is very similar to the sophisticated trader.

INTERMARKET: Any thoughts on traders in general?

SANDOR: An interesting observation about successful traders: You always hear great stories about the people who are successful and very, very flamboyant. My experience has been that the successful traders that I've known have not only been flamboyant, but have treated speculation as a business.

I'm always waiting for a repeat of one of these Joe Diamond (a Chicago trading legend of the 1960's who is alleged to have purchased his multimillion dollar North Shore home with the cash he stored in cardboard boxes in the trunk of his Cadillac) stories for the last 15 years or more. I haven't seen that. I've seen men who are very talented do very well. They tend to be quietly charitable, very disciplined, and you never read about them. Often the flamboyance makes for great press, and the very successful you never hear about.

INTERMARKET: Give me a profile of a successful speculator.
SANDOR: Successful speculators tend to be a lot wiser and a lot more creative and more divergent thinkers than the popular press would lead you to believe. When you put them in a business environment, or discussing political events or in entrepreneurial settings, they tend to be extraordinarily talented. The image of somebody getting lucky making money is one that I just don't see. I have by and large found a tremendous amount of intellectual talent within the exchange community which most people don't associate with this industry. I'm sure you must have found this.

People think, "Hey, they buy it, it goes up, they make a lot of money." It leads the public to think that it is easy. They don't realize there's a whole tier of abilities, both psychological and intellectual —

INTERMARKET: (Interrupting) And emotional.
SANDOR: And emotional, that has led these people to tremendous wealth. And I think that this is the most overlooked thing in the business. It even reaches one step further —

INTERMARKET: That someone at a corporation who hedges well could probably trade well?
SANDOR: An entrepreneurial individual within an entrepreneurial corporation could make a successful trader. And a successful trader can often be a successful entrepreneur. And very often what I look for in a potential client is flexibility, creativity, the ability to respond to new ideas. And those generally are people who are able to restructure a financial institution, turn it upside down, shake it up, and change with the changing times.

These are abilities of successful men, whether they be in the trading, the corporate or the academic world. They're basically comfortable where other people aren't. Most people cannot live with uncertainty. All economic institutions, insurance, etc., are set up so that people can get rid of uncertainty. Those people that are willing and able to cope with uncertainty, society rewards enormously, be they Louis Pasteur, Einstein, a successful trader, or somebody who drills for oil. Those people who can cope with uncertainty psychologically, emotionally and intellectually are those who receive society's psychic and financial rewards. There's a real premium to be paid for that person by society.

INTERMARKET: Could you teach someone to be a great speculator?
SANDOR: I don't think I could teach someone to become a great speculator because I don't think you can teach greatness. I think that I could teach the tools which are necessary for people to learn the art of

speculation.

The rules are not complicated. I once met a man who was a very successful speculator. He was asked what he owed his success to. He walked over to the bookshelves and pulled out one of these rudimentary books describing how to speculate — don't speculate on rumors, follow trends, cut your losses short, let your profits run. He said, "This is why I've become great — I've followed these rules."

I think that very often, the foundations for successful speculation are the simple rules that you read in any introductory book on futures markets and the art of speculation. They're very simple, they're very clear, and almost all of the people who have great fortunes have at least followed those rules. They're necessary but not sufficient. By mastering these rules, plus a little flair, tremendous dedication and a good intellect, you can become a great speculator.

INTERMARKET: Seeing so many wealthy speculators must refute random walk in your mind.

SANDOR: (Pause) No, because people get paid different things to speculate. For example, one of the returns to speculation is that hedgers are willing to pay speculators some amount to be able to transfer risk. Another part is the liquidity function that people provide, which they again get paid for.

Most of the academic treatments regarding returns to speculation always put speculators in one class. I don't think that's valid. First of all, there are different ways to speculate: positions, spreads, arbs. Second, there are two kinds of speculators: good ones and bad ones. The money that the good speculator makes is due in part to the economic function he provides, but also because there are bad speculators.

INTERMARKET: (Laughs) God bless them.

SANDOR: (Laughs) In effect, bad speculation gets transformed into good speculation when the money in the pockets of bad speculators finds its way into the pants of good speculators. No model has ever made these distinctions.

INTERMARKET: Tell me about your art collection.

SANDOR: I collect something that (1) most people don't collect, and (2) in which there is serious debate about its value.

INTERMARKET: A contrarian.

SANDOR: A contrarian — I collect photographs. I collect primarily American photography, both 19th and 20th century. My wife Ellen is a sculptor and has been a continued inspiration. She first interested me in art when she was a graduate student at the Art Institute of Chicago.

I collect photography because I'm struck by the fact that it's an inventive activity which is mechanical. It's very interesting to note that

I'm comfortable where other people aren't. When I was growing up, I went to see films a lot, which most people thought was inferior to reading.

Now film has become a recognized art form. I think photography is getting to be recognized as an art form, too. I also think on a relative value basis, it's probably the best single investment one could make in art.

People think that there are endless numbers of photographs. From the beginning of the 19th century up through the turn of the century, the process for printing was very difficult. There weren't a lot of prints made, since it took an entire day to do so. One day, people are going to realize that there is a far greater scarcity of great photographs than great lithographs. And that vintage photographs — taken, developed, printed and ultimately signed and dated by the photographer — are actually very rare. One cannot reproduce them.

INTERMARKET: Among your favorites?
SANDOR: I have an original photograph of Winston Churchill. I happen to be a great fan of Winston Churchill and again, like all art, you need to know the circumstances. He has the look of a British bulldog. When I saw this Karsh photograph, I was absolutely stunned.

INTERMARKET: Wasn't the story that Sir Winston told Karsh, "I have but five minutes," at which point Karsh removed the cigar from his mouth?
SANDOR: That's exactly the story. And you can see this look. He's just not a man you'd want to fight with. (Laughs) Not at all.

My favorite photographers are Man Ray, Stieglitz, Steichen, Kertesz and Sheeler.

INTERMARKET: Is there an auction market for photographs?
SANDOR: Yes. I participate in it and enjoy it a lot. Sotheby's and Christie's both have them every fall and spring. There is a private market as well.

It's a tremendous release from the tensions of this business. I can go home, look at the photographs, read photography books. I collect sculpture and paintings as well. When you get into that world, every single thing that has to do with the markets seems to disappear.

Much of my collection is very personal. I collect photographs of great artists. You look at the portraits of some great people and you're so surprised by how they look. Aldous Huxley looks very debonair, suave. You would never guess.

I'm also an enthusiastic chess player and I have some photographs of DuChamp by Man Ray, playing in Paris. Just the studious look of these.

INTERMARKET: I remember an amazing picture of Bobby Fischer playing four or five grand masters at the same time.

SANDOR: I played chess with him as a kid. Tournament chess in New York. It's an amusing aside—but has nothing to do with what we're talking about. Fischer was just learning and we were taught by the same grand master. Fischer came in and started playing chess.

He was the most high-strung human being I ever met, and I think I was only 10 years old, so you know, if he struck me as being high-strung when I was only 10, he *really* must have been high-strung.

We used to play something called blitz chess. In blitz chess, you get one second per move. You have to move every second—there's no time to think. If you are any kind of chess player of mediocre quality and you go play blitz chess with a new player who doesn't know enough moves by rote, you automatically will beat him.

And so Bobby Fischer used to come down and we used to play blitz chess. And the guy used to explode, literally—he was a basket case at the end of an hour of either five minute, ten minute, or blitz chess. And he was extremely rattled. He was so unnerved by these experiences of such intensity. It goes back to his pursuit of excellence. When we were in sixth grade, he used to go home, wake up at four o'clock in the morning, and play three hours of chess.

INTERMARKET: With whom?

SANDOR: With himself and a book, going over all the great games. He did this for about two or three months, and by the time a year had gone by, he had developed himself to the point where he could whip everybody.

INTERMARKET: Was he a great chess player because of his genius or because of his determination?

SANDOR: Both. He was extraordinarily dedicated. From what I knew from playing with him, he had a creativity which was amazing. He would go and play a very standard chess game, king's pawn opening, and then do something totally uncertain and shocking. And I think that's what made him a very good player. He was intense beyond all belief, and unusually creative beyond a standard opening.

INTERMARKET: Wasn't his intensity his undoing? I remember in his match against—was it Karpov?—He felt the Russians were sending in codes from the sidelines via the color of the yogurt container.

SANDOR: Wasn't it Botvinnik? No, maybe it was Karpov.

He was an extraordinary kid. I knew him until I was 15. He was just brilliant as a chess player. He was tremendously singleminded. He'd play chess to the exclusion of everything.

INTERMARKET: Sounds like he would've made a great speculator.

SANDOR: I think he would've made an excellent speculator. And I think he would've made a great entrepreneur.

I think he retired to some communal lifestyle. He withdrew from any activities involved with what could be called the real world.

5

David Heuwetter

O n Friday, May 17, 1982, David Heuwetter telephoned Chase Manhattan Bank's downtown office to ask for an extension on a $610 million, uncollateralized loan due Monday to the firm he partly owned, Drysdale Government Securities.

Chase officials were shocked. It was the beginning of four days of negotiations, during which Heuwetter spilled his guts about how Drysdale lost the money. In an effort to attempt to secure his cooperation and to recover some of the losses, Chase is alleged to have given Heuwetter a million dollars of the Drysdale assets for his anticipated legal expenses. According to sources, Chase would end up losing $285 million pretax, and $117 million after tax.

David Heuwetter's story is significant because of the power that a huge Federal deficit has placed in the hands of the relatively few, virtually unregulated government securities dealers who finance that debt.

What follows is the first time David Heuwetter, who traded for Drysdale's house account, has consented to be interviewed about his role in what was considered the most disruptive financial episode of the early 1980s. Heuwetter sums it up in the rhetorical question: "How can someone with $20 in his pocket wind up receiving $10 billion worth of credit on a given day? I can't explain it to you." His is perhaps the ultimate story of a firm with virtually no assets, coupled with a lack of management controls, fragmentary record-keeping and (as Heuwetter admits) outright fraud. It is a story of how leverage can not only bring down a single brokerage, but can shake the entire financial infrastructure.

Heuwetter's involvement in the Drysdale collapse is also a depressing story of blind ambition, of a man who wanted a position larger than the market.

Yet, to put the Drysdale collapse in its true perspective is difficult. While it was a rather insignificant New York Stock Exchange member company, Drysdale

Securities was like most Wall Street brokerages that handle both retail and institutional business. It executed trades on behalf of customers while at the same time trading a house account. The sheer size of the growing government debt means that there is money to be made trading the instruments, and many Wall Street brokerages and even some traditional commodity houses were (and still are) attracted as a result.

Heuwetter himself had come from the sales ranks, serving several stints as a municipal bond salesman at various banks and brokerages including Citibank, A. G. Becker, E. F. Hutton and Chase. Prior to coming to Drysdale, he was trying to market a software program that prices municipal bonds. He has been variously described as charming, dynamic, and intensely dominating. One banker who met him in a Manhattan bar recalls that after a brief conversation, Heuwetter suddenly blurted out, "I don't know who you are. I don't know what you do. I don't know how much you make. But come to work for me and I'll triple it." Then, said the banker, "Heuwetter launched into a five-minute speech on trading that was so fast, I wasn't sure if he was brilliant or crazy."

Starting in December 1979, David Heuwetter joined Drysdale and began trading government securities in two markets: the cash market and the so-called repo market. In the cash Treasury bond, bill and note markets he simply bought and sold government securities with other dealers, trying to forecast the direction of interest rates. The repo market, however, involves complex transactions involving the sale of securities subject to agreement to repurchase them at a fixed price at a later date.

Heuwetter began doing business with Kidder Peabody, First Interstate Bank, and a few others. He in no way intended to be, as he put it, "just another trader" and soon was holding massive positions. From this stage he progressed to repos, the mainstay of many government securities trading desks.

Heuwetter's trading got so big that during the summer of 1981, he and Joseph Ossorio, the owner of Drysdale Securities, considered setting up a separate subsidiary firm to handle Heuwetter's government trading on behalf of the parent firm. In doing so, they would be able to avoid SEC and New York Stock Exchange observation and capital requirements, which Heuwetter said were crimping his trading. From February 1982 to May 17, 1982, Heuwetter was Drysdale Government Securities' treasurer and led its government trading operations. Also he owned all of DGSI's common stock and held its subordinated debt. At this point, Heuwetter ceased to be an employee and his responsibility rose correspondingly.

It was before the end of 1981 that many dealers started wondering about what might develop if Drysdale had the problem that many thought it did — huge trading losses. Many companies refused to do repos with it because of its inordinate risk of default, yet most continued trading with Heuwetter in the cash market.

Hence Heuwetter used the service finders in the repo market, particularly a company named Buttonwood Management Corp. In the normal arrangement, the finder earns an intermediary fee of a few basis points for hooking up owners of government securities with traders who want to do reverses.

During 1981, Heuwetter became adept at playing what is known among government securities traders as "the interest game." According to the SEC, Heuwetter "continually sold in the cash market securities representing the approximate amount by which the securities received in reverse repos exceeded the securities delivered in repos."

In plain English, Buttonwood — for a fee — got U.S. Trust, then Manufacturers Hanover and finally Chase Manhattan, to front for Drysdale, since nobody would question a major institution's solvency. Chase would transact repos with pension funds and other longer-term holders who wanted extra income, and pay cash to receive (borrow) securities which had accumulated substantial interest. Chase would then, for a markup of 25 basis points or so, repo (lend) the securities to Heuwetter on behalf of DGS, again for cash.

Heuwetter's business with Chase made the bank millions. But they were essentially lending — guaranteeing hundreds of millions for Drysdale. If the bond market was stagnate, Heuwetter would be able to sell the securities in the cash market for a gross profit of around 6%.

He was able to do this because, as players of the interest game realize, the pricing of repos was artificially low. Accrued interest is to a large extent ignored by the sellers, the long-term holders who in repoing (lending out) are looking for an added return. Meanwhile, in the cash market the price of coupon securities indicates the interest accrued since the last semiannual payment date. As Heuwetter said, "For every million dollars of securities I repo'ed, I'd get $60,000 of free money turning around and selling them in the cash market." (Minus, of course, Chase's and Buttonwood's markups.)

In this way, Heuwetter was able to generate about $240 million in outflow from Chase to DGS, which was tantamount to an unsecured loan. The trade-off was that once the securities had been sold in the cash market, they would eventually have to be purchased back in cash in order to deliver them at the open reverse repo. Hence, these positions involved the sale of what were borrowed securities, thereby producing a tremendous short position which Heuwetter never discussed in his books. He was borrowing for tomorrow to repay what was owed today, not unlike the government whose debt he was making a market for. By January 1982, Heuwetter was a hamster on a treadmill.

With Drysdale Securities technically insolvent, Ossorio retained Warren Essner, a CPA and audit partner at Arthur Andersen & Co., to assist in establishing Drysdale Government Securities. Ossorio and Heuwetter did not want the spin-off company to be regulated by the NYSE. Essner assembled one tax partner and two audit employees to develop plans for the spin-off. By late January, Essner submitted and Ossorio approved the plan to establish Drysdale Government Securities as a separate entity from Drysdale Securities. Five million dollars in assets — mainly the government securities position — was transferred in exchange for $5 million of preferred stock in Drysdale Government.

Prosecutors alleged that on January 31, 1982, at Ossorio's request, Essner drafted a letter announcing the formation of Drysdale Government Securities, stating a purported capital of $20.8 million. The circular was distributed to

Chemical Bank, and a number of government securities dealers. Interestingly, Heuwetter claims it wasn't necessary to circulate the false statement to obtain credit. The creditors asked for a more formal document — an audit statement from Arthur Andersen — and Essner complied.

In doing so, the prosecution accused him of failing to:

- *examine and attempt to value the transferred assets;*
- *examine company records from February 1 — the date of the drafted letter — to February 22 — when the report was released;*
- *examine the transaction in detail.*

Thus, on February 22, Essner issued a report which prosecutors state "specifically and falsely represented that the assets, including the government securities position, had been transferred from" the parent company to the spin-off and that Drysdale Government "had been fairly valued." Essner subsequently resigned from Arthur Andersen & Co., was indicted by a Manhattan grand jury in July 1983, and was acquitted this past October 31 after a jury trial on charges he issued false financial statements for DGS. In the third quarter ending September 30, Chase had received $49 million in an out-of-court settlement of a suit filed against Drysdale, several officials, and Arthur Andersen.

Having the badly needed credit, from February to the fateful day in May, Heuwetter traded furiously, hoping to trade his way out of insolvency. He took on outright long and short positions often exceeding $100 million per day. His repo positions were at times net long or net short by $1 billion to $2 billion. And he continued to play the interest game in order to raise working capital.

Heuwetter was told in early March by U.S. Trust to reduce his position with them. This put him under pressure to increase his positions with other banks and dealers. In late March, Morgan Stanley refused any repo business with Heuwetter. At this point, the roof began caving in. Drysdale Government was delivering securities late. Heuwetter felt pressure from other dealers as well.

Still, he failed to admit to any problems, nor did he announce the deficit the company was running.

Two and a half years later, numerous questions still abound:

- *Who ended up with the losses? One would assume that it went to the other dealers. But to this day, Heuwetter claims his trading never lost the company money. Several people claim that Ossorio has taken $60 million, but this has not been proven. Many believe the losses ended up as profits on the inordinate interest payments on Heuwetter's huge position.*

- *Did someone commit securities fraud? The government and the SEC believe so. Circulating the fraudulent audit statement was the most easily provable charge. Ossorio was sentenced in July 1984 to eight years in prison for fraud.*

Heuwetter pleaded guilty in March to charges of fraud and tax evasion. As of November 2, he had not been sentenced.

● *Were SEC and NYSE record-keeping laws violated? Again, the government believes so. Heuwetter was responsible for showing Drysdale's government securities positions on its books and records, and failed to do so.*

● *How can the Drysdale episode be prevented from happening again? For this interview, Heuwetter seemed outwardly self-confident, yet inwardly very defensive. He was continually maintaining that his guilt did not involve the loss or theft of money, but rather circulating the deceptive audit statement.*

INTERMARKET: What have you learned from this whole fiasco and how have you personally been able to handle it?
HEUWETTER: Its impact on my personal life has been devastating. Now I'm a criminal. I'll always have that label. No matter how I look at it — reformed or otherwise — I'm still a criminal. I'll always be a felon.

Certainly the fiasco was big enough that it's not one to be easily forgotten. But I'm not about to go change my name. I've done it. I passed out a fraudulent statement, and I didn't have the guts to recall it.

INTERMARKET: Did you do that because you were under Ossorio's influence?
HEUWETTER: I never put that financial statement together, so when it went out, I didn't appreciate totally what it was.

INTERMARKET: You were directly responsible for its contents?
HEUWETTER: No. I knew that being the one distributing it, I would be directly responsible, more so than he [Ossorio]. He arranged for it, put it together and everything, but I was the one who distributed it. Within a couple of days after it was distributed I clearly had the responsibility of blowing the whistle.

INTERMARKET: Should you have gone to Chase?
HEUWETTER: I should have gone to the Federal Reserve Bank and said, "Here's my plight; it just won't work."

INTERMARKET: So you agree with the prosecutor's assertion that you did that because you had to — in order to keep Drysdale Government going?
HEUWETTER: Of course. Absolutely.

INTERMARKET: You thought you could trade your way out?
HEUWETTER: That financial statement really didn't have to be issued. Drysdale had put out a statement in November — an annual

statement that everybody accepted and nobody had a problem with at that point in time. There really wasn't a need to put out a statement. In fact, what it was—[pause] Ossorio wanted to spin it off and get it out of Drysdale. In doing so, you had to put a statement together.

INTERMARKET: To spin it off, he had to show that Drysdale Government had $20 million?

HEUWETTER: I didn't want to have it spun off if we were going to have a $3 million company. [Heuwetter claims not to have known the company had lost enough money to be effectively bankrupt, hence the question of the money.] It doesn't really amount to anything—the issue is the false statement.

INTERMARKET: Had you not issued the false statement, do you think you would have gotten the needed line of credit from Chase?

HEUWETTER: It [the line of credit] was never cancelled! The statement really was not the major contention. Once I had passed out the paperback variety of it, it created a demand for the real thing—an audited statement. But up until I passed out the piece of paper saying, "This is the new statement," [there was no problem].

Everybody looked at this and said, "Hey, we want a copy of this. This will help us. We like this. We'd like to have a copy for our internal auditors." Until I had passed out this statement, I really didn't have an overwhelming demand for one. I created a demand.

INTERMARKET: What about the assertion that other traders weren't doing business with you because they were getting scared about the size you were trading?

HEUWETTER: Morgan Stanley—that's it.

INTERMARKET: Do you think that houses traded with you because they knew that no one on your end was paying close attention to the mistakes that were made in their favor?

HEUWETTER: No. Let me give you my side of the mistakes that were made. Number one, in the government securities business, when you send securities out, if the bank isn't sitting with instructions, they don't take them in. They bounce them. Yet these securities were taken in. In the back of my mind, I feel these so-called mistakes were arranged. Nobody's really examined them to find out where the money is and how it happened. But I know that these things should never have happened. They should've been returned.

I understand that in the securities business, when securities are sent and it's beneficial to hold them, they will hold them. They'll put them in an error account and wait for you to come and collect them. That's standard operating procedure for the business. But by the same token, that's direct delivery into someone's back office.

When you have a clearing bank, and they can't match tickets, boom. Gone. When they're paying out cash, they want to hold on to cash. But when they bounce something for you—you hold the securities and there's a reason to bounce them—and you can hold onto the cash, they'll do it to you every time. Yet these things didn't bounce. There's something that deviated from its normal path. This should never have happened. But it happened, so it leads me to believe that it was arranged—money was stolen. It wasn't accidental.

The cashier has said that he stole $750,000 from my checking account. He put the money into my account, then wired it out. I never caught it because I was too engrossed in what I was doing.

INTERMARKET: Where did you make enough money not to miss that kind of money? I know I would miss that.
HEUWETTER: You've got to understand the insanity that was involved here: Two hundred trades a day. Two hundred repos a day. I did all the back office work. I did all the trading. I walked the bonds through to clear them. It was a 15 hour a day existence. A normal human being couldn't have done it.

INTERMARKET: Were you a multimillionaire before coming to Drysdale?
HEUWETTER: No.

INTERMARKET: Then when would you have earned enough money to lose $750,000?
HEUWETTER: This was my trading account at Drysdale. And these were all pretty much profitable trades. And I had cash flow through it—whether it was accrued interest or profits, today [it] makes little difference. We're not really talking about that money and how it got there. Those were not the charges. The charges were that I created a deception. And that charge is pretty close to the truth.

INTERMARKET: Could the fiasco that you were involved in occur again?
HEUWETTER: Anything could happen again. Somebody will come up with a new twist. Drysdale really wasn't a new twist; it was something everybody in the street did. It was a legitimate way of raising cash. Working capital allows you to make margin on a hedged position.

It [making sure that other companies are prevented from leveraging their way up and defaulting again] becomes knowing your customer and how much credit to advance him. Now they are asking each other, "Who are your major customers?" There are 38 dealers. Does someone have trading accounts with 20 [of them] and are [they] sitting with a $750 million position [thereby holding a reasonable trading position with each dealer, but which adds up to a problem]? I think they've tightened the business up significantly.

INTERMARKET: You've said you were an egomaniac when you were trading at Drysdale. How could you trade successfully with that character flaw?
HEUWETTER: I always traded hedged positions. I'm accused of having huge long positions and everything. It was a large position, but it wasn't a high-risk position. If you look at how the losses occurred, they didn't occur out of the trading positions. I had some near-perfect hedges and was not really looking for a killing. All those things that were attributed to me are really not true. If you look at how it looked ... and like I say, Peat Marwick and Chase's attorney said, "incredibly brilliant trading."

My problem was that I didn't keep an eye on the store. Everybody knew that I was there and that all I wanted to do was trade. Unfortunately, you can't operate that way in the real world. You become responsible for the people you work for.

INTERMARKET: What's the largest position you ever had? Is the $10 billion correct?
HEUWETTER: It approached $10 billion but I don't think it ever actually exceeded it.

INTERMARKET: That would exceed a day's volume in the bond [futures] pit.
HEUWETTER: Basically, yes. If you looked at both sides of the trade, it would be strange. I was long maybe the 10-year on the (Chicago) Board (of Trade) and short the bonds.

INTERMARKET: What kind of a spread would you have to see in the yield curve before doing that?
HEUWETTER: Well, the financing end of the business should have created a problem. Normally, what I did was not a loss leader. The cash was worth more than the coupon at all times.

INTERMARKET: What were the ingredients in your trading that made for doing so successfully or otherwise, and what have you learned since the ordeal? What would you do differently?
HEUWETTER: Hindsight would force me to say that I'd just never do it. In terms of stress, it would be pointless. It was a disease that grew and got out of proportion.

I'm not hiding behind insanity in any sense. But how do you get to trade a billion and a half [worth of] securities every day for on average a two-year period? I don't think anybody's addressed that. Everybody cares about what I did, but what really happened? How did it happen? How does somebody with $20 in his pocket wind up receiving $10 billion worth of credit on a given day? I can't explain it to you. There really wasn't a manipulation; there was no conspiracy. For a good period of time everybody knew who I was and what I was doing.

INTERMARKET: So there's still a fatal flaw in the system?
HEUWETTER: It's still going on, enough so that there could be problems. Lion Capital (a firm whose trading losses earlier this year cost a number of school districts millions of dollars) was small things compared to what's actually going on. There are a couple of billion dollar position traders without the finances to back them being given the credit by some dealers to carry their position in bonds through a third party.

INTERMARKET: So when dealers are willing to take that large risk, one would assume that they are getting better than average interest payments.
HEUWETTER: It's a device to get around the rules. It's still going on. This is not something that I'm aware of. Everybody on the Street's aware of it, but nobody's going to blow the whistle.

INTERMARKET: Is an individual bigger than the market, and can a market be manipulated longer-term?
HEUWETTER: No! Maybe for an afternoon, but reality is still reality. Basically, what happens in the market—there are massive short-term manipulations when a couple of large dealers conspire. I was invited into such conspiracies, so I know they exist. But over the long term, supply and demand always win out.

INTERMARKET: How can you trade the futures knowing that?
HEUWETTER: I just take my little piece first of all, 10 and 20 lots, but I now trade in the Treasury bills, not the bonds. It's like, once burnt, twice shot. I find it very hard to get involved in the bond market for so many emotional reasons which I doubt you can appreciate. It's a constant reminder when I would go into the market of who I was, where I've been, etc.

INTERMARKET: Do you think you'll ever make it back?
HEUWETTER: Not in my lifetime. Maybe if I come back reincarnated. My interest now is in helping my son, teaching him what the real world is about. I'll get my joys from seeing him succeed. Maybe he can straighten out the family name. He will have the problem, if he goes into this business, that people are not going to distinguish him from me. Twenty years from now, people will hear stories and not relate the time to the individual.

INTERMARKET: Did your personal net worth ever exceed more

than one million dollars?
HEUWETTER: I had my own pricing service that probably amounted to $4 million.

INTERMARKET: I assume you are now wiped out.
HEUWETTER: I guess my net worth right now is about $250,000. But I'm sure I will lose it all. A little less than that. My share of the house, my car, those sorts of things. [At this point, he begins to sob, and requests interview to be stopped. After he recovers, he becomes more positive and begins to talk about his future.]

INTERMARKET: How will you feel if you trade your way back to success?
HEUWETTER: I think that if I can get back on my feet, there is a personal satisfaction for having done that. My finances are such that I'll be bankrupt. I'm not hiding anything and no one is accusing me of that. I think it's good that in my lifetime, nobody will be able to say that I benefited from Drysdale. So, if I ever do get back on my feet, it will not be because I stole money.

INTERMARKET: How will Ossorio handle his life?
HEUWETTER: I don't want to address that, and I don't know his circumstances. He and I were never close. Certainly we were never social, and he looked at me as an employee. We never exchanged intimacies of any kind. I never had any insight into how he thought. The only thing I knew about him was that he came in early in the morning and worked hard.

When I read about the things that he's done—they give the dates and the times and the facts—if they weren't giving the facts with it, I wouldn't believe it. Of course my son says I'm the worst judge of character that God ever created.

INTERMARKET: How have you been able to not be very bitter after being duped by your business associate and being persecuted and prosecuted?
HEUWETTER: Well, first of all, I was prosecuted, never persecuted. They [the government prosecutors] were tough in their investigation, tough on the witnesses. They wanted the information and persuaded everybody to come clean.

In fact, I hired an attorney for Ruppert and told him not to worry about me. [Dennis Ruppert joined DSC in April 1978. He was DSC's treasurer and controller reporting to Ossorio.] I told him, "Go down, make a deal for yourself and come clean," not to worry about me. He told that to the grand jury and they couldn't put it together.

With the fall of Drysdale I walked into Chase and tried to mitigate me and would say nothing, I told to cooperate.

It's hard for me to be bitter when I don't have clean hands. I'm not the guy who's accused of doing something I didn't do. I passed out a [false] statement. My moral values were disrupted by my fear of loss of career and everything. I lied, and it's unfortunate. More unfortunate for the people who were injured by it. Logically, how could I be bitter?

INTERMARKET: How has your wife taken it?

HEUWETTER: Very badly. She doesn't like being married to a felon. She's the kind of woman who would never have married a felon in the first place, so having one now really disrupts her life. She's not happy with me. She'll never be happy with me. It's hurt a lot of relatives — more than it's hurt me.

First of all, you're talking to me two years after the shock. I've hit my low in depression and everything else.

Thank God I'm a Catholic and suicide is out of the question. Certainly I've had more than ample reason to do something like that if that were my mentality. But there are some things in my Catholic background that won't allow me to do that. It's a shame my background didn't prevent me from doing some other things — then I wouldn't be here. [Again tears well up, he breaks down, and requests that the interview end.]

6

Brian Monieson

L *ike many successful independent traders, Brian Monieson has a less*
than usual background. A champion bridge and chess player, the
48-year-old made his first winnings at the racetrack. He holds an MBA
from the University of Chicago (1971), a bachelor's degree in business from
Northwestern University (1959), runs a respected clearing and futures research
firm, GNP Financial, and was elected CME chairman in 1983 and again in
1984.

After a stint at Honeywell Corp., Monieson became an independent com-
puter consultant, beginning by doing programming for a race track. From this
initial contract, he was able to found Indecon, a computer consulting firm.
While this does not seem remarkable in today's computer-oriented environ-
ment, in the mid-60's the computer industry was in its infancy, and those who
entered it were pioneers.

It was from his computer programming work that Monieson found his way
into the futures market, developing an econometric model which successfully
traded pork bellies. From there, he bought a Mercantile Exchange member-
ship, opened a brokerage house and was in business. His wealth from trading is
substantial and he claims never to have had a losing year since he began
trading at the CME in 1971.

INTERMARKET: How did you get into the business?
MONIESON: My computer company was doing consulting business
and indirectly was hired to computerize an econometric model of pork
bellies. I was working with my partner and longtime friend, Ira
Rosenthal, and Paul Cootner, a professor of finance at Stanford University. The primary contractor was Commodity Corp. of Princeton,

New Jersey.

We developed an inventory model. Pork bellies really are a commodity that begin production in November, and the marketing season — with few exceptions — begins in June, July and August. The "new crop" starts again in November. Therefore, a certain price will pull out all the inventory, so it lends itself to mathematical analysis as an inventory accumulation problem.

The model at that point was successful — otherwise I'd still be writing computer programs. We formed a group of people — a limited partnership of 10 people — each putting in $5000. We made somewhere in the neighborhood of six to 10 times our money.

INTERMARKET: Over what period of time?
MONIESON: A year or so.

INTERMARKET: What size positions did you trade?
MONIESON: We would build fairly decent size positions.

INTERMARKET: Would you increase your unit size traded as the equity in the account grew?
MONIESON: We increased the unit sizes, yes. We then found that the commission generated on the money we managed was substantial enough to make the brokerage business viable.

INTERMARKET: What year did you start your computer company?
MONIESON: I'd had that business since about 1965 and its first program was an econometric model for the race track — harness racing. The Chicago *Herald American* carried my model's bets as a feature — the three best bets. It turned out that at the end of the year, for every two dollars bet on the system, the individual gained a return of 400-some dollars.

INTERMARKET: What kind of variables did the model take into account? Just the track record of each horse going into the race?
MONIESON: No, it was much more sophisticated than that. Performance was really the major consideration: A horse's performance against better competition was more important than his speed or his time. The racing times became a very slight factor; the speed of the horse wasn't as important as most people believe.

INTERMARKET: So the most important factor was the animal's ability to win?
MONIESON: The ability to compete against better grade horses. Track variability became more important than time. Let's say a race was run on Tuesday at a certain class. This was in harness racing, so let's say a 2:04 won. Let's say a horse wins the same class on Thursday in

2:06 (when presumably the track was in worse shape). Most people wouldn't think that when they met, the 2:06 horse could beat the 2:04 horse.

But they were dead even when you took variability of the tracks into account. The driver meant a lot (to the model); post position also meant a lot. But it was basically a program that involved elements of artificial intelligence, where the computer would reprogram the standards and variables independent of human intervention.

I worked a long time ago on a self-correcting program for chess. Once the person programs it, then you let the computer apply different standards, to see if it can come up with better results. The race track program worked the same way. Eventually, it was no longer captive of the programmer. It determined its own standards to get the best results.

INTERMARKET: How did you work your way into running your own programming company? Did you make money on chess or the horses?
MONIESON: I had worked for Honeywell as a computer salesman and I had always been involved in race horses.

INTERMARKET: I've heard that you are a great bridge player. I assume you play chess and you play the horses—
MONIESON: (Interrupting) I played chess when I was a kid, all the way to third in the state, then I gave up chess—I never finish anything. In bridge, yes, I've won a few national championships, but I've given that up also.

INTERMARKET: What do these things have in common with trading futures?
MONIESON: In some ways, quite a bit. It's been quite difficult to profile people who are going to be successful in this business. Intelligence is not a detriment, but it's not a necessary and sufficient condition either.

INTERMARKET: You're talking about position traders, not scalpers.
MONIESON: Right. Scalping is entirely different. It's more mechanical, like a robot. A scalper doesn't have to know a thing about the fundamentals of a market.

INTERMARKET: Why are most people on the floor scalpers?
MONIESON: I think that your question gets to part of the overall change in this industry. This is going to end up as a pretty rambling conversation ... The industry is evolving from a low-profile environment to a high profile, well-known environment. The Becker brothers (renowned floor traders in the 1970s) have been replaced by Salomon Brothers. And that's quite a replacement.

The value of a membership used to be considerable because being on the floor would permit you to be involved with all sorts of opportunities—runaway markets and so on. That was a tremendous edge. That edge is diminishing, as large institutions and arbitrageurs open these markets up to the world.

Why are most people scalpers? There is always going to be a need for scalpers to create liquidity, but the benefits of being a scalper will not, in the future, be as great.

INTERMARKET: So you never evolved into a position trader, you were one from the start?

MONIESON: I have been a scalper on the floor. I'm a position trader now, though.

INTERMARKET: Are you a scalper when the market moves with you and a position trader when it goes against you?

MONIESON: That's one of the myriad number of platitudes that's thrown out: "Get out when it's going against you. Cut your losses; let your profits run." By definition, when you enter a trade, it should go against you because you are paying the offer. So when are you supposed to get out?

You asked the question whether it's like bridge, racing or chess. I think it is, indeed. What the games teach you is discipline. Discipline is the key—the ability to keep your head when all about you are losing theirs. Everything's euphoric. Soon you begin to learn that when everyone's buying, there's no one left to buy, and that's how markets turn. Markets turn on the best of the news because there is no one left to buy.

That's the real problem with the offers that the Franklin Mint gives you. They say, "Okay, we're going to close this offer in 30 days and then it will be a collectors' item." Except anyone who's wanted it in those 30 days has bought it. If you wanted it, you bought it, and if you didn't want it, you didn't buy it.

The reasoning becomes very simple if you're able to apply it to a lifestyle. The intuitiveness of bridge—if you're able to find queens to finesse—the table feel, so to speak, is the same thing as a market feel. You sniff the air. Try to quantify that to a logical person and he will have a tremendous problem. He will say, "Here are the facts." But a market by definition doesn't work on facts. It has discounted those facts in the past because of the facts that are anticipated in the future.

INTERMARKET: This sounds to me as if you don't take into account high-low-close price action.

MONIESON: I think you have to have a basic scenario of what is going to happen. I think also that charts will become much less reliable than they have been in the past. They were self-perpetuating as long as the money that was using them continued to be dominant. What has happened is that they've leveled off in the amount of money that is following them. This filter gets narrower and narrower. Let's say the charts indicate getting out at 170.00 in the S & P's. Somebody's going to say, "I'll get out of them at 170.10, since if they hit 170.00, they'll hit 170.10." This begins to squeeze the filters down and then you get the choppy markets. I don't think charts and the high-low close indicators are going to be nearly as important in the future as they were in the past, when everybody used them.

INTERMARKET: So you believe where a market turns has little to do with support and resistance as shown in past price action, and more to do with psychology?
MONIESON: Right.

INTERMARKET: So research is obsolete?
MONIESON: Yes. By definition it is obsolete because as theories are published, they are going to be followed. The same way with the contrarian, then by definition, it becomes the normal theory. If everyone is following it, it must be wrong. It's an interesting game, but the reason that people who are highly intelligent often have such a hard time trading is that they apply scientific reasoning to an art form.

INTERMARKET: So you consider yourself more an artist than a computer programmer?
MONIESON: I have a mathematical background, a lot of higher mathematics and computer programming. But I've learned to overcome those obstacles.
     Once again, what I'm talking about is straight speculative trading. There are tremendous opportunities using higher math for arbitrage and to enhance portfolio performance. These allow the portfolio manager to put himself in a better competitive position than his opposition. And as people play the mispricing and arbitrage opportunities in these markets—

INTERMARKET: [Interrupting] The spread gets narrower—
MONIESON: Not only that, more obstacles are put in front of a local whose market cannot go too high relative to the markets now, because some arbitrageur will pound it.

INTERMARKET: On your screen you have a strange mix: cattle, hogs, pork bellies, and S & P's.
MONIESON: Yes. Because I'm not trading currencies.

INTERMARKET: You're waiting for the trend to establish itself?
MONIESON: No. I caught the bottom [of the currencies] 23 times and

each time I get a lower bottom. I've been wrong in the currencies. To me, the macro-economic picture says it is ridiculous for the dollar to be that strong. It doesn't make sense for international trade ...

INTERMARKET: Is the fall in the value of the Merc seats mainly due to communications breakthroughs?
MONIESON: Communications is one part, but the competition in these markets is another part. Obviously, we're dealing in a world market. The institutional players have a lot of research. Although there's a school of thought that says a market discounts news—the efficient market—I don't think they've ever proven that in futures markets.

INTERMARKET: So you don't buy very strong markets that are breaking into new ground and closing on their high?
MONIESON: No. I think there's too much risk.

INTERMARKET: What's the longest you've held a trade?
MONIESON: Three or four weeks.

INTERMARKET: And the shortest?
MONIESON: A few seconds. But this is trading, not investing. A speculator doesn't invest.

INTERMARKET: But if you do happen to pick the bottom of the currencies and they come out strong, won't you want to hold on to that as an "investment" for the rest of the year?
MONIESON: I'll hold it until—well, I have to think, "What's the next thing that's going to pop it?" If you've knocked out the shorts, what's the next bit of news that will pop the market? If I can conceive of some news that is really going to smoke it, okay, fine.
   The one nice thing which you learn at the race track is money management. At the end of the day, when you're behind, if you can look at the last race and walk away from it with money in your pocket, you've learned good money management.
   The fact that you were long the S&P at 165.00 and you got out at 167.00 shouldn't affect you at 173.00. If you like the market you should buy it. Too many people, once they've gotten out of a market, become bearish. They are not bearish because they don't like the market, they're bearish because they missed the six cents.

INTERMARKET: Your trading style seems to be the opposite of several individuals who combined have taken hundreds of millions out of the futures markets. They tend to buy a market. If it does not go with them, that alone is reason enough for them to get out. And they do their best to ignore the fundamentals.

MONIESON: I believe a market going against you is reason enough to get out. If it's going with me, I won't get out for any reason other than to take profits. I need a reason to get out ... although I will get out on pops.

INTERMARKET: Are three points on the S&P considered pop?
MONIESON: Absolutely.

INTERMARKET: So wouldn't your style of trading miss the August '82 and August '84 rallies?
MONIESON: I caught 15 cents on the August '82 rally. But it was a march, not a pop. What happens in a march is that the shorts always wait a little bit longer, whereas a pop runs them out—they give up on a pop. You will lose more money being wrong on a march than you will on a pop—always. A march is insidious. It just keeps ticking, and every day you look at it and say, "Well, I'll give it another 100 points."

INTERMARKET: What's the biggest loss you've ever taken?
MONIESON: You must trade what you're comfortable with. Richard Dennis is reputed to have made nine figures. I couldn't be comfortable with the kind of risk you must invite in order to make that kind of money. I believe that for some reason, people are better at what they do at certain times, and therefore a trader should never press it when he is losing. You learn about how good a trader is when he loses.

INTERMARKET: Because you can't tell when he loses?
MONIESON: No, but it's how he acts. A trader who loses and tries to get back—frantically—what he lost will be a loser in the end.

INTERMARKET: Your analogy of the race track.
MONIESON: Exactly.

INTERMARKET: Have you made more money in the brokerage business than from your personal trading?
MONIESON: I've made more money in the market. I just look at the brokerage as a business. It's an economic opportunity in a dynamic industry. (Pause) It certainly is in a consolidation phase right now.

INTERMARKET: You're interested in selling GNP now?
MONIESON: I'm a trader. Everything's for sale—except Doris and the kids. And I haven't had any good offers for them lately, either. It's a market like anything else.

What GNP Financial is doing is research to bridge the gap between securities and futures. They've developed a yield enhancement program ... dynamic asset allocation.

Mutual funds will ask us to figure out the best way to hedge a certain portfolio—like a utility portfolio. There's not a utility market so do you use bonds? S&Ps? How do you hedge the default risk in junk bonds?

We've done some interesting things. One fund came to us with a portfolio with a beta of 1.5 that doesn't track the S&P at all. We'll design a portfolio with the same beta that does track the S&P, thereby allowing the portfolio manager the flexibility to hedge. That includes dividend yield as well as beta.

INTERMARKET: How do you approach the mindset of the hedger, whose sole interest is beating the S&P, since you trade solely to make profits?
MONIESON: I don't let my philosophy of trading interfere with my philosophy of business. If there's a market for it, I'm not smart enough to say the market's wrong. That's part of being a trader.

INTERMARKET: Has financial deregulation hurt your company? Banks coming in and trying to steal away your clients?
MONIESON: Yes. That's part of the consolidation of the industry. Also, as an outgrowth of that, the cost of running a brokerage is getting so expensive.

INTERMARKET: You trade both the financials and the agriculturals. How do the agriculturals trade differently from the S&P?
MONIESON: Agriculturals trade differently because the agriculturals are a primary market.

INTERMARKET: How do you trade them differently? Do you expect more follow-through after a strong close on the primary market?
MONIESON: No. I basically follow the fundamentals.

INTERMARKET: Do you do the analysis yourself or do you have someone working for you doing it?
MONIESON: That part is difficult to quantify. There's a big swap of information among traders.

INTERMARKET: It amazes me that some of the other very successful traders are not at all computer oriented and yet they have very quantifiable systems, whereas you come from the computer background and yet your approach seems to stress elements that vary—who you swap information with, for instance.
MONIESON: My perception of the market is based on what the fundamentals tell me, mixed in with what I consider a very intuitive feel for what the market seems to be telling me. It's basically watching how markets trade and where people give up.

Traders don't have to be idiots, either. They have to use relative comparison. It's just like the horses. They have to get the best value.

INTERMARKET: So you're saying that whoever can get consistent value over time will win?
MONIESON: Absolutely. Without question.

INTERMARKET: Then how can you boost the unit size you trade, as you did in the pork belly model?
MONIESON: Well, we were new and had a very high confidence level. But right now I wouldn't ... that's my comfortable level of trading. I buy value and when I get it, I'll push it, but never more than 30-40% of the original position. I'll never double up.

INTERMARKET: So if you're long 100 S&Ps and it gives you two points, you might add on 30-40%?
MONIESON: Depending on whether something I'm looking for happens, I might add on.

INTERMARKET: News on the floor?
MONIESON: It has to do with whether something I thought would happen is beginning to materialize. The news on the floor has nothing to do with it. Price action is very important, but the news on the floor is meaningless, almost as bad as for the poor people who read *The Wall Street Journal* and try to trade off it.

INTERMARKET: Let's say the market closed strongly yesterday, gaps opened today, and the daily low, after half an hour into trading, is still the low of the opening range. Is that alone enough to make you add on to your long position?
MONIESON: That alone? No.

INTERMARKET: So you don't look at relative strength—one market against another?
MONIESON: When oil closed down limit, we know from history that when oil goes up in price, the stock market gets killed. So when oil goes down in price, the reverse should happen. That's the type of thing I look at.

INTERMARKET: Do you enter a trade with a certain risk/reward ratio—do you want to only enter trades where your upside is several times your downside?
MONIESON: No.

INTERMARKET: Have you made most of your money being naked long or short rather than spreading?
MONIESON: Yes. Long and short positions.

INTERMARKET: And you don't look at charts?

MONIESON: Yes. But once again, I do have a lot of pattern recognition. I can't explain it to you, but patterns will bother me. If you watch a market for years and years, there will be patterns, just as in race horses.

INTERMARKET: What patterns do you see in race horses?

MONIESON: Let's look at an example of a horse that races well coming from far back with an outside post position. When he gets an inside post position, the public says, "Now he's a lot closer to the front—he's a shoo-in to win." That is probably the worst possible bet you could make. Normally he races real well coming from the back, not from in front.

Another pattern: a horse who's won a couple and then runs an extraordinarily bad race. He normally is a pretty good wager.

INTERMARKET: Do you ever bet on more than one horse?

MONIESON: Never. You can only have one winner.

INTERMARKET: So you make one bet per race, and always to win, not to place or show?

MONIESON: When you bet to show, there's too much money taken out of each pool. Breakage is beginning to cost you. Basically, horse racing is simple. There's 16% taken out of each pool. 4% divided up.

INTERMARKET: When you bet a horse, you don't bet the favorite?

MONIESON: I never touch the favorite.

INTERMARKET: Why?

MONIESON: Value! ... Let's say that your average bet is $2, and the horse is one to five. You win $2.00, maybe $2.20. What's the tendency? You say to yourself, "That horse can't lose. I'll bet $200." If you lose, you've killed all your $2 bets.

You see, horse races, futures, any form of risk management with probability—it's all a value game. Nothing but a value game. What most people don't understand is that I don't care whether my trade wins or loses, or whether my horse wins or loses, as long as I'm getting value. If I am, over time I'll win.

7

Tom Baldwin

*I*n an industry brimming with Horatio Alger success stories, perhaps the most phenomenal is that of Tom Baldwin, a name known to few outside the tightly knit fraternity of Chicago traders. Armed only with an MBA and a stint in the meatpacking industry, Tom Baldwin in two and a half short years has parlayed $20,000 and some talent into a fortune so large that his lawyers want the actual figures to remain unpublished. He has done this by trading large positions in U.S. Treasury bond futures.

His "habit" has been successful to the extent that he now trades $500 million worth of bond futures on an average day. His market operations have gotten so big that many believe he has become one of the dominant forces in pricing U.S. Treasury bonds, which is rare for an independent floor trader. He pits himself daily against Wall Street investment banks, wirehouses, primary dealers, major banks, and the Fed.

To call his trading style intense is an understatement. Baldwin has piercing eyes, a raspy, resonant voice and a commanding physical appearance. He adds to his 5 feet, 10 inches by jumping to shoulder level when the market becomes so hectic that he needs to get off anywhere from 100 to 1000 bond futures contracts at a crack.

Yet Baldwin is also known for his ability to operate calmly and be right about market direction more often than he is wrong. He is described by peers as tremendously self-confident, strong-willed, and occasionally hot-tempered. Many of his floor competitors take into account what they guess is his position before entering the market.

To the old-timers, it seems Tom Baldwin arrived on the Chicago Board of Trade's floor just yesterday. His style of trading is perceived by everyone but himself as tremendously risky. For instance, he will continue to buy while the

*market plunges; he will sell into rallies and let the market go against him
without covering. He remains outwardly composed despite tremendous exposure and an occasional six-figure losing day.*

*Many believe that soon Tom Baldwin's "luck" will run out. His critics charge
that averaging massive paper losses is a bad habit, especially when trading 5000
contracts per day. The following interview took place in November 1984.*

INTERMARKET: How did you get involved in the business?
BALDWIN: I went to graduate school at Santa Clara University, em-
phasizing commodity trading. I always wanted to be in the commodity
business, but I didn't know anything about being a floor trader because
I wasn't in Chicago.

INTERMARKET: Did you trade while in school?
BALDWIN: Yes. I had a class in which we paper traded.

INTERMARKET: How did your trading go?
BALDWIN: I was the best in the class. I bought gold, it rallied and I
kept buying.

INTERMARKET: Did you know then that you were destined to
trade?
BALDWIN: I didn't know then—all I knew was that seat prices were
$250,000, which I didn't have. I didn't know that you could lease a seat.
I didn't know I could really do it.

INTERMARKET: How old are you now?
BALDWIN: 29.

INTERMARKET: And how old were you when you entered grad
school?
BALDWIN: 23.

INTERMARKET: Tell me how you went from trading long-term out
on the West Coast to floor trading in Chicago.
BALDWIN: I worked for Armour and John Morrell, a meat packer, for
three years after grad school. I was product manager for smoked meats
and sliced bacon. I had a staff position, responsible for the profit and
loss, but I had no one reporting to me. It was one of those jobs where
you get blamed for everything—I was responsible, but I couldn't
change things without going through a vice president.

INTERMARKET: Were you saving your money at that point?
BALDWIN: Yes. I wanted to do something entrepreneurial, but I
didn't know what. I was saving money, waiting for the opportunity.

Friends of mine came to the Board. That's how I learned about the

Board and then I came here. I found that my friend traded successfully and I found out how he did it. So I came down about four months after he did.

INTERMARKET: When did you know that this was the thing you wanted to do?
BALDWIN: I saw my friend, talked to him, and a light clicked on. I never even went to the floor; I just know that it was what I always wanted to do.

INTERMARKET: How did you know you'd succeed?
BALDWIN: I'd never failed at anything before, so I thought I'd do well.

INTERMARKET: Were you well capitalized to start?
BALDWIN: I was average. I started with $20,000, just like anybody else. In the three years after I got out of graduate school my wife and I had saved $30,000. So I worked out a budget where I could go for six months to a year without making any money. I couldn't lose any money, but I didn't have to make it. And my wife was pregnant, so she couldn't work. It was really do or die.

INTERMARKET: How were you doing at the end of six months of trading?
BALDWIN: I had turned the corner.

INTERMARKET: You were profitable by six months?
BALDWIN: Actually, I was profitable by five weeks.

INTERMARKET: So you didn't have the usual drawdown of $10,000 or so?
BALDWIN: No.

INTERMARKET: What's the lowest you got?
BALDWIN: At one point early on I was down 19 tics.

INTERMARKET: So by six months had you made $100,000?
BALDWIN: Yes.

INTERMARKET: By the end of 1982 did you have a net worth of over $1 million?
BALDWIN: Yes.

INTERMARKET: Have you been able to keep up with the kind of growth rate you saw your first year?
BALDWIN: No. But my goal is to double my previous year's income.

INTERMARKET: Were you self-taught?
BALDWIN: My friends taught me some things and I then developed my own style. I branched off from their style.

INTERMARKET: How did your trading strategy evolve?
BALDWIN: Just from experience. Purely experience. Basically, my strategy is to reduce my risk. I love trades that have minimal risk. A trade with size and minimal risk allows tremendous profit.

INTERMARKET: What was it like your first month on the floor?
BALDWIN: I was paying $1800 rent for my seat each month.

INTERMARKET: When did you actually start trading?
BALDWIN: My first day on the floor. My goal for my first week was to make 10 trades a day, 20 transactions, all one-lots. That's real hard. I didn't know anybody, I didn't know badges. I was afraid. I didn't know how to follow the market. I didn't know what to watch, who to watch, or anything. All I knew was that when someone was trading with me, I was probably making a bad trade.

INTERMARKET: Because presumably they knew what they were doing and you didn't?
BALDWIN: Right. I spent a lot of time bidding and offering, trying to follow the market, but at the same time watching what was going on, what influenced what. It was very frustrating, because the temptation was to give up the edge. At that point, I never gave up the edge.

INTERMARKET: How long did it take you to learn when it was a good time to give up the edge?
BALDWIN: Between six months and a year—once I started trading 100 lots (worth $10 million).

INTERMARKET: Do you step out when you initiate a position versus only adding on to a profitable one?
BALDWIN: Yes. Now I step out to initiate, but never then. That's because the market has changed. Two years ago, when the market was 5 bid at 6, I could buy it at 5 and sell it at 6 and have the market stay still. Now it doesn't do that anymore.

INTERMARKET: Why? Is the market more nervous now?
BALDWIN: (Pause) It's hard to say.

INTERMARKET: Is it that there are more arbitrageurs?
BALDWIN: (Pause) Yes. But it's not that there are more, it's just that they tend to change the market more often. Also, the traders in the pit don't take positions like they used to. The number of traders with a

position has decreased.

INTERMARKET: So you've seen a shift of power from the locals to the arbitrageurs.
BALDWIN: Yes.

INTERMARKET: Do you put yourself in the league with Plaza (Clearing Corp., owned by Salomon Brothers) and Dean Witter?
BALDWIN: No. They are the biggest.

INTERMARKET: So they make more money than you?
BALDWIN: No. I'm sure they don't.

INTERMARKET: Why?
BALDWIN: They don't have the advantage of volume. They don't trade as much as I do. Suppose they want to sell 2000. They pick their spot during the day, they sell, and it goes their way for 10 tics. They make 20,000 tics (or $650,000). That may be all they do all week.

INTERMARKET: What kind of a trader do you consider yourself?
BALDWIN: A day trader.

INTERMARKET: How did you figure out your style of trading?
BALDWIN: That was the way I started making money. Most locals pride themselves in having no opinion of the market. But I ended up forced to have an opinion because I stood in an area of the pit that had less of a constant flow of paper, so it wasn't always easy to get in and out of trades. I needed a sense of where the market was going.

INTERMARKET: Are you a technician or a fundamentalist?
BALDWIN: I watch both factors, but I'm primarily a technician. I have to be. I have to know where the support and resistance levels are.
  I also have to know what the fundamentals mean. Normally, though, the fundamentals occur outside of market hours, so I don't have the ability to capitalize on new information. During market hours all I'm able to do is utilize technical support and resistance levels.

INTERMARKET: What kind of homework do you do?
BALDWIN: I keep track of all the highs, lows and where the moving averages are. It's real easy. I can remember all the market highs and lows for a week. You have to remember what happened the last time we got down here or how the market behaved when it last rallied to this point.
  Usually the market tends to do the same thing over and over again — or at least two or three times. It tends to go up to a resistance point two or three times before it goes through it, and it also tends to go down to a

support level two or three times before penetrating it.

INTERMARKET: You keep track of high, low and moving averages. How do you use them? When the market approaches yesterday's low, are you selling?
BALDWIN: Yes. But it ends up that at the bottom I get long and at the top I get short. The reason: when the market seems strongest — when it may be at a top — large-sized orders come in to buy and the brokers look to me — and I sell to them. You can't believe how much gets traded at the top and at the bottom of the market each day.

INTERMARKET: You're saying you can tell if it's the top because of the high volume?
BALDWIN: Yes. I can feel it. And a lot of the volume goes to me because I make a market for it. There are a limited number of people who can make a market for 100 lots.

INTERMARKET: Why is it that most of the people who are successful do their own homework?
BALDWIN: If they love the business, then it's not work.

INTERMARKET: What do you usually do after the close?
BALDWIN: I keep track of the number of trades I make per day, plus the number of tics I make per day. I keep track of the percentage of tics to trades.

My philosophy of trading is to trade a lot. A trader who's getting by makes money on 10% of his trades. A good trader makes money on 20% of his trades. An excellent trader makes money on 30% of them. 60% should be scratches, 10% should be losers. That should be the goal.

The more I trade, the harder it is to keep that average. Some trades I scratch, more out of courtesy to the broker — and to keep getting his business.

INTERMARKET: What percentage of your entire net worth are you willing to lose in one day?
BALDWIN: I'd set my limit at 10%. But I don't look at it as if I would lose it. My consoling thought at the end of a losing day is, "It's only 10% of my net worth."

INTERMARKET: Are your winning days a lot more than 10%?
BALDWIN: No. Usually on my winning days I make less than I lose on my losing days.

INTERMARKET: So out of your average month, what number will be winning days, what number will be scratch days and what number will be losing days?

BALDWIN: Two losing days, 18 winning days. No scratch days.

INTERMARKET: What is your standard unit size?
BALDWIN: 200 lots ($20 million). It's pretty hard to trade 500 lots regularly.

INTERMARKET: What's your average profit on that?
BALDWIN: 30%. For example, if I traded a 1000 lot, I should have made 300 tics.

INTERMARKET: And how many contracts do you trade in the average day?
BALDWIN: About 5000.

INTERMARKET: So on an average day you make 1500 tics (or $46,875)?
BALDWIN: For a year's time, that would be average. Sometimes I trade 5000 contracts and I make 5000 tics. Some days I trade 5000 and I lose 3000 tics—though not very often. But overall, I make that percentage.

INTERMARKET: Would $20,000 be a good day?
BALDWIN: Twenty thousand dollars would not be a good day. I have a lot of "good" days, but at the end I consider them bad days if the close went bad. $20,000 is 600 tics. If I made 600 tics and I trade 5000 contracts, I feel like I really worked but I didn't do that well.

INTERMARKET: What is the most number of tics you've made in one day?
BALDWIN: 6000, 7000. $200,000.

INTERMARKET: And the largest amount you've lost in a day?
BALDWIN: 10,000.

INTERMARKET: 10,000 tics in one day? That's $312,500. How did that feel?
BALDWIN: (Pause) I had fun.

INTERMARKET: Did you take a day off?
BALDWIN: No. I don't believe in that theory either. I don't think that if you're in a slump, you have to get away.

INTERMARKET: Do you trade less on light volume?
BALDWIN: Yes, but not proportional to volume. If the volume is down half, my volume may be down a third. All the other big locals leave the pit, but I don't take very much time off.

INTERMARKET: So this is a numbers game for you?
BALDWIN: Yes. It's like shooting free throws. I don't give up the edge, I bid and offer, sell rallies, buy dips, and add on to profits. I work all day long.

INTERMARKET: What is your philosophy on taking positions home overnight?
BALDWIN: I don't like the risk and I almost always have the opportunity to get back into my position the next day.

INTERMARKET: What about gap days?
BALDWIN: That happens so seldom. One out of 60 days. How many times do you have to put on the position before the market takes off? Inevitably, when you do hit it and the market does take off, you're not as long as you want to be.

I'll tell you how I can tell the market will pop. When the market rallies, it tends to rally big during the day—usually a point or more. That's the day I would bring them home. My thought is, if I was short, and I didn't get out, I'd have to get out at the opening the next day. Everyone who was short has to buy it and get out. So bring home the markets that rally or break a point or more during the day.

INTERMARKET: What are some of the problems any large trader, hedger or arbitrageur will face?
BALDWIN: You can't trade large size in the bond pit as easily as you can trade small size. If I want to buy 1000, I have to buy them when the pit thinks they are no good. Anyone who trades size—Salomon Brothers, a major bank, whoever—has the same problem.

Let's say one of these entities wants to get long 1000. They have to buy it when it's no good. For example, if the market gaps open, the only way anyone can get long 1000 if they want to buy it is by hitting the offers. This means that the arbitrageurs want to sell it, the other speculators want to sell it, everyone wants to sell. Now here is one entity whose opinion is that the market is going higher. To me, that's a great edge. Here's one guy calling it higher while the rest of the world wants to sell it.

It's going to go down. You just don't know how far. And all the sellers have to make sure they cover, because as it tends to go down, everyone sells it, and everyone will be buying it back on the way back up.

If Richard Dennis buys his 1000 at 10, and I sell them to him and the market drops to 6, you might say that that's a great trade. But was I able to buy them back in on the way down? If I didn't, it turns around and goes back. All of a sudden it's 6 bid, 7 bid, 8 bid, 9 bid. If I only covered 500 of them and I'm still short, there will be nothing at 11 or 12. That's the problem with trading size. There's a limited market for anyone who only wants to trade 1000 lots.

INTERMARKET: What trading indicators do you use?
BALDWIN: Trading indicators? As a floor trader, I don't have the chance to trade off Fed funds, etc. By the time I find out about it, the opportunity is already gone. Arbitrageurs have already capitalized.

INTERMARKET: When you're in the pit and you know that if the market closes up, all the 10-day moving average systems will be buying on the close, will you fade them?
BALDWIN: If it's on the close, I would never fade them. I would go with them. They are willing to pay more, plus many of the systems get confirmation only after the close, so there should be strong buying the next morning. But the market may open lower the next morning and rally.

I buy in that situation because I have time on my side. There's 30 seconds to go, the systems want to buy, and they'll pay any price.

INTERMARKET: Do you subscribe to the theory that the market is most efficient on the close because day traders don't like to take positions overnight? And, likewise, that Friday's close is the most efficient reflection of value of the week because fewer people like to hold positions over the weekend?
BALDWIN: That used to be the case a year or so ago when the money supply figures were released on Friday. Now that money supply is released on Thursday, everyone gets out of his position before the close on Thursday. Friday's close is not as serious because there are no numbers released before Monday's opening.

INTERMARKET: So the fundamental numbers really move the market?
BALDWIN: Yes. Unless there's a major move in the market underway.

INTERMARKET: When we see a chart of the bond rally and how perfectly it fits into the trendlines—the geometric beauty, so to speak, how can a trader like yourself give much credence to the fundamental numbers?
BALDWIN: I look at the market as such: The technical aspects move the market during the day, and the fundamentals move it at night. Very seldom does the trader have the chance to take advantage of a fundamental number during market hours. They come out at 7:30 a.m. or 3:30 p.m. So the move happens overnight, and you don't have that much chance.

There are very definitely two separate markets—the one during trading hours and then the one from the close to tomorrow's opening. The second market is much easier to read and to trade.

INTERMARKET: Do you like to buy the market when it approaches support trendlines?

BALDWIN: No. I like to sell it there. If the market is able to go through it, it's all over. There's no better feeling than to be short when there are no bids.

INTERMARKET: So Thursday you go home flat, Friday morning the money supply figure is out. What do you do?

BALDWIN: If it opens up 20, usually I fade it right away. Generally, the people who did go home with a long position are going to sell and take their profit. And hence, this is a good way to find whether the market is long or short. However, if there is little selling, I know that most people probably went home short and have to buy to cover, and those longs with profits for whatever reason aren't taking them. So I better get long, and fast.

But if the market gaps up, and comes off the opening, I assume the rest of the world is selling, and I know longs are taking their profits. That is usual and that is why I usually sell gap openings.

INTERMARKET: How far will it have to go down after it's opened up 20 before you really begin selling?

BALDWIN: It depends on how the orders come in, but if it went down to unchanged on the day — which is not unusual — then I really have to sell it.

INTERMARKET: So you might sell 50 or so at the opening to test the water?

BALDWIN: Sure. I'd sell 50 and then I'd buy it. That way, I test the water right away.

INTERMARKET: When do you decide to take profits?

BALDWIN: Feel. Whether I sense the market can continue to go down or not.

INTERMARKET: How do the arbitrageurs and houses like Plaza work? Can you tell what they trade off? Are they weak hands or strong hands?

BALDWIN: I don't know what these investment houses are doing in terms of hedging, so I assume that they are big speculators. Dean Witter and ACLI are the major arbitrageurs. When Shearson wants to sell me 200, I fade them because my first thought is not that the market is going to go against me immediately. When Witter sells it to me, I know it's going to go against me sooner or later. When I see a big rally and the market looks great and all of a sudden I see Witter coming in selling a little, I go with them.

INTERMARKET: Do you ever fade the Fed funds rate or go against other fundamental news?

BALDWIN: Yes. Trading opposite the fundamentalist trades is often a smart thing because the market frequently comes back. I don't think that particular factor is that tremendously important. It only is important insofar as it relates to the trend.

Let's assume the Fed funds rate ticks up. That fact by itself is not so important, especially since the opportunity has already come and gone. It's only important because if Fed funds keep ticking up, then the bond market's downtrend will continue.

You have to be careful, too. I can show you the trend, but it can't help you over the short term.

INTERMARKET: Walk me through the thought process you go through before putting on a major position, let's say buying 1000.
BALDWIN: It depends for one if it is offered or not. Usually it's not.

INTERMARKET: If someone wants to sell you 1000, you don't want to buy, but if no one is selling it, you want it?
BALDWIN: That's right. I just bid for it quietly. If I think I won't have to give up the edge, I won't.

INTERMARKET: So let me understand this correctly. If you're bullish and you want to buy 500, and someone wants to sell it to you, that will make you not want to buy it?
BALDWIN: Well, I'd know that I could get it cheaper.

INTERMARKET: So let's say you just bought and the market doesn't move until you have 300. Now the market ticks up, but you don't have your entire position on. What will you do?
BALDWIN: I would go for it immediately.

INTERMARKET: Would you go "7 bid, 8 bid, 9 bid" immediately or would you go 7 bid until you had all you wanted?
BALDWIN: What happens is I stop getting them. I have a limited number of people who will trade with me. Size and fear. The market moves my way. If I bid 7, the market becomes 7 bid at 8.

INTERMARKET: Do you wait until the majority of the pit is long before you get short?
BALDWIN: No. Despite what a lot of people think, it's pretty difficult to tell what "the pit" is doing.

INTERMARKET: So the pit doesn't generally have a position?
BALDWIN: Right. And that's why an order to buy 100 can change the market. Very few traders carry a position in the pit. It's the traders outside the pit who carry a position.

INTERMARKET: What sort of indicators make you take a position?
BALDWIN: I don't use indicators per se. I like to fade the Fed intervention stuff. Like I say, those tend to come back, unless the Fed's maneuver is really unexpected. As far as trading a position, I like the trend, because I trade around my position and I disguise what my position really is.

INTERMARKET: How do you mean "trade around your position?"
BALDWIN: I might be short 100 and the market might go down, but I might trade 1000 or 2000 contracts in that same period without altering my net short position.

INTERMARKET: So you scalp around your main position?
BALDWIN: Right. Because there's no sense staying out of the market. I like to have a position. As long as I have a position, I'm interested. I'm protected and I'm in tune with the market.

INTERMARKET: About how many times are you in and out of the market?
BALDWIN: I'm in the market most of the time, but I have about 10 different groups of trades.

INTERMARKET: Do you think your knowledge of bond trading would make you successful in any pit?
BALDWIN: Oh, I don't think so. I couldn't trade the size, for one thing. The bond market is the one market in the world where I can trade a 500 lot at the market. That's like 3 million bushels of beans (a position limit). There's nobody who can buy 3 million bean at the market. Nobody.

They're so used to bidding up the market when large orders come in to the pit. Why should a local take that kind of stand? He'll just make you keep bidding for it and watch the market go up.

INTERMARKET: So the bonds are the most efficient futures market?
BALDWIN: Definitely. There's no comparison.

INTERMARKET: Will you ever do what some of the other more successful floor traders have done — move off the floor and trade all the markets?
BALDWIN: If I were away from the pit, I'd find it pretty hard to tell what's a good trade and what's not. I tend to be contrarian more than one who goes with the crowd. So if I see the market move 10 or 20 tics my way, I immediately think that I have to reverse my position. The market never goes one way. It goes up 5, down 4, up 5, down 3.

For floor traders, it's what you do in between there that counts. So if it is falling very steeply, I can buy at the obvious spots — yesterday's high, low and close, wherever the opening range found good support. Yesterday's high is usually a good sell for 4 or 5 tics.

When I move off the floor, that's it. But I love to trade. It's not the money or anything. I love the market. I love reading charts.

INTERMARKET: Are even numbers more often support areas?
BALDWIN: I would say odd numbers — 27, 21, 16, 12, 7 and even. So I think it's a bit more odd.

INTERMARKET: When you're taking a look at the pit and you're thinking of making a move — either long or short — what are you thinking about?
BALDWIN: There are certain brokers to watch and certain traders to watch. The market tends to trade a lot at tops and bottoms — there are many very big size trades at those points. If you watch, when it's over and done there always seems to be a void there — and hence the tremendous opportunity to push it. A lot of traders are afraid to get in because they've seen the market move up or down. To all of a sudden go against that trend is very difficult. But that's where all the money is made — if you can capitalize on it.

Let's say the market is off 10 tics and I just see 500 get sold right at the bottom. All of a sudden there are no sellers and it's gone. The market never goes only one way — it bounces. It works its way back and forth.

INTERMARKET: You put a lot of credence on the size of orders that go by at key areas. How would you trade if you were looking at a screen and were not able to know what size was being traded, but just the price action?
BALDWIN: The key spots are invariably on the charts, the points you should have bought or sold at. It's like the air being let out of a balloon. There's nothing to bid for, there's nothing offered. It's all over.

It happened the other day when it sold off to 20. No one would sell at 21. Then, real slowly, a few people bid 21. But no one would sell that at 22. Then someone bid 22.

INTERMARKET: Does the market go to whatever all the stops are?
BALDWIN: No. It seems like it sometimes.

INTERMARKET: If the market moves to an area where you expect a lot of stops, dips down and then comes right back up, would you buy it?
BALDWIN: No. I'd be looking to sell it because the locals didn't want to hold on to their shorts. I want the market to bounce up and I'll sell it there. It's very rare that a top or bottom is tested just once.

INTERMARKET: Do you see many days where the market is strong all day and becomes very weak at the close?

BALDWIN: No. Generally, if it's strong all day, it may come off a couple of tics at the close, but never enough to make me get short.

INTERMARKET: So on the screen, a bottom will look like "hold, hold, hold, up tic. Hold, hold, hold, another up tic."
BALDWIN: Right. Real slowly. And then momentum builds.

INTERMARKET: So you're saying it's a good buy at the point where the market stops dead, after just falling apart.
BALDWIN: That's right.

INTERMARKET: When would you be a seller in that situation?
BALDWIN: At some point, I have to give up. When my position gets big, I have to get out on strength. When I'm long 300 and someone's bidding for 300, you might say, "Don't sell yet—the market's still strong." It's real easy to wait, but maybe if I wait too long, there's no one to buy.

My only opportunity to get out is when someone else wants to buy. Well, when someone's bidding for 300 and I'm long, that's my opportunity and I have to take it.

In a bull market at the top, people keep getting long, because they've been getting burned by being short.

INTERMARKET: Do you have a hard time selling out your long position, thinking it's going lower, and, when it doesn't, buying it back at a higher price?
BALDWIN: Sometimes. Once I've lost money on a trade, it's very hard to get back into that same trade again. But like I say, a good trader would do it. It's what you have to do.

INTERMARKET: Do you ever panic when you're losing big money?
BALDWIN: No. Never. You lose too much money when you panic. First of all, I don't trade for money.

INTERMARKET: But you average your losses.
BALDWIN: That's because I don't panic. If I've got a bad short position on, I try to buy the dips. Even though I sold it at 4 or 5 and it immediately went to 10, that isn't reason enough to get out. It's probably the top and it's easy, it's so easy to get out. It's what everyone tells you to do. It's a tremendous relief to get out. Phew. But if you hang on just a little bit more—which is very hard to do, your stomach still has that grinding feeling—it will usually come back.

INTERMARKET: Have you been in situations where the market just keeps going?
BALDWIN: Yes. At some point you just say, "This is a bad day." I watch

and I have to say, "Okay, I was wrong." It takes me about all day to throw in the towel. But at the end of the day I just say, "5 for 1000." I just keep buying them. I got my money's worth.

INTERMARKET: It would seem that your way is much less comfortable.
BALDWIN: Yes. But nine times out of ten, it's worked out for me.

INTERMARKET: Is it that the least comfortable thing to do is the best strategy?
BALDWIN: Frequently.

INTERMARKET: Is it comfortable to add on to a profit and hold on?
BALDWIN: Yes. It's easier to take small profits. But I try not to think about it. I just keep thinking that I have to keep buying it or I have to keep selling it. I don't think about my position but concentrate on why it has to keep going.

INTERMARKET: Do you want to get opposite the pit and then run the pit in?
BALDWIN: It's harder to do that than a lot of people think. Generally what's happening when it looks like I'm doing that is this: When I'm opposite the pit and it's going my way, then I'm usually the only trader that the brokers can go to.

All the other traders are the other way, so I have to keep spitting out what they sell me and churning it back in so that I keep that net position of being long. It isn't necessarily that I'm running the pit. It's just that I have to keep buying more than I'm selling if the market's moving up. That's when I have to have a definite market option — it's going to go up. I have to give up the edge, knowing that the market's going to keep going.

INTERMARKET: Are you good at that?
BALDWIN: It depends on the market. I'm a better bear market trader than a bull market trader. That tends to be my style.

INTERMARKET: You move the market at certain points in the day. And a lot of people key off you in their trading.
BALDWIN: Only those who are smart. Traders aren't stupid. I do the same thing. There are certain brokers who put orders on the market and the market will go their way. It's an indication that there might be more to come.

INTERMARKET: A lot of people consider you the biggest local in the bond pit.
BALDWIN: That changes. I have a theory on why traders reach

certain levels. It's because everyone reaches a satisfaction level. Everyone starts as a one-lot trader. Everyone should—if they are to be successful. I traded one-lots successfully, so I wanted to see if I could trade two-lots. When I did that, then five-lots and then 10 lots. It is at this point that most people begin to have trouble.

They freeze when they realize that on one tic, they may lose $312.50 and that's a lot of money. They can't fathom losing it. They're thinking about their trading in terms of money. They begin to have problems because they don't do with the 10 lot what they would've done with a one-lot. They should trade 10 lots like they traded one-lots. Their comfort level isn't that of a 10-lot trader. So they stop.

INTERMARKET: What about speed and aggressiveness?
BALDWIN: That comes with a lot of self-confidence. There's nothing better for the confidence than watching everything going on all day, trading mentally for hours.

INTERMARKET: Have you done that?
BALDWIN: I had to. That's how I became successful. You learn that when the market rallied five tics and a major arbitrageur comes in and sells 50. Even though there's 200 bid for, well, gee, all of a sudden the other 150 are gone. I noticed that time and again. And I capitalized on it.

The next time, you have the self-confidence to know that it looks strong but you sell it anyway. You get speed from self-confidence. You do it once and it works. You do it again, only faster.

I don't trade for money. I don't think that way. I trade for tics.

INTERMARKET: Do you have a high I.Q.?
BALDWIN: I think it's 132. I have a very high aptitude for numbers. Most successful people down here are more scientifically minded rather than artistic. That's not to say an artistic person can't do well. But a person who can associate numbers quickly can do well.

INTERMARKET: Did you do well in school?
BALDWIN: Yes. B+, A-.

INTERMARKET: Did you work at it?
BALDWIN: Not usually.

INTERMARKET: Will you take a winning position home?
BALDWIN: Yes.

INTERMARKET: Often?
BALDWIN: No. Because usually—and some people will disagree with me—usually I can get back into my position the next morning. If I

take positions home, I do that for several days in a row. And when I don't, I don't for several days. My philosophy is that when you can get into your position the next day, the overnight risk isn't worth it.

INTERMARKET: Would you ever take a loser home?
BALDWIN: Yes. If the market sold off 20 tics toward the end of the day and I get caught short and the market rallies two or three tics at the bell. I'll go home short if there's no number [economic report] coming out the next day and if I don't have to take it home over the weekend, because the only reason it will open higher is if there are a lot more traders short than I would think—the outside traders, the cash traders who like to squeeze the futures traders right on the close. Often you'll get a gap down the next morning. It's a calculated risk.

INTERMARKET: You'll be more likely to hold a loser overnight than a winner?
BALDWIN: Yes.

INTERMARKET: On the thought that you should take profits?
BALDWIN: Yes. It also depends on how much you have in the trade.

INTERMARKET: Is this something you would recommend to the beginning trade?
BALDWIN: Oh, no. I wouldn't recommend it for most traders. I think that floor people should go in without a position.

INTERMARKET: What's the largest position that you've taken on initially—all at once?
BALDWIN: 1500 contracts. 500 and then 1000.

INTERMARKET: And the biggest position you've built up to?
BALDWIN: About 1500. And I wouldn't recommend that to everybody either. You don't need to take that kind of risk. For me, I had to satisfy a certain curiosity, a certain feeling that I get when I have 100, 500 or 1000. I don't need to satisfy that curiosity anymore. I did it and I don't need to prove to myself anymore that I could do it.

INTERMARKET: You get credit for much more size in the pit. Does it bother you to be the center of everyone's attention in the pit?
BALDWIN: No. It doesn't bother me. I don't think that any one person is bigger than the market. I just tend to be right more frequently than other people. Nobody's bigger than the market. I don't think many people really understand that philosophy. I think it's been proven time and time again. The market goes where it wants to go, no matter who's in the way or what's in the way. And that's why a person should trade 10 lots like one-lots.

I've learned discipline. I learned that at some point you have to say you're wrong.

INTERMARKET: What is the largest position you've ever taken home?
BALDWIN: Oh, 25% of what I would take on in total. I cut back on my risk.

INTERMARKET: How do you add on?
BALDWIN: In any rally, the biggest size available is right at the beginning. I'd like to add on in equal amounts but equal increments are not usually offered. Once the market gets rolling, the size being offered gets smaller.

INTERMARKET: Is there a best time of the day for you?
BALDWIN: Usually after breakfast. I don't trade the opening. You can get whipsawed very easily without having a chance to get out. I often trade less before 9:00.

INTERMARKET: Why would you wait until 9:00? It's quieter then and I'd think it would be tougher to get the size you do.
BALDWIN: I can shape my opinion more on where I think the market's going to go. Once I have a definite opinion on it, then I can wait to pick my spot. The market doesn't move as fast as it used to. I just have to be patient.

INTERMARKET: You know in advance where you'd like to buy and sell?
BALDWIN: Usually. If what I thought was going to happen does happen, then I go. It just all of a sudden goes. I know it's right. I don't hesitate. If I hesitate, the opportunity is gone.

INTERMARKET: That's part of confidence.
BALDWIN: Right. The other part is, sometimes the market needs a little push, so I have to trade a little bit more than I want to.

INTERMARKET: In terms of size?
BALDWIN: Right. The market is unsure; the other traders are unsure. They need that little extra push.

INTERMARKET: Does it matter who you'll trade with?
BALDWIN: No. But most people won't trade with me. When I trade with a local and the local loses money, he feels bad. I don't want to take another guy's money. If he thinks the market is going up and I think it's going down, fine. He can trade with me. But I don't look for locals to stick them with trades. I tend to trade with brokers. I look for paper.

INTERMARKET: What percentage of your trades are made with outside customer orders [paper]?
BALDWIN: Probably 75%. You don't have the market with locals that I do with paper. There are not many 100-lot locals, but there's a lot of big size paper.

INTERMARKET: Will you take a loss without averaging it?
BALDWIN: Rarely. I do though. It depends. The problem is that I'm not able to take a loss without averaging it. I'd love to, but it's very difficult to take a small loss on a big position. If I could take a one-tic loss on my losing positions, I'd do it in a minute. I end up having to trade around my position and trade my way out of it in order to take the smallest loss possible. It's called averaging, but I'm not doing it to average. I don't have any choice.

INTERMARKET: When will you add to a loss before you call it quits and get out?
BALDWIN: I don't like to think about that usually.

INTERMARKET: Do you add to it?
BALDWIN: Yes. Sure.

INTERMARKET: Let's say the market is at 8, you're very bullish, but you think it may dip to 5. Would you buy some at 8, some at 7 and some at 6?
BALDWIN: I would try to sell some on the way down, and once it rallied I'd buy it back. But you can never be so confident that you know exactly what's going to happen. It's wrong to think you can buy the market at 8, 7, 6, and 5, and then have it turn around and rally 15 points, with you long all of it. If the market's going to go to 5, I might as well sell some, and make it go to 5. I just make sure that at the bottom I'm not short. I can buy it on the way back up just as easily. Why take the risk of it going down? If it goes up, you can buy it, if it goes down you're sunk.

INTERMARKET: Did you ever think you'd be doing this well?
BALDWIN: Never.

INTERMARKET: Could you describe what it feels like?
BALDWIN: I don't really think about it. I don't think of it as money.

INTERMARKET: What do you say to those people who predict you'll blow out? Do you think you ever will?
BALDWIN: I think about it, but I don't think I ever will.

INTERMARKET: If you lost it all, would people help you back in?

BALDWIN: I don't think so. A lot of people would love to say, "I told you so." A long, long line of people would say, "Tom Baldwin, I told you so." The first 100 lot I traded I was almost whipped for.

INTERMARKET: Really? How much equity did you have before you pulled that one?

BALDWIN: That was at six months—probably $200,000. And it was one of the best trades I ever made. As soon as I sold the 100 at 5 the market was 4 sellers. It kept coming down and I unloaded it in staggers, the lower it went. Had I just fallen over as soon as I sold it, I would've had 5 tics on a hundred lot without blinking an eye.

But strangely, everyone thought is was the worst thing I ever did. They told me I was too new and couldn't do that. They had never seen it done before by a novice. They scolded me and I agreed with them and told them that it was a one-time deal and will probably never happen again.

I didn't want to trade 100 lots, but it was just a great edge. The guy bid 5 just as it was about to go to 4 sellers. I couldn't resist. I wasn't nervous. It was completely a reaction. I just said 'Sold.' I knew. He tried to scare me when he saw his error and said '100.' I said 'Okay.'

8

Charlie Andrews

E *very Friday, after the currency futures close at the Chicago Mercantile Exchange, Charlie Andrews heads out to O'Hare Airport for a trip to his 6000-acre ranch in central Kansas. He spends the weekend doing hard physical work, so, as he explains, "I don't lose track of reality and keep straight for myself just what a dollar really is." Before nightfall on Sunday he jets back to his apartment in Chicago, ready for another week on the floor.*

This is the routine of a man who trades for himself as well as both institutional and speculative clients ranging from cattle and ranching millionaires to highly discreet European speculators.

Charlie Andrews is not typical among the gnomes of Chicago, who have gained increased recognition by their impact on the interbank market in the way that their counterparts in Zurich did years ago. Rather, Andrews is the epitome of the trader whose roots are not in futures but in cash. Indeed, while he talks, walks and acts like a cowboy, he has a mind which competes against econometric models, Ivy League MBA's and interbank traders in centers around the world.

Andrews, who advises international banks on hedging, is described as having boundless energy and enthusiasm. He doesn't sleep much. "I've always just operated on two to four hours a night." He talks by phone to Far Eastern contacts from 12:00 to 1:00 a.m. and to European cash dealers in the early morning after 3:00.

INTERMARKET: Where did you grow up?
ANDREWS: I grew up in Kanopolis, a small town in Kansas.

INTERMARKET: How small?

ANDREWS: Small. A town of 700 people. There were 35 people in the high school, and six people in my graduating class.

INTERMARKET: What did you do for fun?
ANDREWS: I grew up milking goats, raising what we'd call bucket calves. I'd dilute the milk down. I could raise several of them off the goats' milk—they'd cost $5 to $10 a head weighing 75 to 150 lbs. This was in the early 1950s. Drought was on and times were really tough for the farmer.
   So by the time I got out of high school and went to college for a couple of years, the cattle market started to firm up. We were in the worst drought imaginable from about 1951 until 1957 and during that time, the cattle market fell in half. It went from about 40 cents to about 18 cents. Calves went even lower.

INTERMARKET: Was the agricultural sector holding up better than today?
ANDREWS: A lot of farms went under. I'd say from 1951 to 1958 there was a period somewhat similar to this one, only the dollars involved today are much greater. The economic situation today is also much worse, but it was a period similar to this. From 1949 through today, I think our farm population has decreased about 50%. But that period, linked with this last five-year period, is probably where the biggest decrease has been.

INTERMARKET: When did you get interested in trading?
ANDREWS: When I was 14 years old, the Union Pacific Railroad gave three counties of kids a ride to Kansas City on a train. When we arrived, we had the choice of three tours, and I chose the Kansas City Board of Trade, not having any idea what they did except that it had something to do with the wheat market. We got there at the close and I looked down from the visitors' gallery and said, "Boy, that's what I'm going to do someday."
   So, I went to the Mexican border when I was 19 years old ...

INTERMARKET: Didn't your father want you to go into farming?
ANDREWS: Yes. He wished for me to stay in agriculture. But I always wanted to trade cattle. My great-grandfather was a cattle trader, a butcher who came over from Scotland and who, among other things, shot buffalo for the railroad and furnished meat to the crews who were building the Union Pacific across Kansas. As he got a stake, he started trading land and then became a cattle trader. He would gather cattle in the country and drive them to the terminal yards and load them on the rail and sell them in Kansas City. My father wasn't involved much in trading. He was involved in small country banking, the cattle business, and some farming.

I had enough cash put together by the time I sold my cattle and then I made some good money tending bar.

INTERMARKET: How?
ANDREWS: At Kansas State a guy who owned the bar had been a baseball hero. He was a big jock and had a big name, so everybody went there. It was just a beer joint and he hated it. He'd rather have been a referee and traveled around the country, so he offered me 10% of the profits to run the bar.

It was probably a better education than anyone in that school received—I learned how to handle people.

INTERMARKET: Both sober and drunk?
ANDREWS: (Laughs) Right. Although I didn't know it then, that was a real good education for someone going into the commodities business.

So when I went to the Mexican border, I had $19,000 in cash saved up. This was not enough to trade two loads of cash cattle. If I bought them and shipped them out, it was two or three weeks before the money would come back to me, and I had no credit.

INTERMARKET: So you'd buy them cheaply in Mexico and sell them for a profit in the states?
ANDREWS: Not necessarily. The duty would equal it out. Mexican cattle were different because they were so thin. I'd buy them and ship them to wherever I could find a home for them and try to make enough money to pay my room and board.

INTERMARKET: So what was the key to trading cattle?
ANDREWS: The key was to find really thin cattle which would grow better than cattle in the States.

Also, there was a difference in the duty for both the under twos and the over sevens (under 200 lbs and over 700 lbs). You could make some pretty good money sorting them right and getting them past the government graders and then unscrambling them. So I got a percent of what I could make sorting cattle, which turned out to be quite a lot of money. On a really good night I'd make $200-$300.

INTERMARKET: So you had to get the more expensive ones past the government inspectors at the cheaper price?
ANDREWS: I'd scramble the cattle. I'd get the real light ones and the real heavy ones on the scale weighing 199 pounds and 701 pounds. I'd save a cent on several pounds of beef, and that would amount to a lot of money.

INTERMARKET: So you accumulated money this way?
ANDREWS: A little. But word got out that I knew cattle, so I got an

offer from one of the big traders down there. He offered to give me a $100,000 line of credit in exchange for 50% of the profits. I also had to post all my cash. But that was all I needed. They might as well have offered me the Sears Tower. It was a big breakthrough for me.

As time went on, I built up a large customer base with companies like Wilson and Morell, which were starting to get into the cattle feeding business to supply their packing businesses. Always remembering that I wanted to trade commodities, I established them as customers — this was in the early '60s. They fed me a lot of good pork information. That was before cattle futures, so I started trading bellies.

INTERMARKET: Day trading or long-term trading?
ANDREWS: Both. Mostly long-term trading because I'd be pretty busy during the day. But I would build positions and liquidate them. I'd carry positions 20, 30 days.

As I got more into it, I would open more personal trading accounts. What I learned was how to trade people.

INTERMARKET: What do you mean?
ANDREWS: No one is always right, but there are people who are almost always wrong. What I'd try to look for is somebody who'd be 90 to 100% wrong. I'd fade them. In November 1964, the Chicago Mercantile opened the cattle contract. By that time, I had a very well-established cash cattle business. I knew where every major cattle string in the United States was. I would know when they were going to go on feed and approximately when they were going to get fat. I would always be trading four to six months out, and I'd be either bullish or bearish, knowing what was going on feed. I would either be a buyer of a few contracts every day or a seller, until I accumulated a position.

INTERMARKET: You'd buy rallies and sell breaks?
ANDREWS: No. You had a 15-cent range, so I'd give a broker an order like, "Buy one at 10:00 and one at 12:00 every day." Just a standing order. I'd buy two a day. Limit positions were 150, so over time I'd build a limit position. Almost every time, the market would move in my favor since I knew the fundamentals so well. I'd make $1.50 on a move, which was good money, but it would take three or four months.

INTERMARKET: On a limit position that would be — ?
ANDREWS: $30,000, $40,000.

INTERMARKET: Was this for any customers?
ANDREWS: No. That was just my own. By that time, the most valuable thing I provided my cattle customers was my belief on where the market was going to go. Plus, my information on where we could make the best deals in the United States buying cattle. By that time I was

covering 21 states.

INTERMARKET: And how old were you at this time?
ANDREWS: 26.

INTERMARKET: Why didn't you continue in the cash cattle business, trading on the side?
ANDREWS: Trading in the cattle business is an art. It's like people — no two cattle are alike. When business got bigger, I couldn't do all the buying personally. I had to rely on the word of other people. Their mistakes started costing me money, because I always stood behind my word. If I told a buyer the cattle was going to be this or that and it wasn't, I'd have to adjust the price. I'd make the errors good, just as I do now.

It got to be that I was making a lot more money trading in futures than I was in my cash operations. Plus, it was getting to be such a hassle. And I smelled that everybody and his doctor and lawyer and dentist friend were getting into the commodity trading business — one, for tax shelter and two, for profit. So I felt that we were headed for a pretty good sized wreck and I wanted to get small again — have a business that I could handle myself. I had already bought a seat, so I decided to get out of the cash end of it.

INTERMARKET: In what year?
ANDREWS: 1973.

INTERMARKET: When the grains started going wild?
ANDREWS: Right. And I was consequently fascinated with the grain markets. I wanted to get into them because there was more opportunity in grains at this time than in the meats.

INTERMARKET: And by this time you'd converted your cash meat customers to futures accounts?
ANDREWS: Oh, I'd say maybe 20% of them followed me into the commodity business.

INTERMARKET: More hedge oriented or more trading oriented?
ANDREWS: Initially more trading oriented, but as time changed they became more hedge oriented. In the beginning it was only a spec market but then it became at least 80% a hedge business. Other than people who just quit or died, I still have the people who started with me.

INTERMARKET: What did you think about the grain markets while you were standing in a dead meat market?
ANDREWS: I became very fascinated. First of all, they were a world

market, so much bigger than the meat market in both total volume done in futures and the total dollar volume. Much larger than livestock. I felt like grains were really something I wanted to get more involved in.

INTERMARKET: From the cash side or from futures?
ANDREWS: Both. I could see that the way it was handled by elevators and by the farmers was in for a drastic change somewhere down the road. I wanted to be involved in exporting.

But then I found out that only a few families control the entire grain exporting business. I could become involved in the country, but no one would let me get involved in the international export of grain. That was about the time when I realized that currencies and grains correlated with each other.

Now in the money business, the sky's the limit—anyone can get in and there's no major international control. They are open markets. I decided it would be much more to my advantage to get involved in the money markets.

INTERMARKET: So you shifted from being a cowboy delving in cattle futures to someone involved in the currency markets?
ANDREWS: Right.

INTERMARKET: Are the principles for trading and hedging currencies the same as those for the meats?
ANDREWS: Absolutely. I could take a cash corn trader, a cash meat trader or a currency or bond trader and switch them. Within a week or so, once they pick up the language, they would be right at home. There is very little difference between trading cash and futures in any market, but nobody knows that.

That was one of my big advantages when I got into the currencies, because I came from a cash business and learned the thought process of the cash trader. In the beginning, the banks never believed that the IMM (the CME's International Monetary Market division, where currencies began trading in 1972) would ever work.

They would hardly even let me in the door to start with. Then, when they could see how wide the cash-futures spread was, they said, "Yeah, well, there's big money in just arbing (arbitraging). Sure, we'll take a shot at it."

I really got my foot in the door when the spread was coming in—the markets were getting more efficient. Then the banks needed someone who could translate cash and futures to their traders. That's where I had the advantage over others. I understood the cash-futures relationship because I did an arb in very volatile markets both in grains and meats. So I had a pretty good advantage in teaching their traders how to get a feel for the difference between cash and futures.

INTERMARKET: What is the difference between cash and futures?
ANDREWS: The difference between a cash market and a futures market is that the futures market moves much faster. Initially — and this goes for any market — cash traders hate the futures. A cash trader is used to making his own market and if he gets hit with a large quantity, he has the tendency to shove it in the drawer and wait until the market comes to let him out. Before futures, a cash trader might go 30 days without liquidating grain or a week liquidating meat. He had time.

INTERMARKET: A cash trader doesn't think of mark-to-market?
ANDREWS: No. He has the tendency to say, "Oh well, the market will come back." In a futures market, the market will recognize if there is an oversupply or a shortage and react very quickly. A cash trader may be short bought (having sold something he has yet to buy) but he can just call around and get something here and there. Most of the time, this will work for him. But the 20% of the time it doesn't work for him will wipe out all of his profits. So what cash traders hate to see is a damn futures market which moves so quickly against their positions.

The futures markets have a tremendous sense of the real situation of the market. What the cash trader hates if a futures market that moves while he's trying to make deals. If he's short bought and making calls like mad, and all he gets is, "Well, Joe, I don't want to sell there; the futures are rallying," it can really screw up his deal.

INTERMARKET: Did this work the same way in the interbank market?
ANDREWS: Absolutely. It moved the market so much faster than the interbank liked to see it move. If a bank gets hit with $50 million or $100 million, the bank would like to take the time to lay it off. Whereas the futures market turned out to be correct and faster when it differed from what the interbank was doing.

INTERMARKET: How has the development of currency futures changed the way a bank does business?
ANDREWS: Of everything I've heard, the finest compliment the futures market has ever been paid was what a very prominent, old European interbank trader told me in his very broken accent. He said the U.S.A. had no credibility in foreign exchange trading until the IMM came along. He said, "Now you do a more precise job of moving the market than the interbank does." What he was telling me was that prior to the IMM, Switzerland and Germany had most of the expertise in FX trading — this goes back hundreds of years.

The only difference between the interbank and futures was one of access — the principles of forward commitment were the same, but the public was not allowed in (the interbank). When the IMM came along, it made moves contrary to what was felt to be correct overseas. All the IMM people who were trading our market were better informed on what the world's supply-demand situation was than the interbank traders were. We made the market move faster and in the right direction. They didn't. It became the interbank following the futures rather than the futures following interbank.

INTERMARKET: Are the spreads in the interbank tighter when the futures are open?
ANDREWS: Oh, much tighter. When I'm trading the interbank after the futures close I may get a five point spread in futures terms. I'll always get at least a three point spread. But when the futures markets are opened, I'll always get a one point spread. From the minute the futures close, the interbank becomes less liquid in terms of a wider bid-ask spread.

INTERMARKET: What percent of the interbank traders use the IMM?
ANDREWS: I think the interbank claims it does $35 billion per day on an average 24-hour day. On a 24-hour day the IMM may do $5 billion. Less than 20%. But there's nothing wrong with that. You go to any commodity except bonds and the volume in the futures is probably 5% of the total cash volume. So I say we do more than our share in any commodity except bonds.

INTERMARKET: You mentioned that you learned to read and handle people tending bar and then trading cash cattle. How did floor trading go?
ANDREWS: Well, I don't particularly talk to many people on the floor. But I talk to a lot of cash traders with ideas. I read them a lot more than I do the floor people. It's so important to read the cash people because some of them are almost always wrong.

INTERMARKET: Aren't there floor traders who are wrong regularly?
ANDREWS: The futures people who are always wrong are not around for long. Plus, your scalper doesn't want to know anything. He has no opinion.
    But I talk very seldom to the fundamentalists on the floor. What I'm talking about is the cash trade. I rely very heavily on those who are 90% of the time dead wrong. They are great to fade. If they have my same idea, I know I'm wrong.

INTERMARKET: So you're saying you shop people versus shopping the market.
ANDREWS: Right. I also can tell by the tone of his voice when the average trader is really secure and confident as opposed to when he is in question or fighting a position. It's very important to know how to read somebody's voice.

INTERMARKET: How do you trade a panic market?

ANDREWS: In a panic market you react; you don't think. Everybody seems to think we have all the news on the floor. Hell, we're the last to ever know why a market did something. Runners come in the pit and ask what happened and we have no idea. Our job is to react. That's where experience really counts.

If you get inundated with buy or sell orders in a panic situation, you cannot panic; you must keep your count. The secret is to keep cool and have your eyes and ears trained on everyone else. You should keep track of how much everyone was long, about where they're going to be done. You never know what created the situation. The Fed may have done something minor or some major world catastrophe could have happened.

INTERMARKET: What have you seen going on in the currencies in the past year—besides a lot of selling?

ANDREWS: What have I seen in the past year? (Pause) Europeans who don't believe in the dollar buy every rally (in the foreign currencies) and double up. And then all of a sudden, they blow it all away when the market continues the downtrend.

INTERMARKET: Not the banks?

ANDREWS: No. European speculators. I don't ever see the banks taking major long-term positions. Give or take a few million dollars, they are flat most of the time. They may day trade, but at night I doubt that they ever carry much more than a $3 or $4 million position.

INTERMARKET: Do you respect the Soviets as currency traders?

ANDREWS: My opinion is that they are overrated. That is not the opinion of most of the people I talk to. They are considered sophisticated, but I feel they are far more sophisticated in grains than in currencies or the metals. What I've seen them do in the grain market has impressed me, but what I've seen them do in metals and currencies has not. Everyone fears them because of their size. Naturally. But I've not seen them do anything very brilliant.

INTERMARKET: What happens on the floor when the Bundesbank intervenes?

ANDREWS: They come into the interbank market and sell dollars and buy marks. Depending on where the market is, the market could move considerably. They usually don't intervene during (futures) trading hours. It's usually before we open.

INTERMARKET: What importance does your frame of mind have in trading?

ANDREWS: I try never to have it affect me. The thing that affects me the worst is a bad outtrade. Otherwise, hell could freeze over and I'll stay calm, collected and level. If I have a bad outtrade, it can't help but affect me. It's the worst thing that can happen to any trader, on or off the floor. It's one thing to lose money trading; you wouldn't be in the business if you couldn't handle that. But when you have a bad outtrade, an error on your part or the other guy's part or both your parts, that bothers the mind and affects the way you do business more than anything.

INTERMARKET: Has the role of technical models changed the currencies?
ANDREWS: Since I've been in the business, it's phenomenal how it's changed things. When I started in the business, we called them graphs. We'd see maybe one graph a year and we'd laugh about them — it wasn't worth the paper they were written on and all that. Actually, very few technicians were prominent until the early 1970s.

Then, as technicians entered the market, technical analysis became a self-fulfilling prophecy — the market would react at given points. A fundamental trader like myself couldn't understand why a market's price action was so important at 65 and not at 60. Why did we have so much activity five points away from another point? That's when I decided that I had to learn what these people were doing and why they were doing it.

The lion's share of the market became technically oriented, so I hired a technician to point out critical support and resistance points. Not that I've ever been afraid to fade a chart, but I have to know where my competitors are at. Is this point where everybody's worried and is this point where no one is? I have to know where I can expect the common man to come in.

A chart is simply a history of how the world perceives fundamentals. The only way we have to guess the future is off history. Technicals have enhanced our markets' volume by many hundred-fold because you could go to customers and show them historical data and show them the basis for your predictions. Without technical indicators we'd still be trading in a small room.

Now in options, the business is completely computerized; predictions are not as relevant. You could figure a lot of these trading indicators — gammas, deltas — by hand, but the computer does it for you within milliseconds. Also, it's strictly a spreader's market on the floor, so charts are not as important when you are trading options.

INTERMARKET: What is the value of a technical model in the meats in contrast to the currencies?
ANDREWS: Well, technically speaking, currencies trade better than any other market.

INTERMARKET: Why is that?
ANDREWS: Currencies trend. Currencies are the best tranding market there is. You have established fundamental situations involving cross rates between currencies. These situations do not change overnight.

Meats are absolutely the worst technical market. Their supply and demand factors change so quickly. Consequently, charts and their readers get ripped right and left in meats. It's just simply that the fundamentals can change so quickly.

INTERMARKET: Why is that?
ANDREWS: Because producers can regulate and change supply quickly. Demand will change at higher and lower levels.

INTERMARKET: Tell me about your most memorable trade.
ANDREWS: I'd developed a European customer who had done very well with me in meats. I convinced him that he wanted to trade the currencies. We did some currency trades and had a decent amount of success. Then, as we became more successful, our quantities became larger and larger.

Anyway, I felt that the dollar had bottomed out. The currencies were showing nice rounding tops. The D-mark and the Swiss had already proven that they were going to go down and the yen and the pound were both hanging in there tough. A very key chart point in the yen was .4989.

INTERMARKET: Previous support there?
ANDREWS: Yes. A lot of long-term support. The yen was trading right around .5000 and had dipped below it just once. And it was Friday the 13th. So I convinced him about 2:00 o'clock in the morning Chicago time that this was the day to break it.

INTERMARKET: Why that day?
ANDREWS: The banks don't like to trade much on Fridays because they like to have their books balanced, and if they trade, it's not much past 10:00 a.m. our time. On top of that, February 12 had been a bank holiday — Lincoln's birthday. So they were out on Thursday and I knew they didn't want to be bothered with the IMM on Friday.

So I told this fellow that we had to use the ninth principle of war: the element of surprise. I felt that we could go in and break the back of the yen.

So he gave me a very large quantity to work with but told me that I better be right. At this time we were trading 1500 yen (contracts) per day and he gave me a substantial percentage of that. We weren't over position limits but it was a real shot.

Twenty seconds before the bell rang for the market to close, I went in and sold. I hit a bank's bid—the only bid at 97. Everyone was bidding off the bank's bid and so everyone backed off. I sold 200 at 94, 200 at 92, 200 at 90, offered 100 at 89 and the yen went immediately limit down.

INTERMARKET: No bids?
ANDREWS: No. Boom. Limit down and the market closed.

INTERMARKET: How many did you get off?
ANDREWS: 600. And the wirehouses came running because they were getting calls out of Europe.

INTERMARKET: Did the other currencies fall as well?
ANDREWS: Yes, some. And the calls were coming out of Europe. Everybody was saying that Charlie Andrews broke the yen; they wanted to know who in the hell Charlie Andrews was. Of course I was rolling with delight. I said, "You tell 'em he's a goddamn old cowboy from Kanopolis, Kansas, who decided to get the Japs instead of the Indians." But that's what made me. My name got out as someone who would go in with size, move the market and usually be right. That's when the banks and those type of people sought me out to do business. They'd hear my name doing large quantities and they'd watch the market continue to go in that direction.

INTERMARKET: How much did this customer end up netting on the yen position?
ANDREWS: That trade could have made $5 million to $7 million.

INTERMARKET: Over what period of time?
ANDREWS: Thirty-some days.

INTERMARKET: What happened to the yen in, oh, I think it was May of 1984?
ANDREWS: March 2, 1984. That was a helluva day. (Pause) Everything had rallied but the yen. They started hitting stops at 21 and took it clear to 85 until it stopped.

INTERMARKET: In 10 minutes?
ANDREWS: Less than that. Then it backed off but within an hour it was locked (limit) up.

INTERMARKET: Banks have been portrayed by everyone but the Administration as the bad guys, foreclosing on a farmer's property. Tell me about your perception of bank executives' understanding of hedging, markets, and so on.
ANDREWS: Well, on the agricultural side, I really take my hat off to the Merc: They've done a helluva job of educating country bankers on

our markets and how they should be used as hedge tools, security agreements, and so on. The country banks that I work with have all their original customers and had no problems. The banks that've taken risk management to heart and have pushed their customers to protect themselves are all in solid shape today. The banks that didn't are the ones with tremendous liquidity problems today.

The threat of country banks going down today is far greater than farms. Sure, there are going to be a lot of farmers who bite in 1985, but I think there is a tremendous concern from people who, like myself, live in rural communities, over whether our banks are going to survive. Can the FDIC stand behind all these banks that really aren't liquid? I think that out of this will evolve much more intelligent lending institutions: market oriented and risk management oriented.

INTERMARKET: What is the real importance of currency hedging for someone who has accepted the risk of doing business overseas?
ANDREWS: Well, any given company that is bidding to do a project in any country can lock up his material, development costs, and pretty much all of his cost except his currency cost. But prior to 1970, very few thought about locking up their currency commitment. If it was a six-month or year contract, the fluctuations hadn't been that great to really get them into trouble. But the movement in the currencies started in the 1970s. Companies who locked up their costs of production and knew their market got caught in some tremendous crunches because you had as much as a 10% movement in the cross rate of a currency in a given year. That 10% would wipe out any profit that they had planned. Volkswagen plainly admitted one year that they would've had a very good year had they hedged the dollar-mark.

INTERMARKET: Why don't companies hedge? And whose responsibility is it?
ANDREWS: Because word gets out that a lot of companies went under or got into dire financial need because of currency speculation, it became a no-no among corporations. They did not know how to control their hedging, how to handle it or have the personnel that understood it. They just said, "That's a no-no and we're not going to do that."

If I were working for that company and they said, "Here's a $50 million project. You're responsible for hedging it," I would form a committee to make the decisions, because if I made a bad decision, I'd get fired and I'd be on the street. If I could say, "There were 10 of us who decided not to do anything," I could pass the burden all around. American corporations do not have qualified people to handle this. Whenever this happens, a committee is formed. No one makes a decision.

INTERMARKET: Do you work with committees?

ANDREWS: In the beginning I did. In the meats it was terrible. When I started out I worked with a seven-man committee to hedge a huge pork position. They never did hedge it and I didn't have the experience to push them into it like I do now. From that point on, whenever I go to an institution, I tell them, "You have to designate one person to handle this situation."

But the currency markets are so important. Twenty-five percent of the money borrowed in this country is going to come from offshore. To give you an example of their importance, for every million dollars I borrowed in 1982 from Switzerland, had I paid it back on January 1, 1985, I would've paid back $835,000 principal and interest—a negative cost of money of 16.7%.

INTERMARKET: So is a big part of your job educating people?

ANDREWS: That's been my job from day one with the farmers, then with the banks.

INTERMARKET: How will the market change in the future?

ANDREWS: Options are obviously going to have a huge net effect to the hedging world. They offer so many tailor-made opportunities for risk management mechanisms. If you're bidding on a foreign contract, you've no idea if you'll get the contract or not. If you want cross-rate protection, a computer can give you seven or eight different possible solutions. They couldn't have picked a better work; it does give you many more opportunities. It opens up such a huge horizon to our business. We'll surpass the stock market in total volume in a few years.

INTERMARKET: Are you bullish on America?

ANDREWS: I think that we've been through a period of negative growth—a very healthy thing. I think we are in a period similar to the early 1950s. In the next two years, we'll continue to climb out of this slow growth, low inflation period. By 1987, 1988, we'll start into a growth period; by 1990 I predict we'll start into an extravagant growth period that will see inflation come back. I see very fast growth in the 1990s. Whatever happens after that, we'll deal with it.

Commodity markets love inflation. That's when you'll see this industry take off.

INTERMARKET: Where have you traveled on business recently?

ANDREWS: The Middle East, the UAE (United Arab Emirates), all over Germany and Switzerland, Monaco and Italy.

INTERMARKET: I've been told you knew John Wayne.

ANDREWS: Yes. I was buying cattle in Mexico. Wayne's Red River ranch was getting a lot of rain. You see, the desert is either feast or famine. When it rains, you want to take advantage of free feed. So he wanted cattle and quick.

The guy who was bankrolling me knew him but didn't tell me anything. He just said, "I've got a man who wants 10,000 of Mexico's worst"—meaning cheap cattle. I went to the Madera Mountains and bought 10,000 corrientes (long horns). I called him and told him I'd get them shipped out in three weeks.

About a day before I was to ship them out, the backer called and said, "My man wants to come and look at them." I said fine. He said, "By the way, it's John Wayne."

INTERMARKET: So what did he say?
ANDREWS: "Where's the tequila?"

INTERMARKET: What was he like?
ANDREWS: All I'll say is this: I was 24 and he was 54, but I went with him on the damnedest two-day party of my entire life.

9

Robert Prechter

*M*any people are in what nowadays can be the very lucrative forecasting business, but relatively few manage to make accurate forecasts. Fewer still can manage a forecasting business while putting their money where their mouth is, trading the markets for profits as well. Robert Prechter is one of the few. In the so-called U.S. Trading Championship in 1984, he posted in four months a 444% profit trading options, then the largest gain of any entrant. His forecasting and trading record makes him a walking contradiction of the Random Walk theory of markets, which says that the market is completely random and arbitrary and cannot be predicted with any degree of accuracy over time.

Prechter's primary tool for forecasting market activity is the Elliott Wave Principle, developed by R.N. Elliott, ... Elliott Wave is a very controversial forecasting method which presumes that the market fits into certain regular patterns or waves indicating the investor sentiment and market direction. Prechter eschews fundamental information, yet the readership of his newsletter, "The Elliott Wave Theorist," includes a good sprinkling of top investment houses. He is based in Gainesville, Ga.

INTERMARKET: Could you tell me the premises or assumptions of the Elliott Wave Principle?
PRECHTER: I wouldn't really say there are premises. There are conclusions that you come to after studying the market and the Wave Principle. Number one, outside events do not really influence stock price movement. In fact, outside events are the consequences of the changes in mass psychological mood which are reflected by the movement of the stock market in the first place.

INTERMARKET: So a comment by Paul Volcker or whoever will not, in and of itself, influence the market?
PRECHTER: It certainly will have no effect on any trends. It may affect the market for 30 minutes, and that's it.

INTERMARKET: So at any one time, is the market reflective of fair value for that particular entity?
PRECHTER: Only in the sense that it's a free market price and that free markets represent the value that people put on them. But the implication, according to a lot of academics, is that forecasting is impossible. Obviously, I think that's incorrect.

You can forecast changes in mass psychological mood. That mood is what determines whether people are optimistic or pessimistic and whether they judge the stock or whatever as worth owning or not worth owning.

INTERMARKET: So you say that the market is only a reflection of a sentiment rather than true value.
PRECHTER: Well, it's a measure of both, really. As I said, value is what people think it is. It can't be measured in any concrete sense without people. People assign value to things. The reasons which influence people to assign such values change, so prices change. But at any one moment, they're always fair. Prices were fair at the top in 1929 and they were fair at the bottom in 1932, because that's what people were willing to pay.

INTERMARKET: Okay, let's go back and define Elliott Waves.
PRECHTER: The Elliott Wave Principle is basically a detailed description of how markets behave. Once that description is written out, it reveals that mass investor psychology swings from pessimism to optimism and back again in a natural sequence. This sequence creates specific patterns in price movement. The most basic pattern is the one in the direction of the trend of one larger degree. The movement you find in that situation is five waves, whether up or down. The five-wave pattern is up-down-up-down-up when the market is moving up to start with.

Each of those five stages has an attendant style of psychology. You can use technical indicators to help confirm that the market psychology at the time fits your interpretation. Each Elliott Wave price pattern not only has its own way of acting, but has implications regarding the position of the market within its overall progression—the first with reference to the past, then looking at the present and also toward the future.

INTERMARKET: Do you see these patterns on both a micro level— daytrading—and a macro level—1908 to 1929 or whatever?

PRECHTER: Absolutely. You can look at a five minute high-low-close bar chart and see the same phenomena occurring. People are going through the same stages as they move from a feeling of optimism back to pessimism. These swings occur very quickly if you're watching the activity in the trading pit on a futures exchange. People are screaming bullish one minute and 10 minutes later they're selling their heads off.

Psychology moves very rapidly, but it's always creating a framework over which larger and slower moving swings are also occurring. That trading upward and downward every five minutes fits into a larger trend which may last five hours, that's all rising or all declining. That in itself will be part of a larger trend which could last a month. And so on.

These trends are of varying degrees. Elliott labeled nine of them, from the smallest that he followed — revealed by hourly charts — to the largest that he surmised, which became clear after looking back at about 100 years of stock market history.

INTERMARKET: To what degree are you a contrarian?
PRECHTER: To the greatest degree possible. I think the expression of contrary opinion is very useful. The problem is that contrarianism is really only a one-way comment. The observation made by contrarians is that at the top of the market, there will be a substantially greater number of bulls than bears. This observation doesn't tell you that because there exists a certain percentage of bulls or bears, it must be the top. Contrarianism doesn't tell you how far the pendulum can swing in one or the other direction. That is why I've found the Wave Principle useful.

INTERMARKET: What other technical indicators do you find useful?
PRECHTER: There are three other segments of analysis that I use. After 10 years of going through every approach I could, I've obviously thrown out more than I've kept. But the three areas that are important and good adjuncts are cycle analysis, momentum and divergence analysis, and sentiment or investor psychology.

INTERMARKET: How would you define cycle analysis? Daily, weekly, 10-week or 10-year cycles?
PRECHTER: All of the above. I think cycle analysis is particularly useful because it trains you, number one, to be patient, and number two, to buy into lows and sell into tops. A lot of approaches do not make that effort.

INTERMARKET: Like a moving average?
PRECHTER: Yes. Trend following, exactly.

INTERMARKET: Are the most precise and regular cycles the shorter term or the longer term ones?

PRECHTER: Cycles are useful whether you're looking at extremely short ones or very long ones. There have been some extremely regular cycles since I've been following them. However, I've found in the markets that if you get shorter than three weeks, there is too much margin for error. The main reason I use cycles is that they aid in Elliot Wave interpretations. They help me decide, for instance, if I'm in a simple Elliott Wave correction or one that may become more complex and extend sideways. If a cycle isn't ready to bottom, I'm willing to wait.

INTERMARKET: How do cycles operate in the practical world?
PRECHTER: There are usually one or two related groups of cycles operating at any one time on prices. And it's quite surprising how precise these cycles can be. In other words, if a cycle is supposed to be X days, it usually falls within one day of expectation.

However, there are two things that cause cycles to be a little difficult. One of them is that occasionally there is a shift in one sublink. If you have, for instance, a 24-week cycle and it subdivides into three eight-week cycles, occasionally you find that there's a fourth eight-week cycle that you can't explain, pushing that more severe bottom out eight weeks.

The other thing, which is apparently quite rare, is a complete shift in cyclic length. An example is what occurred in September 1981. Prior to that time there was no clear and regular eight-week cycle. Following that crash low, all of a sudden an eight-week cycle emerged. It has been just wonderful to trade since then. It's hardly missed a beat. But I expect some year in the future, that cycle will disappear and we'll see the emergence of another one.

INTERMARKET: What do you think about pattern recognition?
PRECHTER: If you're talking about the standard technical chart reading of old patterns, I think it's valid. But it's a little bit like operating in the Stone Age, once you've learned Elliott. Elliott described with great specificity how the patterns subdivided and which ones you should look to for a continued rally and which ones you should look to for imminent breakdown, and so on. But I think that chart reading is valid because it is based on reality versus some ivory tower theory.

Let me just add one thing: I've heard the term "pattern recognition" in reference to computers—teaching computers to recognize patterns which are created by a complicated series of data. I think that's a very promising field of study. If you can get a computer to say that 27 different indicators in certain combinations always lead to certain results, that's great. The mind can't necessarily see them all and come up with the same conclusions.

INTERMARKET: So you're using computers?

PRECHTER: No. I sure am not. I don't use computers and I'm comfortable doing what I'm doing. Rather than try to complicate the issue with too many indicators, I try to keep it as simple as possible with the ones that I am convinced work most of the time. If one indicator does a terrible job at a market turn, I throw it out. I want the ones that I can rely on year in and year out.

INTERMARKET: How do you establish that a specific cycle length exists?

PRECHTER: The best way is to create a series of momentum oscillators which are simply rates of change. In other words, how many points up or down is a particular index — I use the New York Composite Index — in the last X time units? Once you put a series of these oscillators of various time lengths on graphs, just check to find where the deepest oversold conditions occur.

Obviously, I use a shorter time period for shorter cycles and a longer time period for longer term cycles. The point is, the bottoms of cycles create deep oversold conditions in the oscillators and you can pinpoint them. Just go back and check the differences between oversold conditions — not necessarily prices. Because sometimes, upward pushes in cycles in a bear market, for instance, will cause very little movement in prices, but will show up in the oscillators, clear as a bell. Even if the market has made very little upside progress — let's say it's gone from deeply oversold to neutral — it's time to get out.

INTERMARKET: What's your favorite oscillator?

PRECHTER: Just a simple rate of change. Take the current day's close, and subtract it from the corresponding reading X days ago. With longer term rates of change, I use a percentage difference, to make it comparable across all history — back when prices were lower. You can also use hourly rates of change to get excellent short-term signals in real time.

INTERMARKET: Tell me about the contest you won trading options against some other forecasters and financial journalists. What was that like?

PRECHTER: Well, I didn't find the experience pleasant at all. It was very time-consuming and emotionally draining. I had other difficulties to contend with. My wife was flat on her back with our second child. She had been ordered by the doctor not to get out of bed or she would deliver prematurely. So I was taking care of her and our three-year-old daughter at the same time as trading. One trading adage is "Don't trade if you've got personal problems."

Fortunately, my wife delivered our baby on April 29 (1984), and virtually from that day forward I made money again.

The essence of trading is to be disciplined enough to fight your natural humanity. Of course, stock market movement—and the Wave Principle—is a direct reflection of natural human behavior, thinking and sentiment. In other words, to be on the correct side of the turns, you must go opposite to what your personal emotions usually tell you about the market. You have to be a decoding machine interpreting your indicators. To fight your human nature is very tough. The successful traders of the world have learned how to do that. I can do it when pressed, but I find it uncomfortable.

Anyway, it was a lot of fun because I got to put Elliott to the test. I made about 200 trades in four months following short-term moves. It's something I wouldn't want to do for a living, but I think that I could do it for a living if I had to.

INTERMARKET: What were your trading signals?
PRECHTER: Most of the decisions were made watching the fluctuations in the hourly chart of the Dow Jones Industrials and buying or selling puts and calls on index options. A secondary consideration was where the short-term momentum oscillators were intra-day and on a short-term basis. A third consideration was where the time cycles were, though that always deferred to the condition of the momentum oscillators.

INTERMARKET: So you basically looked for situations where momentum oscillators indicated oversold or overbought opportunities?
PRECHTER: I was looking for points at which the wave structure said there's a change in trend imminent. Most of that period was a choppy market. We had a lot of down moves. So if I saw five waves down, I would expect a three wave rally. I would play for that, selling the top of the C-wave and looking for a decline and so forth.

INTERMARKET: What type of options were you trading—at-the-money, out-of-the-money or in-the-money?
PRECHTER: Mostly in-the-money.

INTERMARKET: And were you just buying and selling calls?
PRECHTER: I was buying puts.

INTERMARKET: No liquidity problem?
PRECHTER: I had to manage my money very strenuously, because I started with a small amount of money. The whole point was to show that you could start with a small amount of money and turn it into something. So liquidity was a very important factor, yes.

INTERMARKET: So what did you do?
PRECHTER: A lot of short-term trades. No big hit or a lucky move. I think that's the way to trade options. If you go for the big hit, you

usually get hit.

I made money in February and I made money in May but I lost money in March and April.

INTERMARKET: You came roaring back?

PRECHTER: I was up 300 and some percent after the first month, dropped to up about 189% and finished up 444%.

INTERMARKET: How was your money management?

PRECHTER: One thing to mention is that the safest and the most productive way to play options is to trade deep in-the-money options. They are worth what you're paying for them. They are forced to move if the market goes in the direction you expect. Out-of-the-money options do not necessarily move when the market goes your way. So you're betting on a whole bunch of additional factors when you play out-of-the-money options.

I think the worst options of all to play are at-the-money. You're paying complete premium for something that isn't worth it. Very often they are the most actively traded and have the most premium in them anyway. And that makes for a very difficult time in taking profits. Being late the slightest, you can watch an out-of-the-money option drop 30% as the traders who make a market in those things sense the change.

So I have my ways of trading in order to manage my money. One of them is also never to be 100% long or short.

INTERMARKET: Would you take more than a 10% loss in your account on a single trade?

PRECHTER: I've taken much larger losses than that. If you can't do that, you can't trade options. Sometimes an option can lose 50% of its value in an hour. That's why you need defensive money management techniques.

INTERMARKET: But you didn't have any specific rule on the number of options you'd buy for a specific trade?

PRECHTER: No. The problem is that you can't limit your risk in options. You can't put stops in. You have to pick up the phone and call in. If your option is down 50%, by the time your phone call hits the floor it might be down 80%, in which case you're probably selling the low. So you have to approach options from a little different frame of mind than you would a futures contract. You have to ask, "At what point in my stock market analysis will I come to the conclusion that my assumptions about the next move were incorrect?"

Don't just say, "I'm willing to lose X amount," because if your option drops 50%, it may be a screaming buy. You might want to add to your position so that a bounce back to 75% of the original price will get you even. The whole point is, what does the wave structure say? If it says you're still right—the trend is going to turn in this particular direction—then you want to add to your position.

If the wave structure says, "Hey, you blew it. You're wrong," take your loss and get out of the way. I use my analytical method to tell me when I'm wrong and that's my stop. Any other type of stop is arbitrary.

INTERMARKET: Do you weight your trades?
PRECHTER: Yes. If I have three or four technical indicators all saying the same direction now, I'll make a heavier commitment.

INTERMARKET: Why aren't more market forecasters good traders?
PRECHTER: Forecasting and trading are two different skills. Forecasting may come after some study,whereas if you add the serious and heavy emotional trauma of trading real money, an individual may not be able to think so clearly. That is a different skill—conquering your emotions and being able to act with discipline are two things that successful traders must do that the successful forecaster doesn't necessarily need to perform, at least not to the same degree. Good forecasting helps trading, but it's no guarantee of profits. If you find that you are wrong only one time in five, but that one time wipes you out, you're a lousy trader.

INTERMARKET: You seem to have a pretty good forecasting track record. Why don't all of your subscribers make money?
PRECHTER: I assume most market letter writers would like to say, "All my subscribers are rich," and as a class, my subscribers are probably a higher caliber than most. But I do think it is kind of a sad thing that people—because they are people—are more likely to lose money than to make it. Most subscribe to six market letters and they want all of them to agree at the same time. Whenever it happens that the majority do agree, it's probably the wrong thing to do.

It's people's decisions to buy and sell which make the market move—most people sell into bear markets and buy into bull markets. That's the nature of the situation. It doesn't matter how well I do; there will always be reasons for them either to not follow my recommendations or to follow only those recommendations that they're comfortable with, which will usually make them lose money.

Or they wait until I've been right five times and then go with the sixth one. Or they bet each time, but bet more the more often I'm right. Once I'm wrong they'll be the most heavily invested and then they'll get shy again. There are an untold number of ways for a subscriber or client to follow a very successful forecaster and still end up at the end of the year without any money.

The only way to successfully follow a good market forecaster is to do absolutely everything that the forecaster suggests and do it with an equal percentage amount of capital every single time. If the man has a winning record at the end of the year, so will you. But most people try to bring their own judgment in and when they're the least comfortable, they'll read something in the newspaper or another newsletter which changes their mind at the wrong moment and they'll get out of the position because they never made the disciplined commitment to follow the newsletter in the first place. I think it's impossible — particularly with "The Elliott Wave Theorist," which is really rather difficult to read and is aimed at the market professionals who already know market terminology — for that letter ever to become too popular.

INTERMARKET: You have a substantial institutional following, so I've been told.
PRECHTER: I suppose. Let me just say that I have a pretty good institutional readership. Whether they are acting on what I say or not, I don't know.

INTERMARKET: Good point. Would you find your institutional readers to be a different breed — a better trader than the average fellow?
PRECHTER: Yes. To the extent that anyone has been in the business, he is usually better than the rank amateur. There's hardly ever an exception to that. However, I still find that many, many professionals get extremely emotional when the market makes tops and bottoms. They find themselves making the wrong decisions, even though intellectually they know what they should be doing.

INTERMARKET: Why is that?
PRECHTER: It's not a putdown at all. I understand the constraints under which they operate and I think these restraints are greater than most human beings can stand.

INTERMARKET: What kind of personality would Bob Prechter's perfect trader have?
PRECHTER: I found it very interesting that two of the most successful options and futures traders I know — and I know extremely few — two of them are ex-Marines.

INTERMARKET: The few, the proud?
PRECHTER: That's right. Both! That implies to me that discipline is extremely important.

INTERMARKET: Why is it that most mutual fund managers are not able to beat the S&P 500?
PRECHTER: Well, for one thing, most of them have to operate under the prudent man concept, whereas most successful traders do everything quite differently. In other words, they're slinging around a good deal of money every single day and trading for themselves.

There are laws that say that if I'm managing your retirement money, I have to act prudently. You have to pay attention to rules set up by somebody sitting in some bureau who's never traded a day in his life. I kind of feel sorry for mutual fund and pension fund managers. They have to be able to pull out of the files a report from some fundamental analyst as to why they bought or sold this particular stock, if they're ever challenged because the stock went down. They have to wait until some guy like that thinks it's a buy before they can go into it. An institutional manager has to worry about a whole bunch of things which are outside of the world of making money.

INTERMARKET: You're saying that if he has to wait for some analyst to recommend it, he's not buying the bottom?
PRECHTER: Definitely, although there are a small percentage of independent thinkers in the money management field. You always see that when you see these statistics on how well the funds have done. You find that 80% have underperformed the S&P 500 average, and 70% underperform passbook savings accounts. Obviously, the number of bold thinkers is very small in relationship to the total, but they exist. You can see it because some of the managers have excellent records over long periods of time. They think independently, they do their own research, they are contrarians and they look for value and all the things that you hear people saying over and over but hardly ever see them doing.

INTERMARKET: Let's say you're in charge of writing the regs for money managers. You're now at the head of a new national regulatory agency involved in making certain retirement funds are properly managed. What would you do?
PRECHTER: Well, first of all, I think the whole concept is immoral, anyway. I don't think any government agency should tell people how to invest or who to invest with. The problem is deeper than that because it doesn't even matter.

If I were the head of the agency and I said, "Well, I say you have to be prudent with your investments," but I won't define what prudence is, it still doesn't matter. The average person among the public thinks that in order to buy a stock of a company which sells textbooks, you have to go out and make a case that the schools will have a greater need for textbooks next year. Of course, that just isn't the case. The stock of companies go up and down for a whole host of different reasons. But if a guy who lost money for a client was taken to court and said that he used something other than fundamental analysis, he'd probably be found guilty by the average jury. So, the rules are set whether they are formally proclaimed or not.

The only way to judge prudence in the long run is whether the guy makes money or not. And the truth is that today, 70% of fund managers make too little money or they lose it for their clients. That, I think, is really unfortunate, but is one of the mechanisms of the market. Everybody can't make money.

INTERMARKET: Is it that the wrong types of people are attracted to a career in money management?
PRECHTER: Partly that, but partly that it can't be helped. The cost of running the markets—in other words paying the brokers to do their job—is so great that someone has to pay it. All those transaction costs come out of people's accounts. I don't know how many hundreds of millions of dollars are generated every year from commissions—I'm sure a substantial amount. Everyone can't outperform the averages if all that money comes out of their accounts. People have to pay for keeping the machinery oiled, which means that most people can't make money.

INTERMARKET: On the one hand you're saying that trading the long-term trend makes the most economic sense, but you made a fantastic return trading 200 times in three months.
PRECHTER: I earned twice as much as I ended up keeping. In other words, I paid my broker as much as I made in profits.

INTERMARKET: Would your Marine friends be more long-term as traders?
PRECHTER: Longer-term than I was during the contest. They're short-term when they want to be.

INTERMARKET: What about your background? I heard you were a drummer at Yale?
PRECHTER: I majored in psychology at Yale. I planned to major in economics, but realized that they wouldn't teach me anything that I wouldn't think was false to begin with. They hadn't even heard of Austrian economics, for instance. So I took psychology as a major. As a sideline, I played music with some friends during college. We kept that up a few years after that. I did some recording in New York and basically had a good time.

Then, in 1975, I went to work for the technical department at Merrill Lynch because my avocation and second love—eventually first love—was markets. I knew I wanted to be involved in technical analysis. I went to work for Bob Ferrell (chief market strategist for Merrill Lynch). He turned out to be a wonderful person to work for and was a great influence on me. I left there in 1979 to start my newsletter and that's where I am.

INTERMARKET: You called the summer rally of 1984 right on the nose, if I recall. You were a bit premature in the move you called in the fall of 1984 which occurred in January. What happens when you're

premature versus when you're right on the nose? Were you misinterpreting or did the market not fit into the mold?
PRECHTER: The main thing that happens is that my subscribers get very nervous. As I said earlier, the market must do something to tell me that my overall analysis of where we are in the wave structure is incorrect. As I was saying all during those months, don't worry. We've got our stop in place and from all the evidence I can see—and I hammered this home in every issue in the fourth quarter of 1984—everything I saw led me to believe that the next serious move would be to the upside.

That the big move was going to occur was quite clear to me from the wave structure.

INTERMARKET: When you were premature in the fall were you misreading it or did the market not follow the pattern?
PRECHTER: There are eight types of corrective patterns. Some of those can double or triple, continuing in a sideways trend. That was what happened in the fourth quarter of 1984. We had a simple corrective sequence and there's no way under the Wave Principle that you can decide if that's all you will get, or whether you will get a short rally and another corrective sequence in a back-to-back situation. It's just impossible.

I tried to lean on the time cycles to give me an indication and the time cycles all through that quarter were leapfrogging. We got one low in October, another one in December, and another in early January, whereas in July 1984 we had a confluence of lows in the cycle work, and that was very useful in saying that this was an important bottom.

INTERMARKET: I'm going to ask you to do something that you won't like to do. Can you give me a fundamentalist argument for the market continuing on as you believe it will in the coming years?
PRECHTER: I think mostly we will have a period of increased confidence and that should lead to a speculative environment. The only place that will be showing profits is the stock market. We'll know all the real reasons in 1987 and 1988, assuming we do go higher.

We've had a program of no tax increases for eight straight years, and in fact, some attempts to lower taxes. Every time that's happened in the past, it's been pretty bullish. You've had an administration that's friendly to the stock market. You've reduced the length of time for capital gains from one year to six months. There's even some talk in Washington about eliminating formal and legal margin requirements and allowing the brokerages to set their own. We've got a period of relative prosperity. You can point to a whole bunch of different things—inflation has come down. But I could build just as bearish a case using fundamentals, and that's why fundamentals are of absolutely no value in predicting prices.

INTERMARKET: And how high do you see the Dow going before the crash you expect?
PRECHTER: 3600-3700.

INTERMARKET: And you're very, very bearish in a 1929 type of scenario afterwards?
PRECHTER: Yes. I think we'll enter a long and severe bear market at that time.

INTERMARKET: Do the fundamentals all tie in, in your scenario? Where are the currencies, metals, stock market and the fortunes of Western developed nations headed?
PRECHTER: I think they all tie in. I've got a stock market top at extremely high levels in 1987, maybe 1988. My cycles on gold tell me gold will fall as low as $100 an ounce by 1988. Those two together suggest a period of rising confidence into that time. I think that we will then begin a Grand Supercycle bear market which is something we haven't experienced for 200 years. I think the potential financial calamity is quite great. When I look at the fundamentals behind the debt situation, I think that it's very easy to construct a scenario of collapsing debt structures across the board around the world.

INTERMARKET: So this would obviously have ramifications in the world political situation.
PRECHTER: Right. Politicians always react. They virtually never lead. Politics won't really react until the crisis is deep. Just like the occurrence in the 1930's. There were a whole bunch of sweeping programs once the Depression had reached or passed its worst. No. They won't do anything in advance of it.

INTERMARKET: Any other closing comments?
PRECHTER: Don't be a politician past 1988.

INTERMARKET: Or if you're now involved in the markets, look to retire before 1988?
PRECHTER: That would be a good plan for a lot of people. Some people love bear markets, so for them it will be hog heaven.

INTERMARKET: How is the circulation of the newsletter doing?
PRECHTER: It's doing well.

INTERMARKET: A bull market increases your circulation?
PRECHTER: Yes. A bull market increases circulation just because it attracts a large number of people in the first place. But if you can keep people from losing money in bear markets, I think word of mouth is important.

INTERMARKET: Does your circulation ebb and flow in Elliott Wave patterns?
PRECHTER: I've never charted it. But I suppose there would be an influence. I hope I'm in a third wave and not a fifth.

10

J. Peter Steidlmayer

*P*ete Steidlmayer, a 22-year veteran floor trader at the Chicago Board of Trade, has been drawing considerable interest of late in the Windy City. In a business where success can spell fast wealth and most who achieve it remain secretive, Steidlmayer has taken the insight, observations and approach which he has accumulated over the years (and used to trade successfully), and developed, packaged and donated it to the exchange in the form of a databank and a manual. Working on the project over the last four years with CBOT staff, Steidlmayer has developed a databank which, he claims, is revolutionary in that "it gives the outside trader the ability to understand market activity the way successful floor traders do." The CBOT Liquidity Databank, as it is known, incorporates a comprehensive, integrated and consistent approach to trading which may become standard over time, but thus far has attracted avid interest only among floor traders.

Steidlmayer's approach defies random walk theory — the currently accepted academic viewpoint that market behavior is random and arbitrary. Furthermore, his is probably the first articulate refutation of random walk from a credible source. Steidlmayer steadfastly rejects the belief, which implies that it is not possible to understand market activity or make money trading or investing on a consistent basis over an extended length of time. But for Steidlmayer, his experience tells him differently. "I'm a behaviorist; I learn from observation. Anyone could see what I've learned if they apply themselves to watching the market."

Steidlmayer sees the market as organized by the laws of nature and physics. He says his is "the thinking man's approach to trading," pointing out that it and the CBOT databank are not earth-shattering to people with common sense or "housewives who shop," but only to academics and individuals who trade in

organized marketplaces. ("Trading futures is no different from trading any-
thing from groceries to used cars.") He says that most people who trade in any
organized free market "have been lost from the ground up — they don't under-
stand the basic logic behind the market behavior." Further, he believes that
currently, no one away from the floor is getting the information he needs to
make intelligent trading decisions.

As a floor trader over three decades of vastly different volatility and market
conditions, Steidlmayer's survival is an indication of the flexibility of his
trading acumen through the placid markets in the 1960s, explosive uptrends in
the 1970s, and deflationary and choppy conditions in the first half of the 1980s.
"My approach to trading was good in the 1960s, it has been good in the 1970s
and 1980s, and it will be good forever," he says. His reputation has now spread
beyond the floor, and he was recently invited to outline his theories to a class of
graduate level finance students at the University of Chicago.

Around the floor, few realize the significance of his theories beyond the fact
that he trades remarkably well and does not fit the mold of the typical career
trader. While most floor traders say he is tremendously successful, Steidlmayer
is noncommittal: "Success has nothing to do with money. It has to do with how
you feel about yourself."

INTERMARKET: Let's start out with a tough question. Why do most
people lose money trading and investing?
STEIDLMAYER: First, you have to ask the question, what determines
results in trading? This is a question few people have broken down and
answered correctly. I believe the correct equation for results in trading
is: Your market understanding x (you + your trading strategy) =
results.

So why are people losing? They never give any thought to their
approach and therefore accept a losing approach. They do not make
good trading decisions. Generally, they have a poor trading strategy
that asks too much of them. People fail at trading because they don't
understand the market, they don't understand themselves and they
don't understand the tools they're using. When I use a pair of pliers, I
know I can cut wire but I wouldn't ever try to cut steel plate.

I have a good market understanding. I feel that in the present tense,
I often have a 100% market understanding. I also have a very good
trading strategy. But I lose occasionally because I'm a human being
and at different times in my life I will respond differently to the same
situation. I'm not the same person all the time.

Most people will say, "I trade all right, but it's the commissions that
eat me up." But they're willing to accept that they have a 50% probability when buying something with a predetermined profit and loss point.
They're going to be right 50% of the time, wrong 50% of the time, and
the commissions understandably eat them up. But they are willing to
accept 50% market understanding. I'm not.

Success and failure in the marketplace have always been blamed on the market when in fact the blame belongs with the individual. Individuals will always defeat themselves. Most people make irrational or emotional decisions.

What the databank will do is give people information which will help them make better trading decisions. It will provide a market understanding from which you can devise your own trading strategy. It will help those who have strong discipline and control of their emotions; people who will not defeat themselves. This will open up a tremendous amount of opportunity everywhere.

INTERMARKET: In your equation for success, what do you mean by "you?"
STEIDLMAYER: "You" is something you have to know. You have to be you and you have to be satisfied with what you find. You can try to improve yourself, but you want to know your abilities and stay within them. You cannot be better than you normally are over time and your trading strategy has to reflect this. Most traders ask themselves to be at their peak potential all the time.

INTERMARKET: Tell me, what are some of the assumptions built into the databank?
STEIDLMAYER: Well, to answer that, I have to go back to how I approached the market when I first started trading 22 years ago. The first thing that I did was try to organize the chaos of the market. I felt that while the pit was outwardly chaotic, underneath it all there is a sense of order. Secondly, I tried to connect—I believed that all things in life are basically the same and that trading futures or whatever is no different. I also knew that I had to have a reason for making every trading decision, fundamentally sound reason. And finally, I knew from Graham and Dodd (authors of *Securities Analysis*) that through work, you can assess value. And that price and value are not the same thing, and when they diverge, you have an opportunity. Graham and Dodd said that stocks can be under- and overvalued, and the same goes for futures or anything.

INTERMARKET: This is opposite to the University of Chicago efficient market theory which assumes that market price is market value at any given moment.
STEIDLMAYER: I haven't studied their theories so I don't know if you're representing them correctly. However, from practical experience, I know that price and value are two completely separate things and are very often unequal. They are different in every other market—used cars, groceries, etc.—so why wouldn't they be different for futures? And contrary to popular belief, no organized market like futures or stocks is efficient for more than a fraction of the time. The market isn't efficient, but it's effective. The problem with the academic

community is that they don't understand what the practical purpose of any market is.

The purpose of any market is twofold. Over the short term it's to get trade going. The market will always go to a price area that will allow the most activity to take place. By doing this, the market facilitates the dominant side and advertises opportunity. Everyone who wants to buy in a market can buy. When they do, the market goes too high.

Now comes the purpose of the market over the long term: to self-correct once the dominant side has overextended itself. When there's too much trade, the market has to self-correct — the market has driven up the price so high that it shuts off more buying. OPEC drove up the price of oil so high that it shut off buying — you and I started conserving more — while encouraging more exploration and greater production. The longer-term purpose of the market is to always self-correct and end the overbought or oversold situations. I like to say the market promotes itself through price — meaning lower or higher prices will bring in more or fewer traders — and it controls itself through time — meaning the overbought or oversold situation is corrected over time.

Looking at the market with a large perspective, one finds endless examples of boom and bust. Why? In the short run, while the market is blowing out the excesses and people with the short-term time frame are selling, the market is advertising opportunity to people with a longer-term perspective. They buy. This means that the market is an endless struggle between people with different time perspectives. And this means that the market can be both overvalued and undervalued at the same time for people with different time frames. That doesn't sound very efficient.

For their market theory to be correct, the current market price has to have accurately discounted all the concerns and needs of the market-place in every possible time frame. That just doesn't occur. If it did, the market would just move sideways.

People are basically too lazy to investigate things themselves, so the views of an individual are not really considered, while the views that come out of an economics department of some major institution become gospel. My views are right but they don't carry any weight when they contradict the views of a century-old institution.

INTERMARKET: When did you first realize that price could be away from value in the market?
STEIDLMAYER: Back when I was in school in California (B.A., University of California, Berkeley). I had some statistics — I was pretty good at it. I found that I enjoyed the class and didn't find it boring. I learned a lot.

I took what I learned in statistics and applied it to what I saw. I felt that market activity was organized and that using the law of errors — normal distribution or the bell curve — would bring this out. And in fact, it did.

The law of averages is a common statistical tool which is applied to many phenomena in nature and physics. To apply normal distribution to the pit, I had to figure out what I was going to analyze. I decided to analyze price and time, because I felt that price itself was not very representative of fundamental value.

INTERMARKET: Exactly what do you mean by "fundamental?" I assume you are not talking about fundamental versus technical?

STEIDLMAYER: Well, in all trading — futures, stocks, real estate, used cars, houses, whatever — your buy-sell decisions should be based on the same principles. I believe that there's no difference between trading futures and buying or selling a used car. As I said, everything in life is the same.

In all trading, there is a difference between price and value. What it costs is price, what it's worth is its value. And in all trading, emotional decisions are made by the majority. Whether in futures, used cars, houses, or whatever, the smart trader seeks value and makes his nonemotional trading decision only after some analysis.

Why is it that whenever you sell a house, you paint it first? It's because you know people make emotional decisions when buying, not decisions based on value. In all trading, you have to attach some semblance of value to the market.

When I first came down (to the floor), I noticed that good futures traders consistantly made money but never could explain what they were doing. I always had a very good power of observation and I also am able to reflect a lot. I began to see that I was right — price and value differed on the floor and that these traders who made money were taking advantage of it. So from that observation, I knew that what Graham and Dodd said about stocks was applicable in futures: A trading opportunity arises when price is away from value and the good traders capitalize on this.

INTERMARKET: And how do you know when price is away from value?

STEIDLMAYER: This draws back to the organization of chaos. One of my equations that holds true today and will hold true in the future is that price + time = value. This equation defines value and will hold up forever. This equation defines all free markets and is 100% correct. Time is the constant, and to measure any variable, you need a constant. Price + time = value, or volume. Value and volume are synonymous. Volume = market acceptance = value. Once you know value in any market, you can begin making money.

INTERMARKET: You traded through three decades — the quiet markets of the sixties, the roaring bull markets of the seventies and until

March, the so-called deflation. Since you've seen all types of markets, can you unconditionally say that this approach works in them all?
STEIDLMAYER: Yes. In all types of free markets, this approach will work because if I'm able to capture and define and monitor markets, no matter how the market changes in the future, I'm still going to capture them. The equation will define any free market. The markets will be different, but the databank and the fundamental approach will always work.

INTERMARKET: So when you see a price recur over time ...
STEIDLMAYER: You know that if the price is recurring over many time periods, it's facilitating the market's purpose of creating trade. Hence, if people are accepting it, that area of price activity represents value for that time frame. It's very important to know where this value area is.

INTERMARKET: So every day, you try to buy when price is below the value area or sell when it's above it?
STEIDLMAYER: That only defines the situation. What you really are doing is placing the market's current position accurately.

INTERMARKET: What do you mean by that?
STEIDLMAYER: I am reading the market's opportunities in several time frame perspectives and taking advantage of the best one. The trouble with trading in short time frames is that you don't have time to act. So you relate the short time frame to the next longest time frame. For instance, suppose there's a sale of beer in the marketplace by a new producer who wants to aggressively gain market share. He has a lower price, which over the short term is a bargain. You buy enough to drink over the next weekend, but not your year's supply.

From the perspective of the next longer time frame, it might not be a bargain. If our beer company can gain enough market share to be able to produce more, gain economies of scale in production and thereby turn a profit at this new lower price level, the beer's no longer a bargain — the rest of the beer manufacturer's (prices) will have to come down too.

INTERMARKET: You set up the databank to organize the market into half-hour time segments. What was your consideration?
STEIDLMAYER: The market regulates itself through time. To be in step, you have to monitor yourself in terms of time also. It seems to provide enough time for me to assess the market fairly, to understand where trade is taking place, where the value area is being established, and then give me time to act.

Putting the market into a price-time relationship, the half-hour period stood out. It helped me organize the trends in terms of time: of the marketplace in fast, medium, and the slowest type movement which corresponds with my time risk factor.

INTERMARKET: And you categorize the market in three types of prototypical days?
STEIDLMAYER: Right. A normal day, which occurs roughly 80% of the time; a trend day, about 15%; and a nontrend day which occurs about 5%.

INTERMARKET: Tell me how your approach allows you to spot a normal day versus a trend day.
STEIDLMAYER: In my head I plot the day's price activity over time and that's what the databank does. It breaks up the day into half-hour time frames and uses letters of the alphabet to plot price activity corresponding to the half hour. The letter A indicates that price traded between 8:00 and 8:30, B indicates 8:30 through 9:00 and so on.

What you find is that 80% of the time, markets at the Board of Trade will resemble a bell curve — most of the trade being done in the middle with a low volume price probe at the top and bottom. To describe a normal day, I use the analogy of someone firing on a mortar range. He overshoots, adjusts, undershoots, adjusts, and finally hits the target in the middle and keeps firing. Most of the rounds land in that section.

Usually, a normal day is set up by a market overreaction. You see a large and dominant range in the first couple of time periods. The range within the first two half-hour periods will be at least 80% of the day's daily range. If you have a wide range early in the day, the market overreacts in probing for price level acceptance.

The issue in a normal day is when and why you make the trade, not whether you buy or sell. Both can be profitable. On a normal day, the trading strategy is to buy the break and sell the rally away from value.

INTERMARKET: Why is that?
STEIDLMAYER: Any time there's a dramatic overreaction to the market's probing for new price levels, you will tend to oscillate back and forth like that, consolidating. If there is not that overreaction, that means the market continues to do what it's going to do.

You have to look at what really changes the conditions of the market — we illustrate a lot of them in the manual. Conditions change when price gets so far away from value that when the overreaction occurs, it changes conditions in the marketplace because the shoe is on the other foot. The market has to feature a dominant need, so once the market goes too far in a direction, it now has to satisfy another need and self-corrects in the other direction. In other words, the only way you can really change conditions in the marketplace is to really move price.

INTERMARKET: So if I'm going to hear fundamental news like money supply tonight, I can expect a normal day with a wide range in the first two half-hour segments?

STEIDLMAYER: No. I don't like to predict. But 80% of the time you do have normal days, so it's likely. Money supply could set up an over- or underreaction that would produce the conditions needed for a normal day.

INTERMARKET: So what's a trend day?

STEIDLMAYER: A trend day differs from a normal day because there's no overreaction and so the market doesn't offer equal opportunities to both sides of the market. A trend day puts one side of the market at a tremendous disadvantage. The issue on a trend day is not when and why you trade, but that you go only in the direction of the trend. If the market closes on its extreme low, the guy who is playing the buy side of the market had only one chance to make money — to buy at the close.

On a trend day down, the local floor trader will buy it, take a small loss, buy it again, take another small loss, and on and on. There was never any opportunity for him from the long side. On a trend day, the market doesn't move far enough away from value to change the condition.

To continue the mortar target analogy, in a trend day you fire high, fire a little lower, little lower, little lower and you keep moving in small increments. You don't fire low enough to change the condition of the market. The activity is spread out equally throughout the day.

In terms of equating the two, the normal day price gets far enough away from value to self-correct and consolidate. In the trend day, you see small increments because price never moves far enough to change the condition of the market. The market lulls the trader to sleep so that you don't change your opinion since the individual increments are not that big.

INTERMARKET: Marching on.

STEIDLMAYER: Right. The market's movements never shake you up. In a normal day, when you're bullish and you've been buying breaks, the market will go down far enough to get you to take your loss and go short. Now you're really bullish, but you're short. The market rallies up, you sell more, and you finally buy it back. That's the natural reaction of people who don't understand the dynamics of a normal day.

In order to understand this, people have to understand the floor dynamics of the particular market. Futures, for instance, are a lot different from stocks.

In futures, good brokers basically control the pit on a normal day by the simple fact that they have to move the price to fill their big orders. If the market's trading at six and he's got a big order to buy and he thinks you're a good trader, he'll bid you nine. He's got to jump the market in order to get you to trade — he's got to make it attractive to you. You sell it to him. You might make a point or two out of it, but on balance, he's taking advantage of you by moving the price. Had he bid the market up one point at a time, you would never take his order and when he got to nine, the order wouldn't be completely filled. He has to make it attractive, hence you have normal days.

INTERMARKET: What is it about the market that makes it open quietly when it's setting itself up for a trend day?
STEIDLMAYER: Basically, a market opens quietly because it's at equilibrium and everybody's sort of complacent. No one's real ready for a big break or rally. Usually, these days occur when no one expects them.

INTERMARKET: How did you discover trend days?
STEIDLMAYER: I first discovered that all days don't act alike in terms of having overreaction-consolidation price action. I found that I made money 80% of the time. And the one or two days a month where instead of our normal one or two cent range, we'd have a five to seven cent range — a big day — I'd always barely escape with my life.

INTERMARKET: Because you were used to buying breaks and selling rallies?
STEIDLMAYER: I'd be doing what I was supposed to be doing — being in tune with the way the market normally acted. Anyway, I noticed that all the inconsistent traders made money on that day — people who were playing for the aberration every day. Instead of playing for reality, they played for the one day or two in the month. When they were right that day, they'd spend the rest of the month giving it back.
My strategy was not to get hurt on that day. But I realized that if I could know ahead of time, I'd be able to adjust my style and make good, easy money like the inconsistent traders. Now my whole style is built around identifying and recognizing the type of day — a trend day versus the normal. On top of this I now have a greater selection from which I trade. I monitor and trade 10 different markets so I have 20 trend opportunities out of every 22 trading days. There are an average of two trend days per market per month.

INTERMARKET: How did you realize you could identify a trend day a couple of hours into the day?
STEIDLMAYER: I felt that if the market was there and in the present tense, (then) it was readable. I wasn't asking myself to jump over the moon. There were certain characteristics that had to be there which would differentiate the trend day from the normal day, and so I started

studying the market activity looking for them. I have a strong belief that observation and knowledge reduce risk.

The key to market classification is observing the market. For a trend day, look for small movements. You see, for the market to change condition — overreact and self-correct — price has to really move. You don't get a big move from small movements, so when nothing changes, the market shoots up or down a wide range real fast, it is most likely overreacting, putting you in a normal day.

INTERMARKET: What do you mean when you say that knowledge reduces risk?

STEIDLMAYER: Knowledge reduces risk because it allows you to know what you're working with. For instance, you need to employ completely different trading strategies to profit from trend versus normal days.

While I'm on the subject, people have a lot of false assumptions about risk. One involves risk transfer. Our business is supposed to be built on the ability of someone who doesn't know about the market to have the ability to transfer his risk to someone who'll take the risk.

One of the things that people don't understand about futures trading is that good traders assume no risk. So for the good trader, there is no risk transfer over time. I let the other guy take the risk. If my knowledge and approach hasn't reduced my risk, I discipline myself so that I don't make the trade. Where my knowledge and my approach have reduced my risk, it gives me a winning edge to the point that over a large sample size — 1000 trades or so — the result is a sure thing. I'm sure to make money.

In sharp contrast to many traders who hit a trend, make money and then give it all back, the more I trade, the more I make. I don't have to get lucky. At any given point, I can have a loser or a series of losing trades, but on balance, I know I'm going to make money by the end of the year because I have a disciplined approach to the market that coincides with my understanding of it.

There's another misunderstanding about risk. People feel that the more risk they take, the more they'll make. This is totally false. The more risk you take, the less you'll make. My biggest moneymakers have been when I buy something worth $1.00 for 50 cents and sell it for $1.50.

Think of it in terms of a used car. Everything being equal, if you *know* that this car is worth $2000, are you taking a big risk buying it for $1000 at a bankruptcy sale? If you're a mechanic and you know it's worth that, you are taking virtually no risk. Yet you should make a very large return.

Now let's say you're paying $1800 at an auction, thinking you'll sell it for $2000. Let's say you're not a mechanic. Your risk is much greater and your profit potential is smaller.

The last thing that people have misunderstood is this looking at risk in terms of risk-reward ratios. This is the wrong way to assess risk. Your risk tolerance should not be predicated on price, but on time. How much time do I have to make a decision on this particular trade? The more time I have in which to make a decision, the more data I can look at. The longer I can hold a trade, the less risk I have.

Do I absolutely *have* to sell my car today because I need the money, or can I sell it any time over the next six months and wait for the best offer? Where is my risk reduced and where am I likely to make an emotional decision? This is one of the reasons I organize my daily approach around half-hour time brackets. I monitor and assess the trade, and as the day progresses, I adjust. When I put on a trade, I'll figure out how much time I have to make my decision.

If I'm trading in the instant, I have no time to make a decision. I'm always reacting to what somebody else has done. Chances are, I'm trading emotionally. I don't have time to think. If you don't originate your own ideas and don't have time in which to operate, you will not make money. You no longer control your own destiny. It's that simple.

"Instantism" is what I call this latest fad in futures trading. We've seen this develop because of technological advances in telecommunication. It's fine to get information quick, but you can't work within that instant. So consequently, how good is instantism if you cannot operate within that time frame? No matter how fast you are in reporting prices, you're going to be in the past tense. And you end up analyzing price versus price, which causes all the problems. You need to have a constant so that you can know the variance. A price versus price is meaningless.

INTERMARKET: Define your homework.
STEIDLMAYER: My homework is my learning process. I'm constantly measuring market activity in the various time frames I think are appropriate. I examine the activity which is short run that occurs in too small a time frame to have acted reasonably. I place it into the next succeeding larger time frames for an early alert to the opportunity the market is creating.

One of the things that is key to any trader is such knowledge. That's one of the great things about the manual—it allows the reader a lot of creativity and gives him room to think. I'm not doing his thinking for him. One of the sad things, though not really sad, is that people who use the databank take it back within the framework of their old formats, formats of charting, whatever. What they really need to do is understand market logic to gain insight from this information.

The most important thing in trading is to make your own decisions. You need to have the information to make your own decisions, plus the confidence to make the adjustments that are called for. Most people are cheating themselves by not making their own decisions. By defining, capturing and holding the market, the databank gives the people the ability to understand the market and then the right to think and make their own decisions. That is really tremendous. I haven't really been overbearing in the manual.

Getting back to how I did it before, when I first came to the Board, I came upon a thing called minimum trend. I used to write away for a lot of books. And I asked myself a basic question: Is this guy's basic premise right or wrong? Where is it right or wrong? I was always thinking about why premises were right and wrong — what was going to stand the test of time. I learned that most of them were wrong and that most of them were trying to predict in a market of uncertainty.

INTERMARKET: So anyone you hear predicting . . .
STEIDLMAYER: There are exceptional people, but I'm not one of them. So first of all, I can't put myself in that category. There are 10 or 15% of the people who are going to make money no matter how bad they might look. They are naturals. Your trading style has to be one where a human being can function. That's me, I'd like to operate below my capacity, below my potential, because then I can be consistent. Consistency is the name of the game.

I bought and read a book called *A Treatise on Charting* by John W. Schultz. The price was $2.98. I don't know if it was the same John W. Schultz who used to write a technical column on stocks in *Forbes*, but the column couldn't hold a candle to the book. I got a lot more out of the book, and I don't know if he meant for me to get out of it what I did. The manuscript made me assess what I was going to do.

He introduced me to constants. The idea is that you use constants to measure against the variables. You have to understand the variables. So you don't want to compare variables against variables, or price against price.

He also introduced a concept called minimum trend. Minimum trend is whatever you want it to be, but it's a constant measurement that shows trend variance. That was fascinating to me. It opened up a whole new thing. If the minimum trend was going to signal the change taking place in the market direction, say the price was in the process of moving down from 85 to 81, this minimum sample size could show change enough that even though price is still coming down, the trend had begun to go up already. It has always taken a series of them to make people notice. If I could see the first constant change, I would see the beginning of the mudslide. After there had been 15 constant changes, there was a large enough sample size for other people to see the trend had changed.

INTERMARKET: An example?
STEIDLMAYER: In terms of price and value, initially, the price was changing from 85 to 84 to 83 to 82 to 81, and there are probably a lot of (sell) stops under 80. But if the constant has turned positive, the price

going down would make no difference. So even though you're buying price that was heading down, then you're buying below value. You'd have to suffer bad financial and psychological exposure, because everybody will probably say, "If it gets under 80, it's going in the tank." But that's how I first started. I've developed it into a much simpler thing and in doing so, I've found better ways.

INTERMARKET: Why were you the first one to devise the idea of the databank and the approach it entails?
STEIDLMAYER: It's so simple that no one has ever done it. But the fact remains, it's a tremendous breakthrough in the understanding of markets.

INTERMARKET: Does it transcend everything written about economics previous to this?
STEIDLMAYER: Yes. I don't think the markets have ever been explained, defined, and captured as well as monitored. That doesn't mean that everyone who understands the databank approach is always going to have 100% understanding. I don't always, but at least I'm not trying to predict. I'm not accepting 50-50 odds; I'm working to get higher than that. You can't effectively do more than illustrate what the market is doing and under what conditions it moves.

Furthermore, a practical definition of a free market hasn't been done, so nothing equals it. It can't be done any better, because it's not going to get any more precise. Now what's going to be done better are the enhancements that are going to come off of this idea. But the basic equation, price + time = value, is going to hold true. It's going to stand the test of time.

INTERMARKET: What do you say to the random walk academics who assert that you can't understand the market because its movement is arbitrary and random?
STEIDLMAYER: I'm a behaviorist. I make the observation, record it, reflect on it, and most importantly I evaluate what I've seen. The key is to make the proper evaluation. If everything is arbitrary and random, you can't learn and if you can't learn, you can't make money regularly. I know from my experience that they're not right, and that eventually they are going to come around. I think the academic community has produced a lot of work, but little is practical or ever tested in the marketplace.

INTERMARKET: Could an academic have come up with the theories you assert move the market?
STEIDLMAYER: First of all, I think it would be too simple for them to work on. Secondly, no one would have the experience to know what to look for. I think that when the academic community sees how I define

the market, they will change their random walk philosophy. The market can be understood, and does not move randomly. It moves in an orderly fashion based on the factors I've told you. Once you understand this, you can profit from the market.

INTERMARKET: I sat in on a presentation you made to MBA students at the University of Chicago. I was surprised that after your lecture, they didn't ask any questions. Did everything go over their heads?

STEIDLMAYER: I think the class was good but not one of my best. I tried to cover too much material; perhaps the students were confused. They didn't have a basis to ask any questions. The question most often asked is if everyone uses the CBOT databank, it will no longer work, right?

This question illustrates a total lack of understanding of markets. They don't understand what the databank is doing. In other words, it's not a decision-making system, it's a decision-support system.

What is the world's worst market? The world's worst market is a nominal market where there are no transactions taking place and people are not able to take transactional data and establish some semblance of value. No trades, no information.

Look at the organized exchanges of the world, and ask yourself, "What are the characteristics of these markets compared to broadbased markets where people can take transactional data and make decisions—the housing market, the used car market?" All these are very broad and have a big participation by the public and have transactional data that give you information to determine value.

In other words, if you're transferred to Phoenix, Ariz., you don't pay Chicago prices for the house there. You look at the neighborhoods, you look at the houses, the price history, you see that they are run down or well kept. You ask yourself all these questions: Is this house good for all my needs? Am I willing to pay a premium for it? What is my time frame for making a decision? Is this an investment or for pleasure?

In trading futures, people don't ask themselves the proper questions, the questions that they ask themselves when trading anything else. Most traders have absolutely no understanding of the markets, so when they make money it's happenstance.

So in response to the question, does putting out transactional data which allow people to determine value hurt or self-defeat the market, the answer is, clearly, no. Absolutely, clearly, no. One of the most important things that the random walk people forget is that the market has to advertise opportunity in order to attract trade. You need transaction data that illustrate the difference between price and value to attract people.

The thing you have to ask yourself is whether the supposedly sophisticated centralized marketplaces know what they're doing. Have

they missed something? Do they realize that they have more characteristics of the nominal markets than of the broadbased participant markets? I would say that the organized markets today are nominal in
characteristic.

INTERMARKET: It doesn't seem like many people other than the
floor traders understand the importance of the databank.
STEIDLMAYER: The non-floor community at large doesn't understand the databank because something like this has never been offered
by an organized exchange. It's a new form of information for these
markets. It's going to pinpoint responsibility and make investment
decisions more accountable than ever before. This is not a responsibility that many in the investment community will want to take on. You
can't use the time-tested things that don't work.

If traders and mutual fund managers took their so-called sound
investment approach from the exchange and went into the grocery
store to shop, the store would make a fortune.

Also, having a good market understanding doesn't guarantee you
profits. The key to making money in trading is understanding yourself
and your capabilities—which situation you function best under.

INTERMARKET: So what are some concrete things somebody away
from the market has to do in order to make money?
STEIDLMAYER: First of all, this approach can give a person 100%
understanding of the market in the present tense—sometimes. Your
understanding of the market is going to vary. If you are a 70% effective
person you can come out with positive results.

INTERMARKET: Say you're not a 70% effective person. Say you're a
20% effective person?
STEIDLMAYER: The key here is understanding what you can do. In
basketball, an overused word is the match-up. If I'm guarding a seven-
foot player, I have to foul him before he gets the ball, because after he
gets the ball, he'll make the basket and maybe get the three point play.
If I'm guarding a four-foot player, I can operate differently. I can relax
because I can handle the situation.

So the key to taking good trades is matching up yourself with the
right opportunity. When you have an understanding of the market and
you have an understanding of your own capabilities, you have to
match your capabilities to an opportunity that's suited to what you can
handle.

INTERMARKET: So you're saying that born traders will be helped
and born losers will not become winners, but the trader in the middle
will be helped significantly by the CBOT databank?
STEIDLMAYER: What I'm saying is you're going to see much broader

participation in our markets because the people have a chance. It's going to help decentralize decisions, giving every trader away from the floor the understanding traders on the floor have. That alone will not make them better traders.

The key thing to having an understanding of any market is knowing and understanding value. If your wife goes into the store and buys a box of Wheaties because they're on sale, she knows that the normal price is $1.09 and if she buys at 80 cents, she knows she's buying it below value. So can people take the information currently disseminated and make the same determination? The answer is clearly no.

The other key thing in successful trading other than the market is understanding yourself and your capabilities. People who are great traders can overcome a lack of understanding of the markets. They are fantastic traders. But few people can understand how hard it is to be a fantastic trader. They are very rare. They are like Walter Payton (a star running back for the Chicago Bears, a professional football team). One in a million. Very few people can be as good as is called for in the currently accepted approaches to trading.

INTERMARKET: When today's value area is lower than yesterday's, what will clue me in that I can expect tomorrow's to be lower—a trend in other words? How do I know it won't go higher to get back into equilibrium?

STEIDLMAYER: Before I step onto the floor, I've categorized my bias for every market. Is the market going to continue, change or end? I look at the data when the numbers come out in the morning and analyze the distribution of the volume. Where are the commercials trading? Is the public trading and if so, where? How much volume was in the trend? Did we have a value trend or not?

I ask myself, do we have continuation? Do we have change? Where does the market start out tomorrow? How does the market define itself tomorrow? Does it make a low right away?

Today we opened lower, lower than people thought. Our opening range was basically in the middle of the range. Usually, if a market is real weak, the opening will be the high of the day. Now I ask myself whether the market activity as it develops coincides with my bias. I monitor price over time.

The real thing is, the market is going to go where it goes and it's readable. One of the things you have to realize is that despite the benefits of having a market understanding, sometimes you're not going to have a full understanding of the market. You can be standing in the pit and things aren't dovetailing in or coming together. What I do in this situation is have the patience to wait until I do get turned on to the trade and I do see it. I then monitor the market to make sure I'm right.

INTERMARKET: How did you start trading in Chicago?

STEIDLMAYER: I came to Chicago to trade, willing to take a job in the afternoon and evening to support myself. I made money trading the first day, the second day and the third day. I never had to get the job.

INTERMARKET: Did you enter the pit with the framework of price away from value?

STEIDLMAYER: Yes. Back then I had a different method of calculating price away from value, but I wanted to trade in the fundamental sense. I mentioned that trading used cars is no different from trading futures or anything, and I mean that. Trading in the fundamental sense assumes that in the present, you can determine intrinsic value under current conditions. That is very important.

When I studied this approach, I realized that it is not necessary to *predict* the future of the marketplace. It is impossible to predict the future of a marketplace reliably—although this is what everybody was and still is trying to do. I believe you can understand what is going on in the present tense. Because the characteristics that the market has are going to make things continuous. The market does not stop on a dime.

So when I started, I also wanted to find out how I was going to make money. What formula was I going to use? If I had been systematically wrong and I knew why I did what I did, all I'd have to do was the opposite. I also gave a lot of thought to the process of trading. It's not as difficult as people think.

INTERMARKET: So if you get out based on time, I assume you don't use a stop-loss.

STEIDLMAYER: Right. On any purchase, there are only three possibilities: 1) You buy and the market goes up; 2) You buy the market and it doesn't go up but it doesn't break; and 3) You buy the market and it breaks. If you don't use a stop-loss, you really have a 67% chance of not losing any of your capital. People who consistently put stop-loss orders in are willing to take one event happening before another. This makes their odds 50-50. I felt that by not using a stop-loss, I would pick up a 17% advantage in my favor.

INTERMARKET: So you'll let the market run against you?

STEIDLMAYER: No. I use preventive trading, meaning I don't enter a trade unless it's very attractive. When I'm wrong, I'm not that wrong because I've used sound logic for making the trade in the first place. I stay away from buying overvalued situations—the market being overvalued in several consecutive time frames.

And when I get out of a trade, the question is not, "Is the price going higher or lower?" The decision I am looking for is, "Am I right or am I wrong as to the market's location in the time frame I'm trading?"

INTERMARKET: So you'll be willing to wait if the market hasn't told you if you're wrong?
STEIDLMAYER: That's right. I use time as my exit point, not price.

INTERMARKET: Tell me how your approach gives you an advantage over other approaches.
STEIDLMAYER: The equation is market understanding—which I felt can be 100% in the present tense—multiplied by my trading efficiency or my efficiency as an individual—which is 70%. That would equal a 70% result factor, which is 20% over the 50/50 odds. So I knew I was going to win on the grind. I might lose on any individual trade, but I was not going to lose after 1000 trades.

If the person takes the usual approach to trading—charting and trying to predict the future—he has a 50% chance of being right or wrong. That approach, used by an individual who is 70% effective, yields 35% results. So his risk factor is substantial. He has to overcome 15% to break even. In other words, he has to be exceptional, which is hard to be over time.

INTERMARKET: What do you mean by being 70% effective?
STEIDLMAYER: Not that I can do seven out of ten things, but my consistency level of doing what I'm capable of doing will be seven out of ten. I'll take the garbage out seven out of ten times. In other words, discipline comes into play. For instance, say I want to buy every break in beans. I won't do it every time, but I'll be able to get seven out of ten without much problem.

INTERMARKET: You said in your class that you consider a trend akin to a mudslide and that you are able to identify the slide when if first moves a few inches, while the majority of participants don't recognize it until a few houses have been buried. How do you do this? Are government reports and other conventional fundamentals your key indicators, or is value?
STEIDLMAYER: The biggest mistake people make when trading is that they're late rather than early. I evaluate large samples of data looking for early indicators so that I'll have time to operate. This eliminates 90% of the problem.

Fundamentals are basically your background. For instance, I happen to be a little friendly to gold and silver at this price level (at the time of this interview in late February, gold was around $280). The question I ask myself is, will it break much? What is the trigger that's going to make people buy it? When you do the homework, you know.

INTERMARKET: If you were going to look only at resumes in order to find people you think could become great traders, what would you look for?
STEIDLMAYER: The first thing you need is generosity toward your

fellow man. You can't be a jealous person. A jealous person has a very hard time succeeding. He's always reacting and not thinking. In other words, making emotional decisions. A good trader is not affected when someone's doing better than he is. He's happy that the other fellow's doing well.

I think that there are a lot of people who equate money with success. That's false. Success is being happy, doing what you want to do because you want to do it. Success is not making more money than the next guy. That's ridiculous. When you are glad to be you, you have freedom and happiness. That's when you're successful. If you have to trade to make money to show people you're good, you've got problems.

INTERMARKET: So you look for someone who isn't jealous. What else?

STEIDLMAYER: The successful traders realize that there are people who have greater talents than they. No one can be the best.

I would also want someone with the ability to migrate to where they belong in life. Getting to where you belong in life is very difficult. You get shortstopped along the way. Consequently, the person who can find himself and do what he wants to do has a lot of self-confidence. He's not trying to impress people. He's a low-key, even-keeled individual. He's very self-assured and confident of his abilities, but he doesn't have to prove it.

You have to realize that your net worth really is your ability to function. If you have the ability to function, you don't have to go out and make a lot of money just to show that you're good. You know that you're good. Good faith in yourself and the discipline to do only what you want to do.

You also want to have the ability to think and the ability to apply your thinking. I have what I call a behavioral intelligence. In other words, my observations allow me to see how things work. I can see clearly how things operate in their most basic form. I don't have the intelligence to actually create things. I have more of an applied intelligence. I can apply different principles to areas that people never thought of, but I didn't design the original principles.

With the databank I've done two simple things. One, I've recognized that I can apply the law of errors or normal distribution to any futures market's daily range development because the market is composed of price, time and volume. I didn't invent the law of errors; it's a normal analytical tool. What I did was use it to organize what I saw.

The second thing I did was see the relationship of price $+$ time $=$ volume $=$ value. I've organized what people thought were chaotic, random conditions into what people realize is a natural organization. I've found an equation that is consistent. I feel really good about it. Having price $+$ time $=$ value, I was able to take Benjamin Graham's thesis — the fundamental approach to trading which says that if you can determine value, price is going to be divergent from this occasionally and that will create opportunity for profit. This approach gives me the most important tool in the trading decision.

Not only did I organize chaos, but I found the function of the marketplace, which is to determine value, promote trade and control itself. So I've taken two very simple, very broad concepts and applied them. This allows me to make money because I'm not guessing on anything. In fact, I'm just recognizing market-created opportunities.

INTERMARKET: So if you could only trade from California and without the aid of a quote machine — the only information you had was what you read in the newspaper, could you still profit?
STEIDLMAYER: Why work without information?

INTERMARKET: We've discussed how you've broken down market understanding and its importance to successful trading. Now could you discuss how you work with this in your approach to the market? For instance, improving your trading results?
STEIDLMAYER: I constantly ask myself the question, how can I do better? When I first started, I used to constantly examine my P/Ls to ponder each and every trade. I looked at what I did, why I did it. I looked to improve: What did I do well? What didn't I do so well? And I always tried to find opportunities which I knew I could handle, even though I'd pass up some very attractive opportunities which I felt uncomfortable about.

Statistically, I knew that I could put myself in a position where my year-end results would be better than my overall trading average. Here's what I concluded: In a market of uncertainty, the key is to weigh your trades so that you really load up when you have the most attractive opportunities — the ones that come along only so often where you know you're right.

This window of time where a great opportunity occurred and I was trading very well at the same time wasn't every day — it happened only once or twice a year. When I took such an opportunity I put myself in a position where I didn't have to make an exceptional percentage of correct decisions, since I'd only have a few decisions to make. In other words, these were very long time-frame trades.

If I flip a coin 10,000 times, I'll probably get 50.1% heads and 49.9% tails, maybe a more even distribution than that. If I flip it 100 times, I'll get probably close to 55-45 one way or the other. But I can flip a coin five times and have it come up heads each time. That wouldn't at all be impossible but would be an exceptional result that could only occur on a small sample size.

If each trade is recorded as either a win or a loss, my overall win-loss record for the year will be a lower percent than will be my win-loss record for the really low-risk trades.

The point I'm making in terms of trading is this: you have to distinguish between very attractive situations, attractive situations, and so on, and weigh your trades accordingly. In doing this, my trading strategy is built around my goal of getting heads five times in a row with my major positions.

So, to summarize, I trade three different size positions: my everyday small position, medium-sized positions where I have some conviction over time, and what I call my maximum position. When I'm right on the maximum position, my total results are better than my win-loss record. Like the batter who gets the same number of hits as everyone else but a much larger percentage of homers, especially when it counts.

INTERMARKET: What determines when you put on each size?
STEIDLMAYER: I view the market from the longest time frame, and if I can see when the market is undervalued over the very long haul, undervalued over the medium haul and in the best of all worlds, undervalued in the short-term — maybe I'm buying the bottom of the day's range — that is a very attractive situation. In other words, I put on a maximum position only when I can enter the market, suffer exposure, realize I'm wrong, and still get out with a profit. I can't lose. The opportunity and my timing have to be so good that I could do that.

The second size I put (on) when I have a good idea what's going on over both the short-term and the medium-term. Maybe the market is undervalued over the long and medium term, but overvalued over the short-term. So I put on the medium-sized position when I can enter the market, suffer exposure, realize I'm wrong, and have enough time to get out without a loss. I take my smallest exposure in a situation where I have no conviction other than in the shortest time frame. If I'm wrong, I have to take a loss.

In other words, in the first instance I'm buying something for 50 cents that's worth a dollar. If it goes down to 45 cents, I don't have to sell. If it goes to 55 cents, I don't have to sell. I can sit with that position through time and not be under the gun. For instance, in beans I might have a 10-20 cent loss, but I'm not wrong in my position.

I put on the medium exposure when I'm buying something worth a dollar and I'm paying a dollar for it. I have a shorter period of time to exit the trade and I have less to make.

The last instance — I'm paying $1.50 for something that I think is going to $2.00 but that's only worth a dollar. I can't sit with a loss — I have no time frame to work with if I'm wrong. I have to react to what the market is doing immediately and not think.

In other words, I feel the whole risk factor in the market is being able to utilize time. What this reflects is that all trading opportunities aren't the same and should be treated individually. In the big position scenario, a 10-cent loss in beans shouldn't be a concern, because it's way under value. In the third scenario, a half-a-cent loss you move on because you know you have no time.

INTERMARKET: Could you tell me what you mean by time frame?
STEIDLMAYER: When I first came to the Board, I noticed that the most successful traders were the ones that made the fewest trades. They were trading from the perspective of the largest time frame and, hence, they were making the fewest decisions. This is the approach I adopted and is still my approach today.

A time frame is basically a point in time where you're forced into a decision. Time frames are hard to understand. Every marketplace has them and they dominate the market, especially the long-term time frames. Each person develops his own as does each company or commercial in the market. They are immediate and longer term.

The marketplace reflects two different types of time frames: the time frame of the individual — which only he knows, like "I'm getting out in five minutes," or "I'm getting out right before Fed intervention time." And there's the market's own time frame — the end of the day, the week, a contract expiration, crop reports, whatever. And of course there are options, a product which introduces a totally new time frame.

What determines your time frame is your perspective of the availability of the product. If a product is going to be available later, there's no sense buying it now, unless the price is attractive. When people think there's not going to be a ready supply later, they'll buy more now, satisfying their immediate needs and also what they perceive as some future needs. They also might determine that in the future they'll substitute some new product. If I have a copper mine and you own a wire company, if I tell you I'm going to raise my prices, you'll change to fiber optics. The time frames are based on how long people feel that the time-price opportunity is going to occur.

However, if you know we'll have rationing next week and copper's availability will be in question, you're going to start buying forward. So the participants have different needs and varying degrees of access to information on what might affect their needs.

Your personal time frame is always a forward element. It reflects your expectations and so, taken collectively, time frames represent everyone's expectations. If people expect a price not to hold, thinking it'll go higher, they'll buy a lot.

INTERMARKET: How does this apply to your approach?
STEIDLMAYER: Longer term time frames tend to have a greater influence on market activity. In the longer term, there isn't as much overcommitment as in the short time frame. Long-term time frames are more subtle and those long time-frame participants manage their uses better. Long time frames are also easier to read because they are more stable. Also, they give themselves and me more time to act. Longer time-frame participants have many indicators along the way

that tell them to speed up or slow down purchasing. The longer time frames are more stable because people make less of a total commitment.

Consequently, every time the market dips down, this company is a supporter of it over time. When the price goes so high that the manufacturer knows he can go out of business, management will either have to load up, find a substitute, or go out of business. Both the consumer and the producer manage the situation over time. Events move along, and managed buying and selling decisions made from the perspective of a long time frame have a less splashy market impact.

This is because in a short time frame, there's no choice. There's no room to think in the short time frame. This is one of the problems of an addictive drug. You need it now and you need it later and even if you can't get it, you have to get it. You'll pay anything and so you'll be a lot more volatile in the next couple of hours until you've gotten your fix. So in the small time frame, there will be more volatility because the amount of change will be a large percentage of normal daily movement since such a small sample is being used.

As I said, analyzing your own time frame comes from knowing your needs and sensing the availability of the product or products which can fill those needs. Your time frame depends upon two things: first, if you have to have it now and later, and second, if you need it now but can get along without it later.

In terms of the market focus on the dominant need, it allows anyone who wants to buy, to buy; and anyone who wants to sell, to sell. In every market, there is a dominant concern from either producer or consumer. In any market, there is a dominant set of psychological concerns that have to be neutralized.

If I know that it's hot and dry for the soybeans, the market has to go high enough for me to sell knowing that even if it doesn't rain this weekend, I can't get killed. Markets focus on the fact that two days from now, either it rains or it doesn't rain. They know it's going to rain sometime, it's just a question of when, and whether lack of rain does damage. If there's a drought in June, the intelligent trader knows at some point during summer it will rain. He can take a chance to sell on a rally, saying that if it doesn't rain this week, it'll rain next week and if it doesn't rain next week, etc., etc.

However, if there's a bad drought going on in the month of August, within a week of harvest, the intelligent trader is more careful—there's no tomorrow if it doesn't rain. In early June, he'll be making a short time-frame trade based on observed situations that the drought is neutralized by the rally and the fact that there is a larger time-frame influence.

So the size of the position I put on rests on the amount of data I have and the amount of time I have to work with. The more time you have to work with, the bigger your position can be.

When you have a large sample size, your increment of change is going to be small and subtle and not picked up by everybody. Most people work with a small sample size where a small change is large and over before you can take advantage of it. Or they work with a large sample size with latent indicators.

INTERMARKET: Like a moving average?
STEIDLMAYER: Right.

INTERMARKET: Is that still true today that the most successful traders make the fewest decisions?
STEIDLMAYER: No. Things change and there's been adaptation. I personally have always believed it's better to be a low volume, high markup person, where less decisions are required. There've been other very successful people you've talked to who are high volume and low markup or the best of all worlds, high volume, high markup. It's just a question of the style of trading and one's trading ability.

In the 1960s there was not a lot of opportunity, so you had to be a long time-frame trader. There have been fundamental changes in the marketplace from the sixties until today. The markets are more volatile, and day and swing traders have succeeded in these recent markets. Volatility is not a function of the marketplace, it's a function of the lack of long time-frame influence. Traders always get blamed for the volatility, when in fact, it all points back to people's confidence in the future.

But to answer your question, for myself, I want to make as few maximum trades as possible. In my career, I've only put on about 65 positions of between 500,000 and a little more than a million bushels, or the equivalent, in 20 years. And lately, I haven't even done that. That means an average of three per year.

I should emphasize that there are two things you have to consider before making any trade, and this draws back to the "you" part of my equation for results. One is the market opportunity, and two is how well you're trading at the time that opportunity comes up.

There has been plenty of opportunity, so I suppose putting on only 60 such trades in 20 years' time probably means that I'm lazy. However, the results of this small sample size have been outstanding. I've only been wrong once, and even that was basically a scratch, so I accomplished what I set out to do, which is to have no large subtractions, only large successes.

INTERMARKET: When you put on a maximum position, since you want to make as few decisions as possible, you'll hold that trade?
STEIDLMAYER: Oh, yes. Usually a several-month trade. I've held a few trades for years. I consider them an investment.

INTERMARKET: But you wouldn't hold a medium-sized trade very

long.
STEIDLMAYER: Right. Maybe a month or so.

INTERMARKET: Could you make the differentiation between when you'll put on a maximum position versus a medium-sized one?
STEIDLMAYER: That's a good question. One of the first things I learned on the floor was that most of my design trades—the ones I really dreamed about—never materialized. I feel that the idea comes to you when you're working hard and applying yourself to look for and evaluate different opportunities—then all of a sudden, the light bulb goes on and you see it, right there.

But I have lots of time to make the trade because the market activity begins to change long before the trend turns. I can relax because there are plenty of opportunities to get in with minimal risk. Once I know the train is going out I can relax, but I get on early while it's still in the station. I get a good seat. I guess the analogy would be that most people try to get on after it's pulled out of the station, while it's moving.

To put on a large trade I need a lot of background. I only trade big positions when I think I'm going to make $2 to $3 in beans, $200 or $300 in gold—a large move. That doesn't mean it's going to happen, it means everything is going to be set for that. In a large time-frame boom-bust situation, I'll either be buying the bust or selling the boom in order to put on a maximum trade.

INTERMARKET: Could you be a bit more specific? How do you realize the train's going out?
STEIDLMAYER: I first examine market activity, meaning how price acts over time. Is the market a balanced market or is the bias on the daily range one way or another? Is the market bouncing or is it flat? In other words, is the market facilitating trade, or has it gone too far?

I locate price and measure how far it is from market value in a large time frame. Next, I consider closer time frames that I can take advantage of in order to put the position in a relaxed manner for the larger time frame. For instance, is price undervalued in today's time frame and undervalued towards the next few time frames out? This means I'm early and I only have to wait for developments to unfold—the total situation is undervalued and there's no way that I can lose. This ideal situation would call for a maximum position. Any variation from this I would scale down from.

And one last thing: I always require it to be a demand market rather than a supply market.

INTERMARKET: In other words, market activity always changes before the trend turns around.
STEIDLMAYER: Right. It signals that you can expect change, not continuation. Price gets so far away from value, the conditions are

changing so that the advantage goes to the other side. No one can see it. People are focusing on price, not on market activity. Meanwhile, the market is getting so far away from value that people get overconfident.

INTERMARKET: Is there anything else you do to improve your trading?
STEIDLMAYER: I feel that everyone has to study himself. You have to know if you're early or you're constantly late or what your personal trading patterns are. I'm basically early when I put on a medium or maximum trade. I have an old saying: Fools rush in — and it's always me. I see it before everyone else. When I first was trading, I would suffer bad exposure to the marketplace because I would see the market changing so far ahead of everybody else. I could've waited and still had plenty of time.

INTERMARKET: Weeks ahead?
STEIDLMAYER: In a maximum trade, I may have months to make up my decision. Remember, the market looks bad at some point every day; it makes a low every day and no one who's trading from a short-term time frame wants to be long at that point. One of the things I've found when I take a maximum position is that I have time on my hands to buy the world.

INTERMARKET: So you'd never go out and buy a position limit all at once, but stagger into it, adding on?
STEIDLMAYER: No. I always buy or sell it all at once because I feel I have to make a decision. But the price alone doesn't make any difference because I know I'm right.

INTERMARKET: So you would have no qualms about putting on the entire position at once?
STEIDLMAYER: Right. Because I think that's the hardest thing to do, and you want to train yourself to act on your intuition. I say to myself, "Maximum trade — put it on."
   The worst thing you can do as a trader is to hesitate. Once you have trained yourself to trade only with a good reason, what you constantly have to work on is not hesitating. It's easier in the long run to make the hard decision. It hurts you to make the easy decision. The easy decision is, "I'll wait until I'm absolutely sure." Once you're sure, it's all over. You're cheating yourself if you don't make the hard decision, the correct but hard decision.

INTERMARKET: What would you tell institutional portfolio managers that would enable them to manage money and risk better?
STEIDLMAYER: First of all, I really don't want to be critical of other people, so I'll explain it in terms of what I'd do if I were they. I'd

increase my market understanding by breaking the market down into time frames because I really think succes is a time frame issue in this instance. Second, I would look at the stock not in terms of the total mix of owners, but in terms of the three major participants who have dominant participation in the stock.

My first approach would be to copy some of the people I respect in this business. Warren Buffett, for instance. He finds the right situation by locating value. He trades an economic purpose in the largest time frame where the other time frames have no bearing on the value he's buying.

Most people would say that this approach would make me an investor rather than a trader, so if the parameters I'm discussing with you require me to become more of a trader I'd move to the closer time frame of the market with the same approach.

Looking further, for instance, I see that the specialist definitely has a time frame where he operates profitably, and he has to have time frames where he can't do as well because he's got to make a market. In other words, when he's doing well for himself, he'll make a tighter market, but when he's getting killed, he'll make the spread much wider. He has to — I don't know any of them who've gone broke. I'd get in step with him, since he is the market in the close time frames.

Next thing I'd look at is the time frame of another consistent winning trader who, by necessity of law, has to operate in a longer-term time frame — the insider who owns stock in the company he manages. He has to justify getting in and out of his company's stock for reasons other than his firsthand knowledge. I want to know what he's doing, how much time he's got to operate, and I want to be aware of his time-frame influence on the market.

Lastly, there's the institutional portfolio manager who's a large participant but doesn't have the defined market purpose, i.e., no time frame of his own, but has a known time frame imposed upon him. He normally uses an afterthought approach to the market. His main time frame is a market time frame which makes him vulnerable, i.e., end of quarter. They all want to dress up the portfolio and make themselves look good. I'd want to take advantage of this known behavior. You see, Warren Buffett, the specialist and the inside trader happily go along with the rest of the world's quarterly time-frame of dress-up. These three winners basically call their own tune and I would do the same thing.

The only criticism I'd have of the institutional managers is a strong inconsistency. Whenever they mention someone's credentials, they list the amount of money he manages. But when you read an interview with one of them, the fellow says he trades such large size that he can't get in and out of the market. But if he's managing big money, he's supposed to be able to handle it and not complain about it. Large commodities traders have the same problem, but they never complain.

They have the talent to handle it—the real credentials.

INTERMARKET: How have pit conditions contributed to your market understanding?

STEIDLMAYER: One of the first things I learned is why the daily extremes of every market are made on low volume: I noticed that every day at different times, the pit would empty out. No one would be there. Let's say the market would be down 2 or 3 cents, and we'd all be bearish—but the pit would be empty.

When the pit would fill back up, the market would always get moving in the opposite way. This was an important observation. I realized that the pit filled up because [in this case] it was the higher prices that brought people out of the coffee shops to the pit. So I always felt that the extremes were characteristically made on low volume before I really did a computer study. [The study validates his observation.]

When no one wants a market, it will rally because lower prices aren't creating any market activity. The market had done its job in finding that it had gone too far. The market always seeks activity. When the market comes back up, people react to the higher price and you have the activity.

I was always sure to get even [to have no position] when the market dried up and the traders left the pit. One of the old sayings was, "Never sell a dull one." What that means is, don't go in the same direction as the market's gone to get dull, or when the pit empties out. That's one of the true sayings. Don't go in the same direction the market's going when the pit empties out.

One of the things I was proud about when we first developed the databank was that the accumulation of volume—the first standard deviation which was about 70%—approximates the price-time distribution that occurs in a normal day. I was very proud of that. What that meant was that my basic equation, price + time = volume or value, which has worked well for me over 20 years of trading, was in fact proven correct. I never had the data to work with before—it was only my observation. So it was gratifying that an objective evaluation of my observation proved me correct.

INTERMARKET: How do you spend your energies on an average day? What I mean is, what percent of your energy is spent analyzing the market?

STEIDLMAYER: Most people won't understand this, but I spend 15% analyzing the market and 85% of my time working on myself.

I think that after you have a lot of market experience and you are confident in your analysis, you must teach yourself to do what you know you should do. It is very hard to do this—react instinctively.

A person asked me, "How do I know if I really understand the databank? How can I test myself?" It's like a tennis player who gets an opportunity in the game; he automatically reacts to take advantage of it. It becomes a reflex. When the ball's hit short to the forehand, if you hesitate—"Should I go to the net or not?"—it's too late.

INTERMARKET: How do you know if you are wrong?

STEIDLMAYER: I study price action over time—market activity. Also, I can tell by the way I feel whether I'm right or wrong. I can tell by my outlook—how I feel towards life that day—whether I'm right or wrong on my trade. For instance, I've been working on this Liquidity Databank project for four years for the Board of Trade without one moment of doubt that I was ever wrong, even though there have been lots of problems to solve. The good idea will always win out. Eventually all marketplaces will see the advantages of capturing market activity.

It's hard to explain being right or wrong. When I have a big trade, I may have a large monetary loss on it, but that doesn't even concern me. Other times, when I have a small trade on with a small loss, I'm nervous and edgy because I know I'm wrong.

Basically, my approach differs with most traders' in that I'm never wrong because of price and price alone. I'm wrong because of time and price together. A market promotes itself through price and regulates itself through time. As a trader, to be in step with the market, I have to make sure I'm always regulated by time as well.

INTERMARKET: So you'll never put on a trade and say, "I'll bail out at so-and-so?"

STEIDLMAYER: Right. But I always have a time deadline. Depending on where I'm putting it on, I may put on a small trade and say to myself that I'll get out in an hour and a half if the market hasn't moved in my direction by then.

INTERMARKET: So your style of trading completely flies in the face of the traditional "cut your losses short" approach.

STEIDLMAYER: Oh, no, it doesn't. A basic part of my trade is that you need a strong reason for making a trade.

Say I think the market's going to go up because it's below value. The worst that should happen is that it doesn't go up. If by chance it happens to go lower, it will only be temporary. The break will not be very major. If I think it's going up, at worst it may go against me, but not by very much. I won't be *that* wrong. My way to limit losses is to make good trades. Good trades won't turn into bad ones. I did a working demonstration of the databank last year to show its value to some of my classes. While I was on vacation in Florida I short-term traded away from the floor. I just used my computer and the databank profiles. Nothing else.

I made 20 trades. I promised the class I would trade 25 beans [25,000 bushels or 5 contracts], 50 corn [50,000 bushels or 10 contracts], 25 wheat [25,000 or 5 contracts], 5 gold [5 kilograms of gold], 5 silver [5000 ounces] and 5 bonds. That was all I was going to do. I wouldn't ride my winner overnight, or anything like that, only something easily done by any floor trader on the scene.

INTERMARKET: So what were the results?
STEIDLMAYER: I made 20 trades. I was right on only 12 of the 20 trades. I made $12,900 on the winning trades, my eight losing trades totaled $1,800. I had a strong reason for most trades in the first place. So when I was wrong, I wasn't that wrong. That's the real key to successful trading.

INTERMARKET: With no mental stops?
STEIDLMAYER: Right. I didn't use any stops, I just monitored the markets and got out when market activity indicated that I was wrong. And when I'm wrong, since I understand price *and* time, I don't necessarily have to get out immediately.

As a matter of fact I made more trades than I wanted to. I forced it. I'm usually better than 12 out of 20.

That's what I mean by cutting my losses. I cut my losses using preventive medicine. Don't make the stupid trade and you won't get hurt. There's no need to put stops in. Using stops is absolutely ridiculous.

INTERMARKET: Why is using a stop ridiculous?
STEIDLMAYER: First of all, you're controlling yourself through price, not time. Secondly, you're only giving yourself a 50-50 chance that one will happen before another in this market of uncertainty. Without the stop, you'll have a higher percentage in your favor. Thirdly, you're treating all situations the same when, in fact, they're different. And lastly, if you ask me, people who use stops are using a crutch or buying insurance, like in blackjack. If you don't have the confidence that you're right, don't make the trade. What happens is that people who use stops end up making more trades because they feel they have this crutch that they're leaning against. "Well, it's only going to cost me five cents."

Those attitudes are copouts. They mean you don't have the guts to monitor your trade. You've given up the right to make a decision two or three hours later because you're too lazy to monitor the market. It's a lazy way to trade and will not be successful.

INTERMARKET: How do you follow so many markets?
STEIDLMAYER: First of all, I categorize each market: trending, trading range or consolidation. Each morning when the market opens, I categorize each along the lines of continuation of the previous catego-

rization. For instance, in a larger sample size, a certain market may be trending down and the trend is strong. I come in the morning and size up the market—continuation or change? If I see continuation and I'm not already short, I'll look to sell above value.

You see, markets don't change on a dime. If the market is going to continue, it's going to do one of several things. You could have a normal day only lower, or you could have a trend day down. If you're seeing continuation, the market is not going to get very far away from value, but just erode slowly. The market will give people a lot of encouragement to take the other side.

The first thing I ask myself, if the market is going to continue, what are they continuing? When the downtrend is still very strong, most markets will open, sag, come back part way, and sag some more. The biggest change in market activity is that the market can become more two-sided. They rally the whole way, come back, rally, come back. They have bounce. The market's getting more balanced, in other words.

INTERMARKET: I assume you get no remuneration from the Board for your services?
STEIDLMAYER: That's right.

INTERMARKET: Why didn't you sell the databank rather than donate it to the Board?
STEIDLMAYER: I'm not interested in making money off it. The data are really owned by the members, I'm just repackaging the product.

I believe you set out your goals in life ahead of time. Mine include being a free person. Freedom is what this country is about. Happiness? If I make a lot more money than someone else, that doesn't make me better, smarter, or happier than anyone else. If I'm doing what I want to do and I'm free in life, I've got a lot more than somebody else. Your net worth is basically your ability to function and I have a high ability to function.

I don't know. I think that you're here for a purpose. Getting to where you belong in life is very difficult for most people. I am where I belong in life now, but maybe I won't belong here five years from now. You have to constantly put yourself in the position where you examine how you feel.

So it's a question of how I want to put that net worth to work, i.e., make money by selling my trading approach. That's a goal that I don't choose. I'd rather be free.

INTERMARKET: One could argue that because of the time you've donated to the Board in the last four years, you've given up your freedom.
STEIDLMAYER: Yes, to a degree. I've given up my short-term free-

dom for a good cause. A lot of people would like to make a contribution to society and the world and you can go make a lot of money and turn around and give them the money. I feel I'm giving more because I'm giving people the tools to work with.

There are probably less than 1000 people off the floor that really know how to trade any organized market. I think that's the tragedy. The people who say that you can't make money trading are copping out. They don't have the ability to do it and so they knock it. That disturbs me. People away from the organized exchange markets — used cars, coins, houses, all trade. In every country they trade and barter. But people at the organized exchanges have lost the ability to trade because it has never been developed.

INTERMARKET: Is there still opportunity in trading today?
STEIDLMAYER: There's more opportunity now than ever. There are more products and there's more volatility. It's just mind-boggling. But the opportunities are different.

People are used to opportunities coming from big moves, so that they got away with their sloppy trading practices. But if you learn to trade the everyday situation properly, you find that the big markets are going to be windfalls. That doesn't mean that if I have a good year in 1983, I make more than I did in 1979 when there were bigger opportunities in terms of price fluctuation. But I do very well while I wait for the Olympics to come along.

INTERMARKET: Why were you the first one who invented — we'll call the databank a set of tools.
STEIDLMAYER: I didn't invent the tool. I think every good trader basically had this already. I was the first to define it.

INTERMARKET: Why can't traders talk about it?
STEIDLMAYER: Traders are funny. Several successful ones told me that they wouldn't attend my classes because it might hinder them. A lot of good traders react and they don't know why they do what they do. They do it and they do it for a reason, but they can't express it.

I observe all traders. I enjoy watching young traders coming on to the floor because often they will naturally do the right thing. They are like a seed going into a greenhouse. They adjust to the environment and grow. Very often, the new fellow doesn't know exactly what he's doing, but he's doing it right. I can see basic premises that he holds.

As an older trader, I've had to change with the times. It's very difficult to do that — one of the ways I learn to change with the times is by watching new traders. Not necessarily the biggest moneymakers, but the kid who works hard and consistently does well. He's got to be doing something right, and I can learn by watching him.

INTERMARKET: Give me an example of how you've adapted to the markets.

STEIDLMAYER: It's very difficult. Back in the 1960s I got used to trading from a larger time frame. Then all of a sudden the markets became very volatile due to the society's uncertainty about the future. Mentally, I had to make a tremendous adjustment.

INTERMARKET: Exactly how?

STEIDLMAYER: The adjustment I've had to make was from a long-term trader who made fewer trades to a person who has to make more trades—because that is the trend. I made the statement about when I first came to the floor in the '60s, I realized that the best traders made the fewest trades. That has changed because of the volatile nature of the economy and the world. What used to take the market five or six months to do, it can now do in two weeks. That means you have to make a lot more decisions, and that's why there's more opportunity.

INTERMARKET: What does that say about the economy?

STEIDLMAYER: It means that the economy has matured to the point that nobody cares about long-term consequences. We are in a less stable type of environment. The strong trend in the last few years is for the markets to act quicker and more violently than they'd done in the past. That's an indication that more people are aware of instantism. They change the Fed Fund rate. Boom! It's there, everyone knows it. There's no time to react.

One of the things people are going to do with the databank is to sit back and put instantism in its proper focus—that is, that it's not worthwhile. Although we have trended towards instantism, it's due in part to advances in communications technology. But we're able to put more information out at the Board of Trade to counter instantism and tell people, "You've got plenty of time to make a decision."

Everyone says that trading is a stressful business. This is nonsense; the only stress there is comes when you're wrong and you don't get out of the trade. Stress is living with problems. You don't want to live with a problem, you want to get rid of it. When I have a trade that I get distressed over, I know I'm wrong. I get out of it and I eliminate that stress. You don't want to suffer a lot of bad exposure in the marketplace, because it's bound to affect you.

A baseball player with two strikes and no balls will bat 220, but with no strikes and two balls he might bat 350. If he consistently gets into the hole, he's not going to do as well as he's capable of doing.

INTERMARKET: Do you measure markets against each other?

STEIDLMAYER: No. That's a method that over the last 15 to 20 years has been very successful. I am not a spreader. I don't have the capability to spread. It doesn't suit my personality. Although I follow spreads a lot because I think they give you good indications about the direction the market is moving, I don't trade that way.

INTERMARKET: What is important other than time frames and price in your decision-making process?
STEIDLMAYER: It depends on how you've been doing lately or what your frame of mind is. Am I tired, rested, etc.? The good trader knows the markets, but he also knows where he is and what he has to do as an individual.

When I'm tired, I don't really control myself very well. I tend to make emotional mistakes. Most decisions people make are emotional. As I mentioned, people paint their houses when they sell them because they know buyers make emotional decisions. That's why people buy toward the top of the range—it looks so good.

When you're tired and undisciplined, you won't be able to tell if you're wrong as easily. You want to train yourself to know that you're wrong by the way your body feels.

Controlling yourself is paramount. I don't know if the conscious or the subconsious rules my self. But I always felt that my subconscious was always right. My instinct. When you're a young person, your subconscious basically rules you. Your parents tell you, "Now, don't do this. Don't do that." They are experienced while you don't know what you're doing. That's why young traders can do really well. They are very positive about everything and have no fear.

Middle-aged traders can be just like these middle-aged pro golfers who can't putt anymore. Tee to green they're unbeatable, but they just can't putt. Why not? Because they don't want the embarrassment or the agony of missing.

They're coming up [to the green] and saying to themselves, "I can't miss this."

It's the fear of missing that can hamper your outlook. As a trader, I'm consistently aware of where I am in my life and I have to guard against my conscious self and self-doubt.

Young guys go in the pit, trading like madmen, winning and losing. They know they're going to make money, so they don't mind losing. I don't enjoy the aggravation that losing causes. Consequently, middle-aged traders are too cautious. I told Dave Goldberg—he's one of the reasons that I've been so successful—"Dave, I'm too conservative. I'm tired and I didn't make any of the trades I was supposed to make. I made money and had a good month, but I let too many slip away."

He laughed and said, "You know, Steidlmayer, I've hundreds of customers, and I can't find one that's too conservative. That's never been a problem and it never will be."

INTERMARKET: How does greed influence you or other successful traders?

STEIDLMAYER: It's not really greed, it's that you feel good, just like I felt when I worked on the databank and the manual. Being long beans when they're limit up makes you feel good. Working hard for something and seeing it work out is satisfying. But it's important that when you have this sense of satisfaction, you don't let it overcome you. I don't feel that it's greed that can overcome you, it's your emotional level that causes a lapse in your control. Good traders have control of their emotions. What you don't want to do is be emotional in your trading.

A great analogy can be made comparing great golfers to what every trader should aspire to. I think that if you look at Jack Nicklaus and the way he plays golf, first of all, he doesn't play in 45 tournaments, he plays in seven or eight or 10—he's selective and therefore is making fewer decisions.

Secondly, he prepares himself for each one so that he's not mentally worn down. Next, he doesn't shoot 64, then 78. He's consistent. He shoots 70, 69, 71 and so he's not riding an emotional rollercoaster. He's playing well within his capabilities. He doesn't try to kill each shot because he knows consistency is what counts.

And unlike most traders, he doesn't try to predict where his shot is going to land. He doesn't care where it lands, because wherever it goes, he's going to handle it. He doesn't worry about it.

I'm no great golfer. So I go up to the tee and worry, "I don't want to hit it in the trees, I don't want to hit it in the lake. What if I hook it?" I've got negative thoughts. Nicklaus goes up there, squares off, hits it, and wherever it lands, he hits it again. He's got confidence that he can handle the situation, no matter what happens.

It's the same thing in trading. When I'm trading well, I don't care if I have a monetary loss on, because I'm going to handle it. Nothing could ever hurt me, because I can handle whatever can happen.

INTERMARKET: What kind of size did you trade when you first started on the floor?

STEIDLMAYER: When I first started trading, I came to the floor considering myself as a developing factory. In other words, I wanted to get the product out of the factory easily and efficiently before I tried to boost production. Once I was able to take the raw materials—the market, my understanding of it, and myself—and show consistent profits over 12 months, I would boost my volume. That's what I did. I spent my first year only trading one-lots. Only after that did I up my volume.

But I'm always conscious of what I'm asking of myself—I want to trade at or below my capacity most of the time. Every trader is like a factory; he has a potential, a capacity, and an operating level. If you're trading below capacity at your operating level, you'll make nonemotional decisions. And like the market, and factories, a person's potential fluctuates. This ties into what I said about jealous people.

Don't worry about the next guy's operating level. Don't worry about the richest guy in the pit or the guy who trades the most.

If I would've explained to people what I did when I started, they would've put me away in the nut house. I did't ask anybody's opinion of the market. I just did my own thing. I wanted to know whether I was right or wrong over time. When I found out I was right, I upped my volume.

INTERMARKET: When was that?
STEIDLMAYER: My second year.

INTERMARKET: Did you feel more nervous with more at risk?
STEIDLMAYER: No, but when you up your volume, you will lose. It's good for you.

I remember the first time I traded big, I think it was my third year and I was at Oak Street Beach over the weekend thinking about it. Monday it was either, "Be a man or be a mouse." We'll find out one way or another. I came down and sold 500 corn [500,000 bushels or 100 contracts] to Milt Kirschbaum on the opening.

He was a very good broker and was shocked that this little trader hit him with 500. He thought he was off the market or something. It was like I hit him in the face with a right hand. He bounced his head back and took a look around the pit—he was checking to see if he made a mistake. He looked around, he knew I was wrong, and he bid higher. The market closed 6 cents higher that day. I had a $30,000 loss, but I didn't cover a pound of it because I felt I was right on the move, but wrong on my timing.

The next day the market was 2 cents lower, so I got some of it back. The market within a couple of months caved in and I ended up making 20 cents on my trade.

INTERMARKET: On 500?
STEIDLMAYER: Yes.

INTERMARKET: Nice. But what really stopped you from taking your loss on that day?
STEIDLMAYER: I didn't think I was wrong. I was right in the big picture but wrong in the small picture. My timing was way off—fools rush in. Like I say, I'm always too soon. I always see the market activity signaling change before the price turns. So I'm usually ahead of everyone else.

INTERMARKET: What did you see before everyone else?
STEIDLMAYER: I can't remember the particulars. It was humbling.

INTERMARKET: [Pause] How was it that you came to terms with your success?

STEIDLMAYER: You need some instance which points out what money is and what financial success really is—nothing.

When I went out to visit my dad in California after I began trading here, I'd always have breakfast with him real early in the morning. Now, he was against my coming into this field because no one he knew ever went into the commodity field and ever made money. He didn't want a black mark against the family name.

INTERMARKET: Seriously?

STEIDLMAYER: Oh, yes. He thought it was the wrong thing to do. He wanted me to go to work for a big company. This was in a boom economy; guys were getting hired out of my class for $500 a month and company cars, benefits. This was appealing to many people But I knew I'd rather make my own, take less and be free. Once I'd made my decision and he understood why, he supported me all the way. That's the way he was.

Anyway, after my third year I calculated my profits and I was real proud. At breakfast one day I casually mentioned to him, "Yes, I made more this year than the chairman of General Motors." He was reading the paper or something and without changing is expression, looking up or anything he said quietly, "Well, I'm sure you're doing fine."

I was let down. So I wondered whether he heard me correctly. The next morning at breakfast in a roundabout way I said the same thing. He gave me the same answer: "I'm sure you're doing fine for yourself."

After that I started thinking about what he said. I realized he's right. No big deal. What he was saying was, "I'm sure you're doing all right. If you're happy, that's what's important."

INTERMARKET: So monetary success isn't really important to you?
STEIDLMAYER: Right.

INTERMARKET: What is?
STEIDLMAYER: I don't have any monetary goals. I do the best I can all the time. I figure that my net worth is my ability to function. Money itself doesn't really mean anything to me. It never really has. It just means things to me in that it can buy things I'd like to have. It's a means to an end.

I would never have a goal to make dollars per se. Just because I have the ability to make money doesn't mean that's what I should be doing. If I have a year five times as successful as other years, I don't feel any better. I know that I've done a good job. I know that if I trade, I'm going to follow ten markets and I'll make money. I'm going to catch my share of the opportunities if I work hard. There's nothing wrong in my foundation. I have a sound approach, and I work hard. So I don't have any fear of not making money. And I'm very strong, also. And I have a good mind. I can make a decision and not worry about it. I'm able to observe a lot and interpret it and I'm not afraid to act on my analysis.

INTERMARKET: So you come from a rural background?
STEIDLMAYER: Yes. I grew up in Colusa, California.

INTERMARKET: Your father was a farmer?
STEIDLMAYER: Yes.

INTERMARKET: And you put yourself through college?
STEIDLMAYER: Yes. University of California at Berkeley.

INTERMARKET: How do you feel having pulled a lot of separate concepts together to develop a cohesive and consistent approach to all markets?
STEIDLMAYER: I really feel successful for accomplishing this, not for its results, but for having been the first to think it through logically. I'm extremely satisfied. People don't realize that anything will work 50% of the time in a market of uncertainty. The key is to consistently perform better than this.

Risk Is Not A Four-Letter Word

Today more than ever, risk is a fact of life. Avoiding risk is impossible. Recognizing the opportunities it presents is the mark of a smart investor. Managing risks and taking advantage of them is what futures and options trading at the Chicago Mercantile Exchange is all about.

The CME is the world's most diverse marketplace, offering actively traded futures contracts on Standard & Poor's stock indexes, short-term interest-rate products, foreign currencies, cattle, hogs, pork bellies and lumber. The CME also offers options on S&P 500, interest-rate, currency, cattle and hog futures.

These contracts, along with the background on how to use them effectively, can help investors and businessmen alike treat risk as other than a four-letter word. With CME contracts, it's possible to take advantage of short-term market moves, both up and down...manage interest-rate volatility...or even hedge the value of an equities portfolio.

To learn more about futures and options trading at the CME, contact your broker. And call the CME toll-free at 1-800/331-3332, Dept. "HC," for free literature that explains in clear language how these markets work—and how they can provide exciting trading opportunities. ▪

CHICAGO MERCANTILE EXCHANGE®
FUTURES AND OPTIONS WORLDWIDE
International Monetary Market
Index and Option Market

30 South Wacker Drive   Chicago, Illinois 60606
312/930-1000
67 Wall Street   New York 10005   212/363-7000
27 Throgmorton Street   London EC2N 2AN
01/920-0722